T0367685

POWER OF
PERFORMANCE
MANAGEMENT

POWER OF PERFORMANCE MANAGEMENT

How Leading Companies Create Sustained Value

André de Waal

JOHN WILEY & SONS, INC.

New York • Chichester • Weinheim • Brisbane • Singapore • Toronto

Library of Congress Cataloging-in-Publication Data:

de Waal, André.
    Power of performance management : how leading companies create
sustained value / André de Waal.
        p.   cm.
    ISBN 0-471-38347-3 (cloth : alk. paper)
    1. Corporations—Valuation.   2. Industrial management.   I. Title.
HG4028.V3 D4 2001
    658.15—dc21

                                                        00-043586

Foreword

The concept of how a successful company operates in the information age is undergoing a historic shift from "make-and-sell" to "sense-and-respond." Make-and-sell is an industrial-age model centered on transactions, capital assets, mass production, economies of scale, and product margins. It emphasizes predictability and efficiency, with the head office formulating strategy and controlling most actions while frontline managers implement agreed plans. Sense-and-respond is an information- and service-age model emphasizing client relationships, intellectual assets, mass customization, economies of scope, and value creation. It emphasizes knowledge of customer behavior and organization adaptability with frontline managers accepting the primary burden of performance responsibility. With customer preferences increasingly determined by the click of a mouse, the need to embrace the sense-and-respond model is ringing alarm bells in many industries. The implications for the traditional performance management model could not be clearer. Indeed these changes challenge the fundamental assumptions that have underpinned management and measurement practice for the past 75 years.

How is the accounting and measurement community responding to these changes? With characteristic caution, is the answer. Although they may listen sympathetically to the problems of the frontline troops, they have found few reasons to depart from their traditional methods of analysis and reporting. They are naturally suspicious of the clarion calls for change and see virtue in caution, consistency, and control (mixed, it must be said, with a degree of creativity). That they hold these views with such conviction is perhaps not so surprising in a world of management fads and short-term fixes that dazzle one minute and fizzle the next. While the introduction of the balanced scorecard, activity-based costing, and value-based management in the 1990s has demonstrated that accountants can be innovative, few companies have really used these tools to challenge the hegemony of the make-and-sell model. The more typical approach is to improve the old model by making it operate at greater speed and efficiency.

The CAM-I Beyond Budgeting Round Table (BBRT) is a management research group that has done some groundbreaking work in this field. Its thesis is that for firms to compete effectively in the new economy, they need to break free from the make-and-sell business model. This means deemphasizing and in some cases dismantling altogether the apparatus of traditional planning and budgeting systems and replacing them with more appropriate performance management processes. Understanding what these processes are and what you need to do to adopt them is likely to determine whether your company is able to compete effectively in the new economy.

The trouble is that while many senior executives talk about focusing on customers and becoming a knowledge-based company, few really understand how their performance management processes are holding them back, and they do not know what should replace those processes. It is as much a battle of ideas between the old economy product-centric world and the new economy customer-centric world as it is one between alternative structures and systems. Key to success is changing management behavior.

"What you measure is what you get" is a favorite aphorism of many a management writer. As most practicing managers know, measures drive management behavior, especially if they are reinforced by reward systems. But few organizations have understood the importance of this connection and dealt with these issues in a holistic way. It means building new performance management systems in parallel with new management structures and redefining responsibility boundaries. This is not an easy message for a measurement industry that believes it has the complete solution. This book faces these issues head on. Not only does the book deal with the key measurement issues, but it also tackles the organization problems concerned with aligning strategy and behaviors. Few books have attempted this challenge, and even fewer have done it so convincingly. André de Waal has succeeded in producing a compelling guide for managing performance in the new economy. His book is not just a book of new ideas. It includes a number of new, interesting, and well-researched cases that lend much credibility to his thesis. Its timing could not be better. As many large companies have begun to see the new economy less as a threat and more as an opportunity, they will need good roadmaps. This book will help businesses build the new performance management and measurement systems and processes that will increasingly be seen as essential to success in the new economy.

Jeremy Hope
Program Director CAM-I Europe,
Coauthor of *Transforming the Bottom Line*
and *Competing in the Third Wave*

Acknowledgments

This book would not have been possible without the willingness of the organizations featured throughout the book to share their knowledge and experiences. Especially the way in which management teams took precious time out of their schedules to provide me and my fellow consultants with candid insights into their performance management processes is much appreciated. A big thank you to you all!

Many people helped in preparing and finalizing this book. Special gratitude goes to the following stars: Megan Salch for proofreading the book and for providing assistance whenever I needed it; Felicienne Bloemers not only for writing two case studies but also for providing the framework for the book setup; Morel Fourman, Kobien Mijland, Mick Fernhout, Huibregt Ribbens, Paul-Jan Linker, Nicole van Dijk, and Hans Fermont for providing me with drafts for case studies; Melissa Raczak for proofreading several cases; Elyan Zegers and Ton de Waal for proofreading the complete book on very short notice (sorry for spoiling your holidays, but it was worth it!); and my editor, Sheck Cho, for believing in this project and for granting me respite and extending the deadlines (we made the last one!). Finally a big thanks to my wife, Linda, for helping me write important parts of the book (and for sticking with me throughout).

Contents

Introduction

WORLD-CLASS INTEGRATED PERFORMANCE
MANAGEMENT PROCESS: THE BENCHMARK

> In the New Economy, winning will spring from organizational capabilities such as speed, responsiveness, agility, learning capacity, and employee competence. Successful organizations will be those that are able to quickly turn strategy into action, to manage processes intelligently and efficiently, to maximize employee contribution and commitment, and to create the conditions for seamless change.
>
> *D. Ulrich*[1]

Contemporary trends in competition, technology, and management and the rise of the New Economy increase the pressure for organizations to develop cutting-edge strategic plans. These plans need to be executed in a superior way to stay ahead of competition and to consistently create value for the organization and its stakeholders. Organizations today are creating value in ways not envisioned a decade or even a few years ago. But on their road to added value, they are facing roadblocks not thought of until recently:[2]

○ *Organizations have to deal with the new business models that are emerging.* Intangible assets, like knowledge, brands, people, and systems, are becoming increasingly important for creating value. These intangible assets have to be combined with the traditional assets to arrive at new business models that are ready for the new way of doing business. The management and measurement systems of organizations are not yet aligned with the new business models and the new way of doing business, which creates control risks. The New Economy itself is also creating new risks because of new transactions, new markets, new technologies, new competitors, and new relationships.

○ *Organizations have to plan for breakthrough performance.* The performance management process needs to be structured to consciously plan for breakthrough performance. Today, too many planning processes focus on running business improvement rather than breakthrough performance. Organizations have to focus more on planning "outside the box." In this respect, the concept of value-based management is becoming increasingly popular. However, more attention is required to define practical techniques and tools to link value-based strategies with tangible short-term activities and targets.

○ *Organizations have to develop new processes and tools.* Organizations need new processes and systems to manage the combination of tangible and intangible assets. The degree of success in managing these assets stipulates the degree of success the organization will have. Not only is excellence in each performance management subprocess important, but also excellence in the overall, integrated process. The matching and alignment of the information used by the individual subprocesses are critical for an organization in becoming a best practice. New technologies, like the Internet and Intranet, are making more information available faster. Managers, therefore, have to recognize that the old model of keeping as much information as possible to themselves is passé. Organizations have to make their information sources transparent to both the internal world and the outside world, especially to their stakeholders.

○ *Organizations have to look out from the inside.* Organizations are increasingly forced to shift from the traditional inward-looking focus toward a more outward look on the business environment, market trends, and actions of competitors. The challenge is to combine external business intelligence with internal information and then to integrate the combined data into the performance management processes.

○ *Organizations have to take into account their employees' view.* Even the best-designed performance management process can only be effective if it is appropriately aligned with the management style and culture of the organization.

This book examines how the performance management process supports organizations in overcoming the above mentioned roadblocks. A superior performance management process enables managers to develop high-quality strategic plans, to set ambitious targets, and to track performance closely. This ensures the achievement of strategic objectives and thereby the sustained creation of value. This book describes new ideas and developments in the area of performance management that help managers to rethink and reshape the performance management process in their organizations. The book is based on the results of a benchmark study recently conducted by Arthur Andersen at prominent, global companies and on the results of projects that Arthur Andersen undertook in the area of performance management at various clients. The ideas are illustrated with case studies that describe how companies have applied the ideas in a practical way.

The benchmark study was part of a strategic study into the performance management process that a prominent multinational organization, supported by Arthur Andersen, recently conducted. Internal and external developments caused this multinational company to reconsider and change its performance management process and related management reporting infrastructure. Such developments included a recently introduced new business model for managing the organization, the changing role of the controller as the driver of value creation, and new developments in information technology, including the company-wide introduction of new enterprise resource planning systems. Objectives of the strategic study were to develop a vision that would ensure that the multinational organization's performance management process was state-of-the-art, integrated, simple, flexible, and high quality, while at the same time generating the appropriate information required at the different management levels in a timely, user-friendly, and fully transparent way.

HOW TO USE THIS BOOK

In Chapter 1, a summary of the challenges that organizations face on their way to world-class integrated performance management is given. From Chapter 2 onward, each chapter starts with a detailed description of a specific challenge that organizations face on the road to a world-class performance management process and then describes ideas that deal with these specific challenges. For each idea the benefits of its implementation are listed along with possible considerations and the behavioral implications to be taken into account during this implementation. Each chapter concludes with one or more case studies that exemplify ways in which organizations applied one or more of the best-practice ideas.

The chapters in this book do not need to be read consecutively. At the end of Chapter 1, you may identify the challenges in which you are particularly interested (maybe because your organization faces issues in that area) and therefore go directly to the pertinent chapter. Remember, however, that all the challenges are related to each other. Implementing one idea in a certain area of the performance management process might affect other parts of the process, requiring a revisit to the ideas for that area. Therefore, make sure to read Chapter 8, which deals with the integration of all the ideas.

This book describes ideas that prominent organizations have implemented to improve their performance management process. These ideas can be very valuable to other organizations, but they should not be adopted and copied indiscriminately. An excellent performance management process is unique to each organization, and it must be tailored to the specific needs and nature of every organization. Also, some ideas can be contradictory to each other or even exclude each other. In that case, the organization has to choose carefully the ideas that it wants to implement. The ideas should be used to incite managers to rethink the design and effectiveness of their own performance management process. Then the ideas have to be further adapted to and aligned with the organization-specific situation and the desired level of improvement. During this process, the integration of the ideas into one coherent and consistent design of the entire performance management process is crucial.

KEY POINTS

- ☑ Contemporary trends in competition, technology, and management and the rise of the New Economy force new business models, new risks, new processes, new tools, and new types of information onto organizations.
- ☑ A world-class performance management process supports organizations in addressing these challenges.
- ☑ Innovative ideas, found at prominent, global organizations, improve the performance management process.

NOTES

1. Ulrich, D., A New Mandate for Human Resources, *Harvard Business Review,* January–February, 1998.
2. Arthur Andersen Business Consulting, *World-Class Performance Management, Results of International Benchmark Study,* Netherlands: Arthur Andersen, 1999; Boulton, R.E.S., B.D. Libert, and S.M. Samek, *Cracking the Value Code, How Successful Businesses Are Creating Wealth in the New Economy,* HarperBusiness, 2000.

1

Challenges for Performance Management in the New Economy

ON THE ROAD TO WORLD-CLASS PERFORMANCE MANAGEMENT

There is a statement attributed to ice hockey great, Wayne Gretzky: "A good skater skates to where the puck is. A great skater skates to where the puck is going to be." And this statement says it all. As an organization and as leadership, you don't want to be where the puck is because that does not give you enough advantage over your competitors, who are also where the puck is. You want to be where the puck is going to be. And you want to get there long before your competitors do. In today's dynamic competitive environment, only the companies which are first on the scene will reap the true benefits of competitive advantage. The others are too late and will be overtaken quickly because the lead times of new ideas are going down rapidly, a phenomenon caused, among other things, by the Internet.

How do you get there first? Your organization has to become world-class and stay world-class in everything it does, especially in the crucial performance management process. This has all to do with "knowing where the puck is going to be." You have to be able to anticipate changing circumstances in your industry. You want to have the right information at the right time to make the best decisions and to take the best actions. You need to know if strategic goals are going to be met and if you are able to satisfy the share-holders and the stakeholders of your organization.

To become a world-class organization, a world-class perfor-mance management process is a must. *Performance management* can be defined as the process that enables an organization to deliver a predictable contribution to sustained value creation. A world-class performance management process consists of excellent strategy de-velopment, budgeting/target setting, performance measurement, performance review, and incentive compensation subprocesses. These subprocesses are integrated in a simple way to create the transparency of information needed to become and to stay world-class (Exhibit 1.1).

   o *Strategy Development.* This process leads to clear strategic objectives and action plans for measurable performance im-provement. These are based on a thorough understanding of the key value drivers that are aimed at achieving a com-petitive advantage.

      Business issues that drive organizations to improve the strategy development process are the focus of the strategic plans and the quality of the strategic targets. The strategy development process is often too focused on calculating detailed future financial results rather than on planning

Exhibit 1.1   Sequence of the Subprocesses in the Performance Management Process

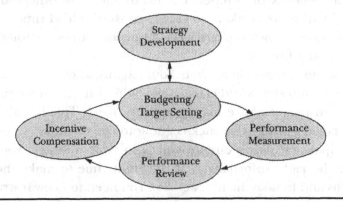

for value creation. Strategic plans tend to look inward, resulting in unrealistic long-term views that do not take environmental developments into account and that are not sufficiently focused on competitive advantage and true differentiation. Strategic targets are not clearly defined and measurable. They also do not sufficiently focus on concrete actions to achieve the strategic targets.

○ *Budgeting/Target Setting.* This process leads to clear operational action plans for improving the key value drivers, for committing resources, and for setting financial targets for the coming year.

Business issues that drive organizations to improve the budgeting process are the reliability and the detail level of the budgets. The reliability of the budget needs to be addressed because of the volatility of the business and the business environment and because of the early start of the budgeting process in the year. The budget tends to be too detailed, containing too many parameters on all management levels.

○ *Performance Measurement.* This process collects, processes (including consolidation), and distributes data and information to allow for an effective execution of the other subprocesses.

Business issues that drive organizations to improve the performance measurement process are the quality of the management information and management reports. Current management information is not fully satisfying management needs and does not incur proactive behavior because nonfinancial information is not included in the reports, reports are not sufficiently exception based, and reports do not include corrective and preventive actions.

○ *Performance Review.* This process periodically reviews actual performance, targets, and forecasts to ensure timely preventive and corrective action taking to keep the company on track.

Business issues that drive organizations to improve the performance review process are the quality of the forecasts and the timing of the performance reviews. The added value of forecasts is relatively low because the reliability of the forecasts is insufficient. The forecasting process is too time-consuming because the forecasts are too detailed and too often prepared manually. Furthermore the forecasts are not used sufficiently as a basis for preventive action taking. Performance review meetings take place on a regular basis rather than on an exception basis, thereby taking too much time and not sufficiently focusing on performance issues and problems.

○ *Incentive Compensation.* This process links strategic and operational actions for key value drivers, in a way that is balanced with compensation and benefits policies. The benchmark study did not focus on this process, therefore only a limited number of ideas and examples are given in this area.

The main business issue that drives organizations to improve the incentive compensation process is that this process is not sufficiently aligned with the other subprocesses, thereby not instilling a performance-driven behavior in the organization.

Information technology is an important enabler for executing excellent performance management subprocesses. It is crucial in realizing information transparency—the ability for management to have online access to necessary management information in a timely and user-friendly way. During the benchmark study, those trends in information technology and ideas from software companies were collected that specifically have an impact on future information-sharing possibilities and performance measurement efficiency.

IMPORTANCE OF WORLD-CLASS PERFORMANCE MANAGEMENT

More and more it becomes clear that the quality of the performance management process enables companies to perform better.

The professional literature and case studies clearly show that companies who have implemented and are using a good performance management process perform better, financially as well as nonfinancially, than those companies that are less measurement driven.

In a research study, senior executives from organizations with a structured performance measurement system in place and operational were asked how their organizations were ranked, compared to their peers in the industry. The same was asked of senior executives from organizations without a structured performance measurement system.[1] The executives' opinions were checked against the three-year return on investment of their organizations (Exhibit 1.2).

In another interesting study, which was conducted over a span of four years, the performance management processes and financial results of 437 publicly traded firms were analyzed.[2] Of the sample, 232 companies said they did not have a formal performance management process, and 205 used a formal process. The study looked at three-year financial performance of these companies, showing a strong favorable result for the performance management focused organizations (Exhibit 1.3).

In that same study, the average changes in financial ratios of a performance management focused organization, before and after

Exhibit 1.2   Comparison between Types of Organization with and without Structured Performance Measurement System

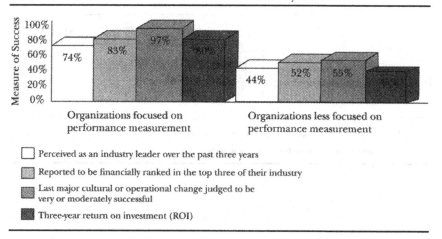

Exhibit 1.3   Comparison of Nonperformance with Performance Management Focused Organizations

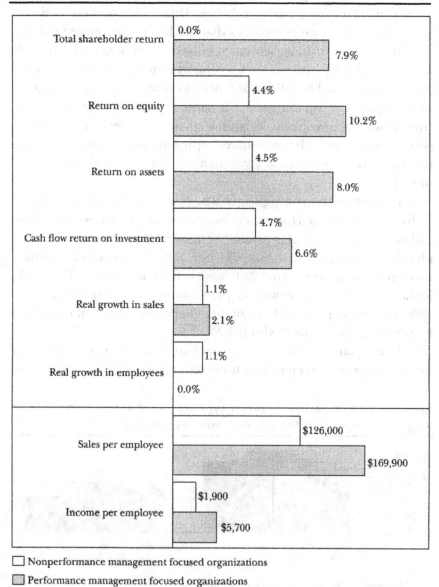

Total shareholder return   0.0%
                            7.9%

Return on equity   4.4%
                            10.2%

Return on assets   4.5%
                            8.0%

Cash flow return on investment   4.7%
                                  6.6%

Real growth in sales   1.1%
                            2.1%

Real growth in employees   1.1%
                            0.0%

Sales per employee $126,000
                            $169,900

Income per employee $1,900
                            $5,700

☐ Nonperformance management focused organizations
▨ Performance management focused organizations

Exhibit 1.4   Changes in Financial Performance, Before and After
Implementing a Formal Performance Management System

Financial Ratio	Average Before	Average After	Average Change
Total shareholder return	−5.10%	19.70%	24.80%
Stock return (relative to market index)	−0.13%	0.18%	0.31%
Price/book value of total capital	0.03%	0.26%	0.23%
Real value/cost	−0.06	0.13	0.19
Sales per employee (in $1,000)	98.8	193.0	94.2

the implementation of performance management, give compelling evidence in favor of implementing performance management (Exhibit 1.4).

In a recent academic study,[3] personnel managers from organizations with a formal performance management process were asked how effective this process was in improving the overall performance of their organization (Exhibit 1.5).

The majority of the respondents rated the effectiveness of the performance management process positively. This effectiveness was found especially in the achievement of financial targets, the development of skills and competencies, and the improvement of customer care and process quality. The conclusion of the study was that the majority of the people polled believed it was well worth the effort and expense to make their organization performance management oriented.

Exhibit 1.5   Degree of Impact of the Performance Management Process
on Organizational Performance

Effectiveness of Performance Management Process	Percentage of Organizations
Very effective	7
Moderately effective	41
Slightly effective	29
Ineffective	8
Don't know/not stated	15

In addition to these quantitative research studies, the professional literature lists many qualitative benefits from installing a world-class performance management process:

○ The strategy is translated into tangible and qualitative objectives and measurements throughout the organization. Management reports are more complete and give a clear picture of the crucial business activities. Effective planning and budgeting subprocesses are supported because the relations between functions and activities on the one hand and performance on the other hand are clear. Management focus is therefore better aimed at issues that are important to the organization, and this has a positive effect on the performance level and the organization's results.

○ A good performance management process functions as an early warning system, giving signals about potential issues before these actually happen or become real problems. Managers can therefore better anticipate new developments because they receive better information at an earlier stage.

○ The availability of high-quality information at all management levels makes management by delegation possible, which speeds up the decision-making process. Better reporting enhances managers' self-management and self-control. People are more motivated because they are clear on what their goals are and on how they are expected to behave and perform, and they get regular feedback on how they are doing in these respects.

○ The concept of the learning organization is supported by focusing people's attention on continuous improvement and development and by continuously raising performance expectations. Total quality management is enforced by ensuring that the expectations of external and internal customers drive the activities and the performance of the people in the organization.

○ The culture of an organization is impacted because the performance management process ensures that consistency exists between what an organization says it values and what is actually measured and rewarded. Also, information is more standardized, providing a better basis for discussion at all levels of the organization.

PERFORMANCE MANAGEMENT CHALLENGES

Clearly it pays off to install a world-class performance management. But will it be a smooth ride from here on? Probably not. You may expect to encounter barriers that need to be overcome. After all, even our world-class hockey player runs into barriers—other hockey players. So what are these barriers that need to be overcome to become transparent and to obtain a world-class performance management process? You need to deal with seven challenges, which are depicted in Exhibit 1.6.

1. *Establish a consistent responsibility structure.* Set clear expectations and foster accountability for action taking. The roles and responsibilities of each management level must

Exhibit 1.6 Seven Performance Management Challenges

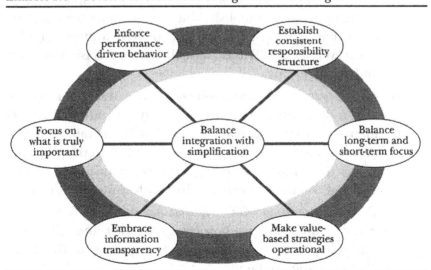

be crystal clear, and these have to be consistently applied throughout the performance management process.

2. *Balance the long-term and the short-term focus.* When you are able to do this, your strategic plans are actionable and are being translated into tangible short-term targets. You have more insight into the future, using nonfinancial value drivers as leading indicators for future performance.

3. *Make your value-based strategies operational.* Your strategy has to be aligned throughout the organization by using a common language to measure and to manage value throughout the organization. In order to be able to focus on the future, nonfinancial leading value drivers become more important. And your strategy has to be linked with operations, using both financial and nonfinancial value drivers.

4. *Embrace information transparency.* This allows you to have the right information at the right time, to make the best decisions, and to take the right actions. You are challenged to deal with the varying management information and reporting needs of the different management levels and with the level of standardization that is required. Information technology is an important enabler in this respect.

5. *Focus on what is truly important.* This sounds simple, but it is a challenge to accomplish. You need to start focusing on exceptions, analysis, and actions. You have to stop trying to know every detail. This focus will improve decision making and action taking.

6. *Enforce performance-driven behavior.* Can you say your organization does this to improve overall organizational performance? In that case, management "walks the talk" and acts on what it agrees to. Accountability and proactivity are key values that apply to your organization, and individual targets and compensation are in line with strategic objectives.

7. *Balance integration with simplification.* Linking the performance management subprocesses together and still keeping the processes simple and transparent is the final challenge you are facing.

This book will tell you more about these challenges and how to deal with them. Learning from best-practice experiences and discussing these in your organization enables you to create a transparent organization with world-class performance management.

KEY POINTS

☑ A world-class performance management process enables an organization to deliver a predictable contribution to sustained value creation.

☑ Performance management focused organizations perform better, financially as well as nonfinancially, than nonperformance management focused organizations.

☑ Your organization will encounter seven performance management challenges, which need to be addressed in order to become world-class.

☑ Challenge 1. *Establish a consistent responsibility structure:* to set clear expectations and to foster accountability for action taking.

☑ Challenge 2. *Balance long-term and short-term focus:* to make strategic plans actionable and to translate these plans into tangible short-term targets.

☑ Challenge 3. *Make value-based strategies operational:* to align the strategy throughout the organization by using a common language to measure and to manage value creation.

☑ Challenge 4. *Embrace information transparency:* to have the right information available at the right time, to make the best decisions, and to take the right actions.

☑ Challenge 5. *Focus on what is truly important:* to focus only on exceptions, analysis, and actions, not on every detail.

☑ Challenge 6. *Enforce performance-driven behavior:* to have management "walk the talk" and act on what it agrees to.

☑ Challenge 7. *Balance integration with simplification:* to integrate the performance management subprocesses in a transparent way.

NOTES

1. Schiemann, W.A., and J.H. Lingle, *Bullseye! Hitting Your Strategic Targets through High-Impact Measurement,* Free Press, 1999.
2. Gubman, E.L., *The Talent Solution, Aligning Strategy and People to Achieve Extraordinary Results,* McGraw-Hill, 1998.
3. Armstrong, M., and A. Baron, *Performance Management, the New Realities,* Institute of Personnel and Development, 1998.

2

Establish a Consistent Responsibility Structure

CHALLENGE OF CONSISTENCY

The best organizations everywhere pay close attention to consistency and alignment.

J.C. Collins and J.I. Parras[1]

Develop a flexible leadership style. Executive leadership styles are evolving from a "command and control" approach to a style that focuses on a clear purpose, common values, and innovation.

S. Hartz[2]

Trust in management requires consistent behavior. Therefore, the roles and responsibilities of each management level must be clear, and the chosen management style must be applied consistently throughout the performance management process. How satisfied are you with the consistency and alignment in your organization? Do your managers and employees know what they are held accountable for? Based on their accountability, do they set up action plans for their own area of expertise? And is the management information in your organization aligned with the responsibilities of the people? How often do you ask ad hoc questions of your managers because the information you need is simply not there? And how often do these managers frown on you, because they did not expect you to be interested in this information in the first place?

To establish a world-class performance management process, it is essential that there exists throughout the organization consensus on the responsibility structure of the organization—there is a clear answer to the question "Who is responsible for what?" in the areas of strategy development and strategy execution. Only a clear responsibility structure will lead to true value creation for shareholders and stakeholders of the organization.

Goldsmith and Clutterbuck[3] remark that in their research of the characteristics of high-performing companies worldwide, several common factors became visible:

○ Clarity of role and responsibility between corporate headquarters and business units.
○ An absence of corporate headquarters' bureaucracy.
○ Consensus between corporate headquarters and the business units about what should be controlled where.
○ An emphasis on "no surprises."
○ Structures that maintain the benefits of smallness and simplicity.
○ An emphasis on speed of information and decision making.
○ A balance between strategic and financial control.

Goldsmith and Clutterbuck conclude that high-performing companies promote autonomy by being very clear about what they want and consequently about what they do not want to control from the corporate headquarters. In this way senior management at corporate headquarters has more time for long-term tasks, such as strategy development, for coaching and for developing the next generation of managers they can trust. After all, the more trust that exists, the less need to monitor and control.

Trust in management requires consistent behavior on all management levels. The roles and responsibilities of each management level must be crystal clear, and the chosen management style must be applied consistently throughout the performance management process. The information requirements from management must be predictable, instead of causing a constant stream of ad hoc information requests and regularly changing information requirements, as is customary in many organizations.

CHOOSE AND APPLY A CONSISTENT PARENTING STYLE

A management control model gives the answer to the question of how an organization should manage and control its businesses. This control model forces an organization (1) to make choices about the roles and responsibilities of corporate headquarters, of the divisions, and of the business units and (2) to determine how the performance management process has to function within the organization.

For this purpose, the three parenting styles as described by Goold,[4] and depicted in Exhibit 2.1, are used:

1. Financial control
2. Strategic control
3. Strategic planning

These three styles differ in the extent to which corporate headquarters influences the strategic planning processes of lower levels in the organization and controls and manages these lower levels.

The influence on the development of the strategy and the strategic objectives of lower organizational levels depends on the frequency and the intensity with which corporate headquarters involves itself in the strategic development process of these lower levels. This influence stipulates the degree to which important decisions are made top down or bottom up.

The manner of controlling the lower organizational levels depends on the way, the frequency, the content, and the level of detail of reporting from these lower levels to corporate headquarters. Procedures stipulate when corporate headquarters can intervene

Exhibit 2.1   Corporate Headquarters' Influence on the Strategic
Development Process of Lower Organizational Levels and Manner of
Controlling of These Levels, Depending on the Parenting Style

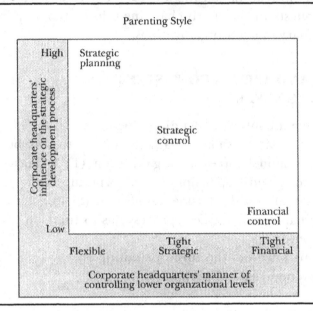

on lower organizational levels and what control tools (sanctions, incentives, promotion/demotion of managers) are available for corporate headquarters to do this.

The Three Parenting Styles

The three parenting styles are discussed here and summarized in
Exhibit 2.2.

- ○ *Strategic planning.* Corporate headquarters plays an active
  part in the strategy development process of the divisions
  and the business units. The planning process is heavy and
  time-consuming. Because corporate headquarters is so
  close to the divisions and the business units, it is at all times
  informed about their status. Therefore, the control focus
  lies mainly on achieving longer-term strategic objectives.

Exhibit 2.2   Characteristics of the Three Parenting Styles

Definition	Strategic Planning	Strategic Control	Financial Control
Type of industry	Rapidly changing, fast growing, or fiercely competitive industries.	Mature industries and stable competitive situations.	Wide variety of industries.
Parent role	Closely involved with business unit in formulation of plans and decisions. Clear sense of direction.	Planning decentralized to business units. Parent role is checking, assessing, and sponsoring.	Insists that all decisions are "owned" by the business units themselves.
Business role	Seeks consensus with headquarters and other units for business initiatives (in line with strategic targets).	Own responsibility for strategies, plans, and proposals.	Independent entities, sometimes working together to achieve mutual benefits.
Organizational structure	Large or powerful functional staffs at center. Shared service departments (marketing, R&D, etc.).	Decentralized with focus on individual business unit's performance. Headquarters operates as strategic controller.	Minimal staff at the headquarter level, focused on headquarters' support and financial control.
Planning process	Resource allocation driven by requirements of long-term strategies. Planning influence of headquarters is high.	Negotiation of financial and strategic performance targets. Planning influence of headquarters is medium.	No formal strategic planning, process focuses on business unit annual budget and financial targets. Planning influence of headquarters is low.
Control process	Low priority on monitoring monthly financial results. Control by headquarters is flexible.	Regular monitoring of actuals against planned, on financial and nonfinancial targets. Control by headquarters is strategic.	Concentrates on financial targets and results (contracting). Control by headquarters is strictly financial.
Value creation focus	Creation of new business units for long-term business development.	Long-term strategies and goals of the business units (facilitating + coordinating).	Operating improvements and financial control.

Corporate headquarters will only officially react on large deviations of operational results, which makes the control process flexible, taking second stage to the planning process. The size of the staff departments needed to support corporate headquarters in this style is relatively large. In short, corporate headquarters is heavily involved in developing, deploying, and monitoring the execution of the strategy at the divisional and the business-unit levels.

○ *Strategic control.* Corporate headquarters issues strategic guidelines, but the divisions and the business units make their own strategic plans independently. These plans are evaluated and prioritized by corporate headquarters. Focus in the plans lies on defining both short- and long-term financial and nonfinancial objectives, which are regularly checked by corporate headquarters. The size of the staff departments at headquarters is average. In short, corporate headquarters monitors the execution of the strategy, while the development and the deployment of the strategy is left to the divisions and the business units themselves.

○ *Financial control.* The responsibility and the authority to develop strategic plans is totally delegated to the divisions and the business units. Corporate headquarters in principle does not evaluate these plans but is only interested in whether the divisions and business units achieve the financial targets as forecasted in their strategic plans. Corporate headquarters de facto manages a portfolio of businesses. The size of the financial department at corporate headquarters is relatively large, the other staff departments at headquarters are small. In short, corporate headquarters only manages on key financials from the divisions and the business units.

During the definition of a new management control model, it is of the utmost importance that an organization chooses one parenting style and applies this style consistently throughout the performance management process. Consistent application results in clarity about the roles and responsibilities that the different management levels in the organizations have, consistency in managing and controlling the various organizational levels, clear expectations about responsibilities, clarity about which strategic objectives should be achieved by whom, and consensus about when higher management levels can intervene in the management process of lower management levels.

Several Parenting Styles at the Same Time

In spite of the earlier statement about choosing one parenting style, in practice one often encounters within a large and complex organization several parenting styles at the same time. In principle, organizations should indeed strive to have one consistent parenting style, sending a clear signal to the organization. However, if an organization operates in heterogeneous business environments in a wide variety of industries, several parenting styles may be found. This is fine as long as the chosen parenting style for a specific division is applied consistently throughout that division and its underlying business units.

For some divisions, corporate headquarters will apply the parenting style of financial control. This style is used within divisions that meet financial targets consistently over a period of time. These divisions are mainly managed on the basis of financial figures, and their business units have a fair amount of freedom in their strategic planning processes. Divisional management only gets involved in business unit management if a particular business unit shows serious deviations from the agreed-upon targets.

In other divisions, corporate headquarters will apply the strategic planning style. This is the case in divisions that operate in a highly dynamic, volatile, and competitive environment, in divisions that are young and/or have a young, relatively inexperienced management, and in divisions that consistently do not achieve their targets. In these cases, experienced senior management has to step in to coach divisional management.

CHOOSE AND APPLY A CONSISTENT PARENTING STRUCTURE

The parenting style of the organization, and thus the responsibilities of the different management levels, has a great influence on the desired parenting structure of an organization. The parenting structure stipulates the way in which the control process between corporate headquarters and the division and its underlying business units is structured (Exhibit 2.3). It also forces choices about the desired relations between senior management and divisional and business unit management with regard to the control and information processes.

The three parenting control structures described here are summarized in Exhibit 2.4:

1. *Simple reporting.* Corporate headquarters stand directly above the business units, so there is direct and frequent contact between the two management levels.

Exhibit 2.3   Structure of Corporate Headquarters' Control on Lower Organizational Levels, Depending on the Structure

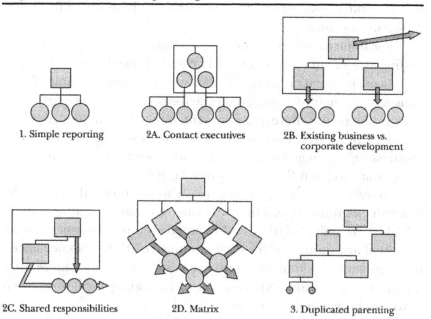

1. Simple reporting   2A. Contact executives   2B. Existing business vs. corporate development

2C. Shared responsibilities   2D. Matrix   3. Duplicated parenting

(2 = Divided parenting)

Source: Adapted from M. Goold, A. Campbell, and M. Alexander, Corporate level strategy, creating value in the multibusiness organization, New York: John Wiley & Sons, 1994.

Exhibit 2.4   Characteristics of the Parenting Control Structures

Definition	Simple Reporting	Contact Executives	Divided Parenting			Duplicated Parenting
			Existing Business vs. Corporate Development	Shared Responsibilities	Matrix	
Organization structure	Single parent level above business units.	Portfolio specialization of individuals within a single parent level.	Two parent levels: one for development and one for parenting portfolio.	Two parents both with active role in influencing businesses.	Parents on two dimensions: regional and product/brand/service grouping.	Multiple parenting levels.
Company size	Small companies with few business units.	Mostly medium- to large companies.	Mostly medium- to large companies.	Mostly large companies.	Large companies.	Very large companies.
Relation business unit with corporate	Direct formal and informal contact with corporate.	Formal contact with corporate. Frequent informal contact with contact executives.	Direct formal and informal contact with second parent layer.	Formal contact with corporate for strategic and budget control. Regular contact with division.	Direct relationship with different parenting groups for different purposes.	Repetition of basic tasks, at different levels of aggregation.
Advantages	Simplicity.	Single parent level.	Parent close to important business issues.	Distinct roles for divisional and central levels.	Specialization of parenting.	None.
Disadvantages	Difficult to expand.	Lack of clarity about position of contact executives.	Duplication risk.	Overlap of influence on business units.	Lack of clarity/excessive overlap.	Cash/time costs of duplication not justified by additional value creation.

2. *Divided parenting.* Specialist groups are created at corporate headquarters, thereby increasing the managing capacity of corporate headquarters. There are four substructures:

   ○ *Contact executives.* At corporate headquarters, there are representatives appointed who are responsible for one functional or organizational area in the organization or for part of the portfolio. Business units will still go to corporate headquarters to get approval for their plans and budget. However, in the remainder of the year they will have frequent (in)formal contact with their contact or sponsoring executive.

   ○ *Existing business vs. corporate development.* The management levels in the organization are split in order to be able to focus on different sources for value creation. Corporate headquarters focuses on corporate development and external relations. The next layer focuses on managing the portfolio.

   ○ *Shared responsibilities.* The management levels in the organization are split in order to be able to focus on different sources for value creation. However, corporate headquarters not only focuses on corporate development and external relations, but is also heavily involved in influencing the business units in the portfolio. The next layer focuses on managing the business units and the linkages between these units.

   ○ *Matrix.* Business units report to the division on two aspects, most often a regional geographic side and a product or services side. Corporate headquarters settles disputes between the two sides of the matrix and further focuses on corporate development and external relations.

3. *Duplicated parenting.* This structure involves repeating the same basic tasks at different levels of aggregation. Each level parents the level below and exhorts influence beyond that level. An example is the case of both the division and corporate headquarters directly controlling business units.

Once a clear parenting style and parenting structure have been established, and once the rest of the organization has been aligned to this style and structure, consequences on the performance management process can be analyzed. The parenting style and structure have consequences for the subprocesses strategy development, budgeting, forecasting, reporting, and review subprocesses, as well as for the layout of reports and for the systems supporting the performance management process. For example, look at how the chosen parenting style influences the components of the information and communication technology (ICT) strategy and architecture of an organization (Exhibit 2.5).

The chosen parenting styles stipulates how the information architecture of an organization has to be organized. The responsibilities for various tasks with regard to ICT are determined by the chosen parenting style. In this way, it becomes clear which management level(s) is(are) responsible for purchase and maintenance of hard- and software, for drafting the detailed information planning, and for managing ICT projects. Will this be done centrally, in the business units, or both?

Exhibit 2.5   Elements of an Organization's ICT Strategy Can Be Filled In, Based on the Chosen Parenting Style

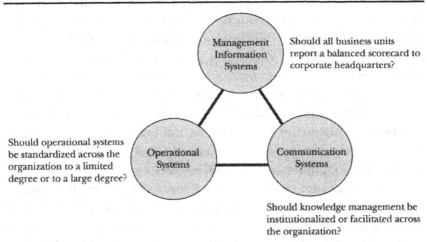

SET STRICT CORPORATE STRATEGIC
GUIDELINES AND TARGETS

In many organizations, corporate headquarters issues strategic guidelines, strategic companywide targets, and targets for each individual division. These are used by divisions and business units as input and guidance when they formulate their strategic plans. Corporate headquarters also set the time horizon of the strategic plans. The time horizon can differ each year, depending on the predictability of the economic environment, the anticipated volatility of the business, and the risks the divisions and the business units run. With the corporate guidelines as a starting point, each division prepares a strategic action plan and breaks down the divisional targets to the business-unit level. Divisions are autonomous in this process, as long as they adhere to the corporate guidelines. Corporate headquarters is not actively involved and does not give formal approval to the divisional strategic plans. The guidelines and targets are clear and strict, making expected strategic performance explicit and measurable. In this way, instead of divisions and business units either spending too much time trying to interpret the guidelines or trying to negotiate or renegotiate the targets with corporate headquarters, they can focus on the actions that should achieve the strategic objectives and targets.

In some organizations, corporate guidelines and targets are rigorously applied. All divisions receive the same strict corporate guidelines and targets, which are not subject to negotiation. Examples of guidelines are "Operating profit should improve by more than x percent over the next y years" and "Inventory turnover should improve by more than x percent over the next y years." However, using the same set of guidelines and targets for all divisions may not be realistic because divisions and business units can be diverse in nature, competitive environment, and maturity. Corporate headquarters should take these differences into account.

The targets are challenging and cannot be achieved by simply improving current business processes. Therefore, divisions and business units are forced to generate new ideas and actions themselves, aimed at both cost improvement and revenue growth.

Strict, explicit, and measurable strategic guidelines and targets, which are not subject to negotiations, enable divisions and business units to spend more time formulating strategic actions aimed at achieving the guidelines and targets. This increases the quality of the ensuing strategic action plans and initiatives.

BEHAVIORAL IMPLICATIONS OF CONSISTENCY

To every challenge, there is a hard side and a soft side—organizational/systems versus people. You need to deal with both to arrive at a solution for each challenge that really works.

When looking at the challenge of establishing a consistent responsibility structure, the most important behavioral implication is that every management level has to stick to the chosen and communicated style and structure—it must consistently "walk the talk"! Setting strict corporate guidelines and targets facilitates this attitude because it does not leave room for uncertainty. After management has developed a shared vision on the desired parenting style and parenting structure, it plays a key role in communicating the responsibility setup to the people in the organization. Then, every manager has to align his or her managing style with the chosen style and structure so no discrepancies will occur between these two, resulting in conflicting signals to the organization. But lower management levels should also walk the talk, by showing perseverance when higher management levels are deviating from the agreed-upon style and structure. These lower levels should stand up and hold higher management to their promises and agreements.

CASE: A CHANGE IN PARENTING STYLE AT AVR

This case study is an example of an organization that had to change its parenting style and parenting structure to be able to deal with internal and external forces. This particular organization, AVR, operates in a rapidly changing industrial environment with many opportunities but also with many threats. The management team has spent a lot of time restructuring the organization to make it more agile and ready to take advantage of the changes. Arthur Andersen has provided assistance to this organization in establishing a management style and structure needed to manage the organization in these turbulent times.

Organization's Background

AVR is currently the biggest waste management organization in The Netherlands. The organization services the complete chain of waste treatment: from collecting the waste at the point of origin to the end processing and disposal of the waste, including pretreatment and recycling. AVR also provides consultancy: organizations and municipalities are taught how to deal more efficiently with their waste.

AVR management aims to belong to the top three waste management companies in the Benelux (Belgium, The Netherlands, and Luxembourg) area and to the top companies in Europe. At the same time, the organization is changing its image from a mere incinerator company to a full-service waste management company. The main strategy of AVR to obtain its goals is to work in partnership with governmental agencies and industrial companies. Through these partnerships, AVR stays closer to its customers and, therefore, can offer better-tailored services. The organization can also show its reliability and its innovative strength. Moreover, AVR wants to grow by means of acquisitions and alliances and through cooperation with other waste treatment companies.

In general, the waste management industry deals with two main categories of waste stream (Exhibit 2.6). The primary waste stream consists of untreated waste, which is produced by industrial companies, governmental agencies, municipalities, and households. Efforts to reduce the amount of waste (prevention) take place mainly in this stream. The untreated waste is collected, sorted into different types, and then processed by waste treatment companies. The secondary waste stream consists of landfilling, or storing in depots those residues that cannot be recycled or incinerated.

Exhibit 2.7 gives an idea of the magnitude of recycling that can take place nowadays.

In the past few years, the waste treatment market in Europe has developed into a fierce marketplace. Competition is getting

Exhibit 2.6   Schematic Overview of the Sources and Streams of Waste

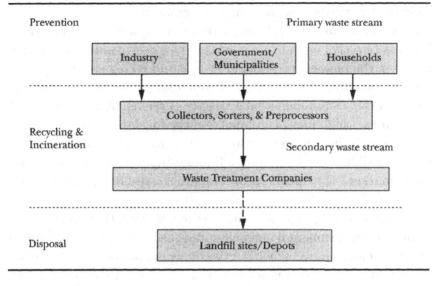

Exhibit 2.7   Types of Recycling That Take Place Today

Type of Waste	Recycled As
Domestic waste	Glass, compost, paper
Glass, paper, carton, batteries	Glass, paper, carton, batteries
Selected hazardous waste (e.g., mercury)	Chemicals
Building and demolition materials	Wood, iron, paper, bricks
Vegetables, fruits, garden materials	Compost
Domestic appliances	Domestic appliances
Silt, sludge	Compost
Car wreckage	Cars

Type of Incineration Waste Products	Recycled As
Steam	Energy
Ashes	Road construction material
Scrap	Metal industry components

Type of Dump Products	Recycled As
Dump (decomposition) gas	Electricity
Organic waste	Compost

stronger, margins are getting thinner, legislation is becoming stricter, and customers place higher demands on the services they receive. There are several concurrent developments that are causing this fiercely competitive market. The government is withdrawing from the physical treatment of waste and is concentrating more on environmental legislation and controlling compliance with the rules. Waste treatment is now strictly carried out by specialized companies, which may originate from the local domestic market or may come from a foreign country. Foreign participation has become possible due to the rapidly liberalizing European waste treatment market. The specialized companies are no longer only the traditional waste disposers. More and more, national and international energy companies are joining the act. Also, there is an obligation for governmental agencies and cities to put large waste treatment jobs out to bid within the European market. All these developments increase competition significantly in the waste treatment market.

Many waste treatment companies are reacting to these developments by merging with other companies or by setting up strategic partnerships. In this way, they can offer services for treatment of all types of waste—become a "one-stop shop" for waste treatment—and increase convenience to customers.

Establish a Consistent Responsibility Structure: Making the Change

While the external environment was changing rapidly, AVR experienced several internal developments, which threatened its ability to react agilely. For instance, because of a number of recent acquisitions, AVR had to pay more attention to internal processes. Also, the workforce had to obtain even more skills and competencies tailored to the increasing and changing demands of the customers. This meant a stronger focus on human resources and training, which required more management time and attention.

AVR reacted to the internal and external developments by changing and streamlining the organization around its main services. AVR's services are now rendered by five divisions (Exhibit 2.8),

Exhibit 2.8   AVR's Divisions, Aligned with Types of Customers and Types of Procedures

	Customers		
Services	Governmental agencies	Waste collection companies	Industrial companies
Collection & transport	AVR Government		AVR Industry
Recycling	AVR Recycling		
Processing & disposal	AVR Waste Treatment		AVR Chemical

which are tailored to the needs of the various types of customers. There are two commercial divisions aimed at selling services to specific markets—AVR Government and AVR Industry. And there are three waste treatment divisions that specialize in specific treatment techniques—AVR Chemical, AVR Waste Treatment, and AVR Recycling. The latter three divisions work for the commercial divisions, but they can also receive waste directly from preprocessing companies. In the divisions, various business units are responsible for rendering the services or disposing of the waste (Exhibit 2.9).

This new organizational structure makes it possible for AVR to develop an integrated service called the MAMS (modular waste and environmental services) concept. Through this concept—a one-stop-shop service—AVR can take care of all the waste of its customers. Offering this kind of service means that close cooperation is needed among AVR's divisions. It also demands strict coordination over these divisions. The availability of timely and relevant information throughout the process is a critical success factor. In order to make this MAMS concept possible, AVR needs a clear picture of the responsibilities and the tasks of the several management levels in the organization. Arthur Andersen was asked to help with making the parenting style and the parenting structure of the organization more clear.

Exhibit 2.9   Overview of the Alignment between Waste Streams and AVR's Divisional Structure

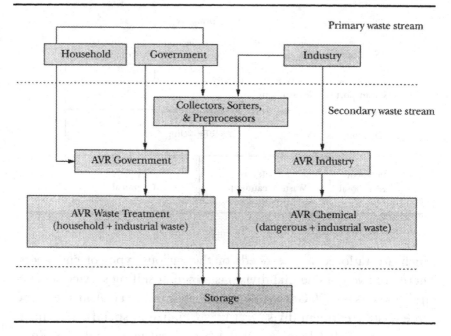

When Arthur Andersen looked at the current situation, it quickly realized that the various acquisitions and subsequent restructurings had caused some vagueness about responsibilities in the organization. Drafting a clear strategy and developing the MAMS concept had helped a great deal in setting out the course for the organization for the next few years. Still to come was improving the information flow, improving the internal controls, and aligning the vision of managers with the role and the responsibilities of corporate headquarters and its divisions.

In the old, more stable days, AVR was a centrally managed organization in which corporate headquarters had the most important voice. In the new environment, it was not yet clear who had responsibility for which process. AVR management and Arthur Andersen decided to conduct two workshops. In the first workshop, senior management at corporate headquarters discussed the current parenting style and structure of AVR. They also discussed the *desired* parenting style and structure, which would support AVR's strategic ambitions. The results of this workshop were presented to management from the divisions during a second workshop. Consensus was then reached between corporate headquarters and the divisions on the changes needed regarding the parenting style and parenting structure. All participants of this second workshop were confident that the organization would now be really ready for the future.

Shift in Parenting Style: Implementing the Change

Formerly, AVR was centrally managed because it was a small organization, which operated in a relatively stable environment. Management could still be very close to the operation and was thus well informed. However, external pressures (as described in the section "Organization's background"), which occurred at the same time that the organization was growing, meant that this central management style was no longer tenable. A change in management style was needed.

During the workshops, the different parenting styles were discussed and a choice was made for each aspect—which style best described AVR's situation for that particular style ($\sqrt{}$ in Exhibit 2.10).

With the objective of arriving at a parenting style that would enable the company to live up to the present and future challenges, AVR's management expressed a clear preference for the strategic control style. This style would enable the company to be managed in a more hands-off manner, with more entrepreneurship in the divisions. Consensus was reached that senior management at corporate headquarters and divisional management should start acting according to the guidelines of this control style ($\rightarrow$ in Exhibit 2.10).

Legislation has a high impact on the waste treatment industry. Production processes of waste management companies have to be aligned with the standards that are defined by law. Continuously changing and updated legislation mean that AVR is in a rapidly changing environment, forced to react quickly. Additionally, the external developments all compel the corporate team to stay closely

Exhibit 2.10 AVR's Parenting Styles

Definition	Strategic Planning	Strategic Control	Financial Control
Type of industry	Rapidly changing, fast growing, or ✓ fiercely competitive industries.	Mature industries and stable competitive situations.	Wide variety of industries.
Parent role	Closely involved with business unit ✓ in formulation of plans and decisions. Clear sense of direction.	Planning decentralized to business ✓ units. Parent role is checking, assessing, and sponsoring.	Insists that all decisions are "owned" by the business units themselves.
Business role	Seeks consensus with headquarters and other units for business initiatives (in line with strategic targets).	Own responsibility for strategies, plans, ✓ and proposals.	Independent entities, sometimes ✓ working together to achieve mutual benefits.
Organizational structure	Large or powerful functional staffs at ✓ center. Shared service departments (marketing, R&D, etc.).	Decentralized with focus on individual ✓ business unit's performance. Head- → quarters operates as strategic controller.	Minimal staff at the headquarter level, focused on headquarters' support and financial control.
Planning process	Resource allocation driven by requirements of long-term strategies. Planning influence of headquarters is high.	Negotiation of financial and strate- ✓ gic performance targets. Planning influence of headquarters is medium.	No formal strategic planning, process focuses on business unit annual budget and financial targets. Planning influence of headquarters is low.
Control process	Low priority on monitoring monthly financial results. Control by headquarters is flexible.	Regular monitoring of actuals against ✓ planned, on financial and nonfinancial targets. Control by headquarters is strategic.	Concentrates on financial targets ✓ and results (contracting). Control by ← headquarters is strictly financial.
Value creation focus	Creation of new business units for long-term business development.	Long-term strategies and goals of ✓ the business units (facilitating + coordinating).	Operating improvements and financial control.

involved in the strategic directions of the various divisions and business units. Budget planning can be decentralized to lower levels with control and sponsorship from the corporate level.

Although all divisions have their own clients, a situation that makes them relatively independent from each other, the MAMS concept forces the divisions to work closely together. It also ensures that information flows over divisions so that business units are not hampered in their activities.

Today, there is still a relatively large staff at the corporate center as a remnant from the centralized past. In the near future, this staff will move to the divisions because the main operational processes take place at that level. Corporate staff will then be decreased.

The new, more decentralized structure of AVR gives the divisions and the business units more accountability for their own planning and control processes. Although there is still a heavy emphasis on looking at detailed financial figures, in the near future this will shift to a more hands-off control by corporate headquarters. The recently introduced balanced scorecard will get a central place in the review process between corporate headquarters and the divisions. Finally, the value creation process is initiated and controlled by the divisions and the business units themselves, focusing on strengthening their own organizations.

Another Shift?

Changing circumstances almost caught up with all the hard work described in the preceding sections. External developments in the waste industry and internal developments at AVR moved so rapidly that within two years AVR's management had to take another good, long look at the organizational structure and the corresponding parenting style.

An analysis was made of the product-market combinations AVR offered. It turned out there were several overlaps in the products, and in the related business activities, that the divisions carried in their portfolio. Also, the characteristics of some of AVR's target markets were virtually the same, and some of AVR's clients bought services from several divisions. These findings prompted another analysis, this time of the internal processes. Several opportunities to improve the efficiency of these processes were found, mainly by grouping related processes together. It was decided that the concept of Porter's value chain would be introduced, resulting in a new setup of the divisions (Exhibit 2.11). In future, similar clients are to be grouped, and the chain of processes needed to service these customer groups will consequently also be clustered. There is one account manager per customer to take care of relations with that customer and to manage the processes needed to service that particular customer. This new setup should better support the MAMS concept.

After arriving at a consensus about the new setup, management looked again at the parenting style. The conclusion was that the choice of strategic control was the right one for the success of the new organizational setup. This is because in this setup, management of the divisions needs to be empowered to be able to react quickly to the demands of their customers and the process chain. It was decided to go ahead with the implementation of the new managing style throughout the performance management process: authority will be delegated, and information supply will be aligned and customized to the requirements of the chosen parenting style.

Exhibit 2.11   AVR's New Organizational Setup, with a Focus on Grouping of Customers and Grouping of Related Processes

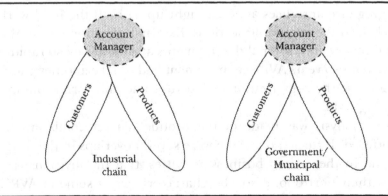

Shift in Parenting Structure

The workshops led to the realization that AVR's current situation involved a hybrid mix of parenting structures. This mix consisted of the "contact executives," "shared responsibilities," and "matrix" structures as detailed in Exhibit 2.12.

The current status is best described by the "contact executive" structure (Exhibit 2.13). Two corporate senior managers each have the responsibility for two divisions. It is the senior managers' job to make sure that enough information about their divisions is shared with the other senior managers at corporate headquarters and that directives from the senior management team are communicated to their divisions. Because of the relative newness of the organizational structure, in practice, these senior managers are quite involved in the day-to-day operations of their divisions and the underlying business units. However, the senior management team is of the opinion that divisions have to take a stronger and more visible role in managing and controlling their underlying business units in the near future. This will move AVR more toward the "shared responsibility" structure. The MAMS concept makes yet another structure viable— the "matrix" structure. Because AVR is divided into customer-oriented and product-oriented divisions, there is a strong need for a matrix organization to ensure that the customer-product relations are managed well.

The changing organizational setup forced AVR's management team to also take another look at the parenting structure (Exhibit 2.14). Because there are now two main organizational chains, each with a great deal of autonomy, the management team decided that the contact executive structure is the best suited choice.

The process of deciding the best parenting style and parenting structure was by no means an easy process. Next to the regular workload, which was ever increasing because of the dynamics of the industry, management had to attend workshops and management team discussions. These commitments took time and demanded flexibility because, during the process, things happened that made it necessary to look again at the choices made. This second look resulted in the decision to stick to the original choice with respect to

Exhibit 2.12   AVR's Current Mix of Parenting Structures

Definition	Simple Reporting	Contact Executives	Divided Parenting			Duplicated Parenting
			Existing Business vs. Corporate Development	Shared Responsibilities	Matrix	
Organization structure	Single parent level above business units.	Portfolio specialization of individuals within a single parent level.	Two parent levels: one for development and one for parenting portfolio.	Two parents both with active role in influencing businesses.	Parents on two dimensions: regional and product/brand/service grouping.	Multiple parenting levels.
Company size	Small companies with few business/units.	Mostly medium- to large companies.	Mostly medium- to large companies.	Mostly large companies.	Large companies.	Very large companies.
Relation business unit with corporate	Direct formal and informal contact with corporate.	Formal contact with corporate. Frequent informal contact with contact executives.	Direct formal and informal contact with second parent layer.	Formal contact with corporate for strategic and budget control. Regular contact with division.	Direct relationship with different parenting groups for different purposes.	Repetition of basic tasks, at different levels of aggregation.
Advantages	Simplicity.	Single parent level.	Parent close to important business issues.	Distinct roles for divisional and central levels.	Specialization of parenting.	None.
Disadvantages	Difficult to expand.	Lack of clarity about position of contact executives.	Duplication risk.	Overlap of influence on business units.	Lack of clarity/excessive overlap.	Cash/time costs of duplication not justified by additional value creation.

Exhibit 2.13   AVR's Current Parenting Structure: Two Senior Managers Are Contact Executive for Two Divisions

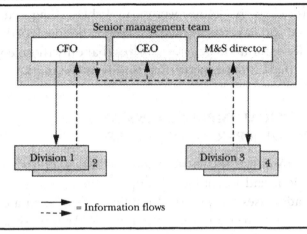

Exhibit 2.14   Logical Choice for a Contact Executive Structure in the New Organizational Setup

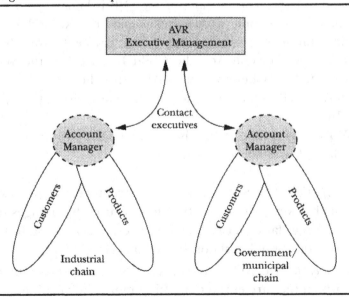

the parenting style but to amend the originally chosen parenting structure(s). In the end, management felt it was a worthwhile process because clear guidelines were established along which AVR's performance management process could be designed and installed. AVR senior management realizes that only those companies will survive that can restructure as rapidly as the market changes.

CASE: PRACTICAL IMPLICATIONS OF UPDATING SVB'S PARENTING STYLE

This case study describes an organization that, as a result of a major reorganization, had to change and update its parenting style. The case study addresses the practical implications of such a change in style, for the organization and its managers. Arthur Andersen has assisted the organization in choosing the parenting style needed to manage the organization in the twenty-first century.

Organization's Background

The social security bank SVB is the oldest authority in the Netherlands which implements laws and regulations concerning social security and welfare. The product of the SVB is benefit payments to over four million people within and outside the Netherlands. The authority administers, among other things, payments from the General Retirement Pension Act, the Child Benefit Act, the Widow's Pension Act, the Asbestos Victim Act, and the Chronically Sick Support Act. SVB's main activities are depicted schematically in Exhibit 2.15.

SVB's strategy is to administer the benefit payments in an effective, lawful, and efficient manner:

- ○ *Effective:* The SVB organizes its structure and processes in such a way that new instructions, caused by changes in laws and regulations, can be administered, according to the demands of the legislator, in a client-friendly way.
- ○ *Lawful:* The SVB pays its clients exactly the amount to which they are entitled, nothing more and nothing less, in a timely manner.

Exhibit 2.15   Simplified Overview of SVB's Main Activities

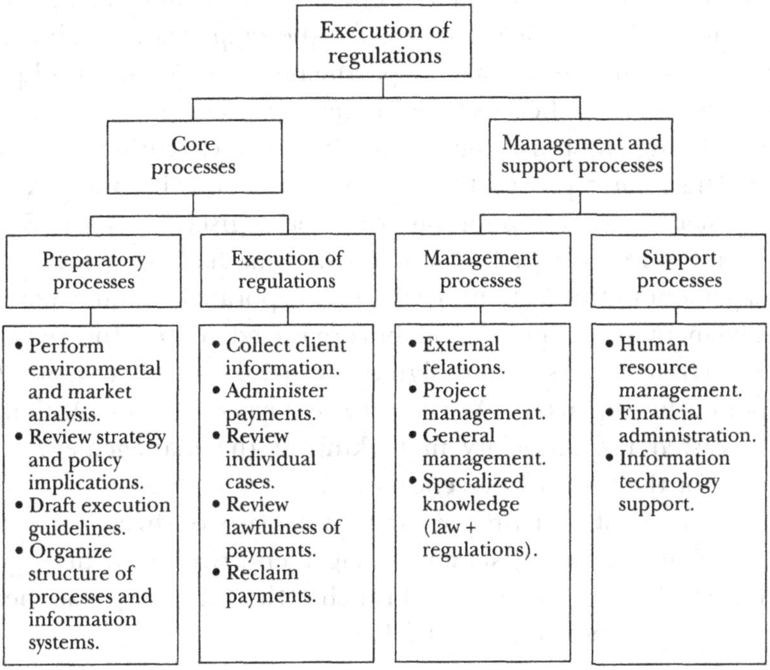

Execution of regulations			
Core processes		**Management and support processes**	
Preparatory processes	Execution of regulations	Management processes	Support processes
• Perform environmental and market analysis. • Review strategy and policy implications. • Draft execution guidelines. • Organize structure of processes and information systems.	• Collect client information. • Administer payments. • Review individual cases. • Review lawfulness of payments. • Reclaim payments.	• External relations. • Project management. • General management. • Specialized knowledge (law + regulations).	• Human resource management. • Financial administration. • Information technology support.

○ *Efficient:* The SVB performs its activities in a cost-efficient way.

SVB was established in 1988 as the result of a merger between various labor counsels and the predecessor of the SVB. The purpose of the merger was to make the execution of the social security laws more efficient and more standardized. However, the parties in the merger did not have the same management tools and techniques and were still autonomous. This resulted in regulations that were by no means uniformly implemented in the 23 districts of the newly founded SVB.

Since the merger, the SVB has been working diligently on its unification: an organization in which regulations are executed in a standardized, uniform manner. Considerable investments were made in knowledge management, employee quality, and information technology. The 23 districts were combined into nine branch offices. The unification process has been a major operation that demanded a lot of attention and energy from senior management and that entailed radical changes for the employees. During this period only parts of the staff departments at corporate headquarters were adjusted because senior management gave priority to standardizing and to raising the quality of the execution of regulations. This choice proved to be a good one, and the organization has gained a good reputation with the legislator. When SVB's processes were more or less settled, the time had come for senior management to think about how SVB's corporate headquarters and management functions should be organized in the future. SVB asked Arthur Andersen to design a new management structure for corporate headquarters. As part of this project, Arthur Andersen also assisted the authority in looking at the management style needed for the twenty-first century.

The current structure of the SVB consists of three layers: the board of management; senior management, who each manage a part of SVB's portfolio; and the branch offices and corporate headquarters departments (Exhibit 2.16).

Exhibit 2.16   SVB's Three Organizational Levels and Two Control Levels

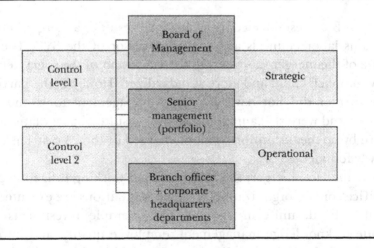

The SVB is governed by the board of management (BoM), which is responsible for managing the SVB as a whole, with the main focus on strategic planning and execution (level 1 in Exhibit 2.16). The BoM consists currently of three senior managers: the president-director and two vice presidents. Each senior manager is responsible for part of SVB's portfolio, which means each manages several of the processes described in Exhibit 2.15. The operational execution of these processes takes place in the branch offices and in the departments, located at corporate headquarters (Control level 2 in Exhibit 2.16).

Establish a Consistent Responsibility Structure: The Final Piece of the New Organization

After the major parts of the unification were completed, the SVB reviewed its management style. It turned out that it had become a hybrid, having characteristics of all three parenting styles: financial control, strategic control, and financial planning.

SVB operates in a relatively stable environment. The extensive and voluminous social security laws (General Retirement Pension Act, Child Benefit Act, Widow's Pension Act) do not change frequently, and consequences of potential changes in the social security legislation can in general be anticipated ahead of time. This stable environment, together with the major impact of the reorganization and the subsequent unification, allowed the SVB to be centrally organized, with senior management holding a tight grip on the execution of the processes at the branch offices. Corporate headquarters needed a large influence on the rest of the organization in order to safeguard the quality of the processes. The departments at corporate headquarters were responsible for designing the core processes and for monitoring their execution by the branch offices. This meant that branch offices did not have much say in the strategic development process of the SVB. Their main influence was on operational deployment of the strategy and operational planning of their activities.

The SVB is a production organization, which means that the contribution of senior management mainly consisted of ensuring that operational processes were performed efficiently and effectively. This, combined with the work involved in guiding the unification process, meant that senior management had to focus on achieving financial targets and improving the operational core processes, leaving little room and time for strategy development (Exhibit 2.17).

The BoM was of the opinion that such a hybrid style was not desirable for managing the authority in the twenty-first century. Consistency in parenting style and consistency in the performance management processes were needed to deal with the following major challenges that the authority would be facing in the near future:

- ○ Society is individualizing rapidly, with people getting more independent. This means that the social security laws and regulations will be tailored more and more to the individual needs of clients. This also means a higher level of contact between employees from the SVB and the clients, for which an increased client orientation is needed. The individualization also gives SVB the opportunity to solicit for the assignment of the processes related to new regulations.

- ○ The available workforce throughout Europe is expected to reduce significantly in the next few years. Also, the young people who are available are better educated and more mature and independent than young people used to be and will, therefore, look for empowered jobs. The SVB has to be the kind of employer that can attract these new people and retain current employees. It also requires a coaching attitude from senior toward junior management.

- ○ New forms of information technology, like the Internet, will change the traditional ways of dealing with clients. This also means that the SVB has to invest not only in new technology but also in knowledge management to increase the organization's capacity to think of new ways to execute regulations in efficient ways.

- ○ Supervision from the legislator will increase in the near future. There will be increased pressure to be more cost

Exhibit 2.17   SVB's Hybrid Mix of Parenting Styles

Definition	Strategic Planning	Strategic Control	Financial Control
Type of industry	Rapidly changing, fast growing, or fiercely competitive industries.	✓ Mature industries and stable competitive situations.	Wide variety of industries.
Parent role	Closely involved with business unit in formulation of plans and decisions. Clear sense of direction.	✓ Planning decentralized to business units. Parent role is checking, assessing, and sponsoring.	Insists that all decisions are "owned" by the business units themselves.
Business role	✓ Seeks consensus with headquarters and other units for business initiatives (in line with strategic targets).	✓ Own responsibility for strategies, plans, and proposals.	Independent entities, sometimes working together to achieve mutual benefits.
Organizational structure	✓ Large or powerful functional staffs at center. Shared service departments (marketing, R&D, etc.).	Decentralized with focus on individual business unit's performance. Headquarters operates as strategic controller.	Minimal staff at the headquarter level, focused on headquarters' support and financial control.
Planning process	Resource allocation driven by requirements of long-term strategies. Planning influence of headquarters is high.	Negotiation of financial and strategic performance targets. Planning influence of headquarters is medium.	✓ No formal strategic planning, process focuses on business unit annual budget and financial targets. Planning influence of headquarters is low.
Control process	Low priority on monitoring monthly financial results. Control by headquarters is flexible.	Regular monitoring of actuals against planned, on financial and nonfinancial targets. Control by headquarters is strategic.	✓ Concentrates on financial targets and results (contracting). Control by headquarters is strictly financial.
Value creation focus	Creation of new business units for long-term business development.	Long-term strategies and goals of the business units (facilitating + coordinating).	✓ Operating improvements and financial control.

efficient, while at the same time maintaining the high level of quality in the execution of the regulations.

○ The performance management process has to be adapted to the increased need of SVB's managers for nonfinancial, integrated information from the departments and the branch offices in order to produce better analyses.

○ Increased clarity about the roles and responsibilities of the various organizational and management levels in the organization is needed to be able to react with agility and flexibility on local and SVB generic developments. This might mean that the execution of supporting processes will be more integrated with the core processes.

Choosing a New Parenting Style: The Practical Implications

After the analysis, several workshops were held with the board of management, members of the project steering committee (in charge of the analysis), and Arthur Andersen consultants. Consensus was reached on strategic control as the future parenting style. The following considerations were made in this respect:

○ *Relatively predictable environment.* SVB expected the environment to stay relatively stable, with minor competition. Changes that may have a strategic impact could be detected at an early stage.

○ *Role and added value of senior management as board member and as individual manager.* In the light of the developments described in the previous section, the BoM had to focus more on developing long-term strategic guidelines and plans and on making the effects measurable. The execution of these strategic plans should be done by branch offices and departments, under the responsibility of the senior portfolio managers.

○ *Planning and control process.* The effects of strategic and operational plans had to be made measurable by means of financial and nonfinancial indicators, and the effects should be tracked with exception and action reports.

○ *Organizational structure.* Policy-making activities should stay concentrated at corporate headquarters. Branch offices should get more autonomy in planning and executing the operational processes.

Changing from a hybrid style to a uniform style had some important implications: roles, responsibilities, and activities had to be examined and, if necessary, changed (Exhibit 2.18). A consistently applied strategic parenting style has several consequences for the roles of the various organizational and management levels, as depicted in Exhibit 2.19.

There will be a clearer separation between the role of senior managers as board members and as portfolio managers. As board members, they will have to spend more time on setting strategic guidelines, making long-term plans, and managing external relations. This means that the time they currently spend on operational management activities will reduce significantly. As portfolio managers, they are responsible for the translation of the strategic plans into operational plans and for subsequent execution of these plans. The responsibility for the actual realization of the various plans is placed at lower organizational levels: departments and branch offices. Senior managers, in their role as portfolio manager, are accountable for the results of their portfolio to the BoM as an entity.

In the current planning process, setting financial targets is an important event. However, the renewed interest in strategic planning requires the use of financial and nonfinancial indicators. After all, the targets that have to be achieved are both financial and nonfinancial.

With regard to the organizational structure, there will be a shift from an influential corporate headquarters toward a limited number of specialist managers at headquarters. The departments and branch offices will in future translate strategic plans into operational plans themselves. At the same time, the BoM will need more strategic support and also highly skilled staff members to perform the "lookout" function that is necessary for quick response to any new regulations or modifications to existing regulations.

Exhibit 2.18   The Change to One Consistent Parenting Style Means Changing Several Aspects

Definition	Strategic Planning	Strategic Control	Financial Control
Type of industry	Rapidly changing, fast growing, or fiercely competitive industries.	✓ Mature industries and stable competitive situations.	Wide variety of industries.
Parent role	Closely involved with business unit in formulation of plans and decisions. Clear sense of direction.	✓ Planning decentralized to business units. Parent role is checking, assessing, and sponsoring.	Insists that all decisions are "owned" by the business units themselves.
Business role	✓ Seeks consensus with headquarters and other units for business initiatives (in line with strategic targets).	✓ Own responsibility for strategies, plans, and proposals.	Independent entities, sometimes working together to achieve mutual benefits.
Organizational structure	✓ Large or powerful functional staffs at center. Shared service departments (marketing, R&D, etc.). →	Decentralized with focus on individual business unit's performance. Headquarters operates as strategic controller.	Minimal staff at the headquarter level, focused on headquarters' support and financial control.
Planning process	Resource allocation driven by requirements of long-term strategies. Planning influence of headquarters is high.	Negotiation of financial and strategic performance targets. Planning influence of headquarters is medium. ←	✓ No formal strategic planning, process focuses on business unit annual budget and financial targets. Planning influence of headquarters is low.
Control process	Low priority on monitoring monthly financial results. Control by headquarters is flexible.	Regular monitoring of actuals against planned, on financial and nonfinancial targets. Control by headquarters is strategic. ←	✓ Concentrates on financial targets and results (contracting). Control by headquarters is strictly financial.
Value creation focus	Creation of new business units for long-term business development.	Long-term strategies and goals of the business units (facilitating + coordinating). ←	✓ Operating improvements and financial control.

Exhibit 2.19   New Role of the BoM and the Related Planning and Control Flows

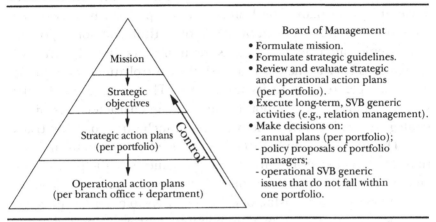

Board of Management
- Formulate mission.
- Formulate strategic guidelines.
- Review and evaluate strategic and operational action plans (per portfolio).
- Execute long-term, SVB generic activities (e.g., relation management).
- Make decisions on:
  - annual plans (per portfolio);
  - policy proposals of portfolio managers;
  - operational SVB generic issues that do not fall within one portfolio.

A Single Parenting Style?

The choice of a single management style is a matter of principle. In practice, there will be instances in which it is probable and maybe even necessary to deviate on certain aspects from the chosen management style. There are two main types of deviations:

○ *Incidental deviations.* These deviations can occur at all times. The why and the how of the temporary deviation must always be made clear to the organization. Usually, when the situation has normalized, the organization will return to the originally chosen management style.

○ *Structural deviations.* These deviations force a structural adaptation of the parenting style to better satisfy the specific needs of the organization. Whether a structural deviation from the chosen style is needed has to be assessed regularly by senior management.

The following two examples illustrate the differences in types of deviation. The first example discusses the need for an incidental deviation. The regular reporting shows that one branch office performs unsatisfactorily, in relation to important performance indicators.

The senior manager, who is in charge of the portfolio in which this branch office is placed, will therefore ask that branch office to make an action plan. The branch office's performance is closely monitored for improvement by means of instituted action reporting to the senior manager. As soon as the indicators show that the performance is back at the desired level, the control attention of the senior manager returns to its usual level. This is an example of a senior manager who temporarily uses some characteristics of the strategic planning style to help get the branch office back on track.

The second example discusses the need for a structural deviation. The starting situation is much the same as in the previous example: The performance of one of the departments at corporate headquarters is unsatisfactory. The responsible senior manager asks the department for an action plan to improve its performance. However, after a certain amount of time, there are still no signs of improvement. The situation gets even worse: other departments also start to perform significantly below target. The problems are spreading, and solving them can no longer be the responsibility of just the senior manager. At this stage, the BoM has to step in because risks are mounting that can affect the entire organization. The senior manager is asked to hand in an action plan and provide action reporting and to inform the BoM of the progress in relation to the improvement plan. A consequence might be an organizational or a portfolio reshuffle or even a change to the strategic planning style for quite a while for this portfolio, until the problems are structurally solved.

By choosing one single parenting style, the SVB expects to achieve several important benefits:

○ *Transparency of roles and responsibilities.* There will be more clarity about how senior managers operate toward the various organizational levels in their roles as respective board members and as portfolio managers. Because of this clarity, which extends also to the other management levels in the organization, managers are better able to focus on specific activities. Also, it will be easier to discuss and to agree on the way to monitor the organization's strategy and operational processes.

○ *Transparency of information.* There is a direct link between the planning and control process and the demands made on it by the chosen parenting style. This will lead in the management reporting process to transparent and accessible information for all management levels.

○ *Trust of the organization in management.* Management and control are accomplished based on agreements known to everyone involved. This condition makes the management process more predictable and diminishes the element of surprise. It also has a positive effect on the organization's trust in the way management operates.

KEY POINTS

☑ Trust in management requires consistent behavior. Therefore, the roles and responsibilities of each management level must be clear, and the chosen management style must be applied consistently throughout the performance management process.

☑ Choosing a parenting style and a parenting structure defines and clarifies the relation between the organizational structure (roles and responsibilities) and the performance management process.

☑ The parenting style stipulates the extent to which corporate headquarters influences the strategic planning and operational control processes on lower levels in the organization.

☑ The parenting structure stipulates the way in which the control process between corporate headquarters and the division and its underlying business units is structured.

☑ An organization can set clear and strict strategic guidelines and targets, making expected strategic performance from the divisions and the business units explicit and measurable.

☑ Every management level has to stick to the chosen and communicated parenting style and structure—consistently "walk the talk."

NOTES

This chapter is based on the theory of M. Goold, A. Campbell, and M. Alexander, as described in their book *Corporate Level Strategy, Creating Value in the Multibusiness Organization,* John Wiley & Sons, 1994.

1. Collins, J.C., and J.J. Parras, *Built to Last,* HarperCollins, 1997.
2. Hartz, S., PR Newswire, 12-8-1998.
3. Goldsmith, W., and D. Clutterbuck, The Winning Streak Mark II, How the World's Most Successful Companies Stay on Top through Today's Turbulent Times, Orion Business, 1997/1998.
4. Goold, M., A. Campbell, and M. Alexander, *Corporate Level Strategy, Creating Value in the Multibusiness Organization,* John Wiley & Sons, 1994.

3

Balance Long-Term and Short-Term Focus

CHALLENGE OF A DUAL FOCUS

Nine out of ten companies do not succeed in implementing their strategy.

R.S. Kaplan[1]

Managers at visionary companies simply do not accept the proposition that they must choose between short-term performance or long-term success. They build first and foremost for the long term while simultaneously holding themselves to highly demanding short-term standards.

J.C. Collins and J.I. Parras[2]

Although high-performing companies have a very strong emphasis on delivering promised results today, they maintain an equal emphasis on delivering results tomorrow.

W. Goldsmith and D. Clutterbuck[3]

Why do CEOs (chief executive officers) fail? *Fortune* magazine published an interesting article about research into the reasons that prominent CEOs were fired from their jobs.[4] According to the article, the main reason was not that these CEOs did not have a strategic vision for their organization or that they did not know which way to go with their organization, but that they failed to execute this strategic vision. These CEOs could not get their organization and its employees energized enough to turn vision into reality. In the end, these CEOs could not deliver the results they promised.

The results of the *Fortune* research tie in with other recent research[5] that indicates that organizations have difficulty in turning their strategic intent into activities that achieve strategic goals. Although they often have a good strategic plan in place, more than half of the companies polled said they were not able to articulate and to communicate this strategy effectively throughout the organization. And 90 percent of the companies polled confessed they were not able to deliver on their strategy consistently. However, the majority of companies polled confirmed that clear, action-oriented deployment of their strategy significantly influences their success.

Translating strategic plans into short-term action plans seems to be the main difficulty for organizations. The strategy development process is too focused on calculating future financial results in detail, instead of planning for value creation and looking at the effects of nonfinancial indicators on the business. Strategic plans do not sufficiently focus on concrete actions to achieve the strategic targets. Strategic targets are often not clearly defined and measurable. Furthermore, the link to the short term (i.e., the budget) is often obscured. The budget process is mainly an exercise of revisiting last year's budget, instead of truly connecting the strategy with the budget.

So the challenge of balancing a long-term focus with a short-term focus has to do with the execution of actionable strategic plans: long-term plans should be translated into realistic short-term actions. Long-term expectations should be more realistic so that organizations (finally) deal with the "hockey stick" effect. This infamous effect causes organizations to make financial projections for future years that are unrealistically positive and that do not have a really clear basis—the projections are "coming out of nowhere." The increased focus on the future should also become apparent in the balance between nonfinancial indicators, which look to the future, and financial indicators, which look at the past.

SPLIT THE STRATEGIC PLAN

> An organization needs continual enhancements of its existing products and services, but also some breakthrough products or services.
>
> *R.S. Kaplan*[6]

Strategic plans often focus simultaneously on new growth opportunities and on running business improvement opportunities. "Running business" relates to the current operations of an organization. However, strategic actions to achieve both types of opportunities are different in nature and require different time spans and resources. Often, it is difficult for managers to distance themselves from the day-to-day operations, causing the innovative part of the strategic plan to get shortchanged.

To allow an organization to better focus on each type of opportunity, the strategic planning process is split into two different processes, each of which addresses an opportunity separately (Exhibit 3.1).

The Strategic Growth Planning Process is focused on actions that create breakthrough growth opportunities. The Growth Action Plan focuses on new markets, new or revised products, and new distribution channels. The Growth Action Plan results in new sources of revenue for an organization in the next one to five years.

The Strategic Operational Planning Process is focused on actions that improve the running business. The Operational Action Plan focuses especially on cost reductions and on sales growth with current products and current market channels. The Operational Action Plan leads to incremental improvement in the next one to two years.

Splitting the strategic planning process into a profitability part and a growth part entails two separate processes, different timing of the plans, and involvement of different people (mainly manufacturing in the profitability part and marketing and sales people in the growth part); resulting in two distinct strategic action plans.

Now, the link between the strategic plan and the budget can also be adapted and improved. As shown in Exhibit 3.2, the budget for the first year (Y1) is created from a combination of the latest

Exhibit 3.1   Strategic Development Process Leads to Two Separate
Plans: Growth Action Plan and Operational Action Plan

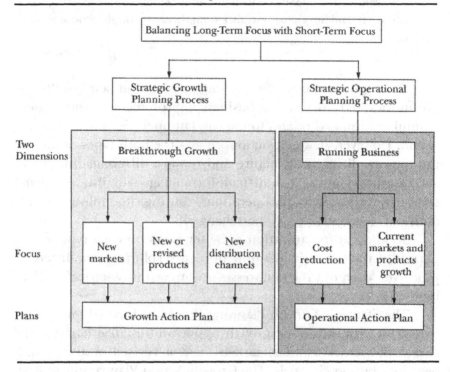

Exhibit 3.2   Budget Is Composed from Input from the Latest Status of
the Organization Plus the Results of the Strategy Development Process

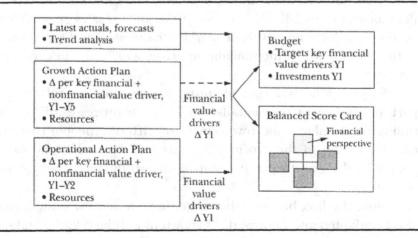

actuals, the latest forecasts, a trend analysis, and input from the Growth Action Plan and the Operational Action Plan.

For each action in the Growth Action Plan, the expected positive effects on the key value drivers are calculated for the next five years. These effects are each given a certain value Δ (delta). Also, the resources needed to execute the proposed growth actions are calculated. The same is done for the actions in the Operational Action Plan (now for the next two years), resulting also in Δ values and needed resources. The Δ values for Y1 are combined with the trend analysis done on the latest actuals and the latest forecasts to arrive at the budget for the coming year. This means that the development of the two strategic action plans have to follow each other closely in time, because Δ values from both plans are needed for the budget calculation. The needed resources are also combined, to arrive at the investment plan for the coming year. The Δ values are also an input for the balanced scorecard's financial perspective for the coming year.

A split in strategic attention for improvement of the running business and for strategic growth opportunities has the benefit of forcing management to focus more on each of the aspects of strategic planning, thus enhancing the content of these plans. Management has to think "out-of-the-box" to look for new growth opportunities and subsequently has to clearly articulate strategic actions solely aimed at achieving these opportunities.

Management gets a clear view of the boundaries of the strategic goals because the Operational Action Plan represents the minimum performance required of the business. Because the budget is based mainly on the Δ values from the Operational Action Plan, the budget targets are more realistic. They no longer include the uncertainties that are embedded in targets derived from ambitious growth plans. Therefore, the hockey stick effect cannot happen anymore. In the budget, some Δ values from the Growth Action Plan can be incorporated, but only for those growth actions that already have an effect in Y1 (the dotted arrow in Exhibit 3.2). Because of the nature of growth actions, most effects are expected over the longer term, when they will become part of the Operational Action Plan anyway. Conversely, the Growth Action Plan represents the realm of possibilities, the turnover and revenue that can be obtained when the organization's creativity gets going.

SPLIT THE FORECAST

The forecasting process proves to be for many organizations a time-consuming, overly detailed, and overly complicated number crunching exercise. The forecasts lack relevance because organizations try to forecast in great detail over a long period, which is difficult and results in many inaccuracies because of the nature of looking into the future. This makes managers, used to detailed accurate figures, uncomfortable. Because of the diminished relevance, the forecasting process lacks ownership in the organization, and therefore nobody wants to be accountable for the forecasts.

The first step to remedying these problems is that an organization should forecast only on a limited set of key financial indicators. These are the key value drivers that have been identified in the strategy development process. They are also the indicators that are used in the budgeting process (see Chapter 6). An organization should only analyze the differences between forecast and budget for these key financial indicators, in order to formulate preventive actions for improving the results on these indicators.

The second step is to split the forecast into two types: short-term and long-term. At the middle of the quarter, an outlook for quarter-end is made. This short time span enhances the accuracy of the forecast. At the end of each quarter, a forecast is made that predicts four to six quarters ahead. This forecast can be used for external purposes, to give year-end predictions.

Quarterly Flash Forecast

In the middle of the quarter, a Quarterly Flash Forecast is made by the business units. This forecast is made for specific key financial indicators only. The business units might calculate more detailed predictions only for their main products to have a good basis for the flash forecast. When the forecast does not equal the quarter-end budget, the business units have to formulate short-term preventive actions, aimed at achieving the quarter-end budget.

The flash forecast can be made halfway through or at the end of the second month in the quarter, depending on the systems support available. It is made four times per year. The leading non-financial indicators are not included in the flash forecast. The Quarterly Flash Forecast is a steering mechanism for the business units, meant to formulate and to execute preventive actions early enough to still improve the quarter-end results and to stay (at least) within the contingency area (see Chapter 6 for a description of contingency areas).

The division totals the flash forecasts of all the business units and adds division specific items to put together a divisional fore-cast for quarter-end. If this forecast does not equal the divisional quarter-end budget, the division has to formulate short-term pre-ventive actions, aimed at still achieving this budget. These actions can be consolidated from the business unit actions or can be sepa-rate actions.

The division reports the divisional flash forecast and the pre-ventive actions to corporate headquarters. The Quarterly Flash Forecast will be discussed with corporate headquarters only when the forecast hits the corporate intervene area (see Chapter 6 for a description of intervene areas).

Strategic Rolling Forecast

At the end of the quarter, a Strategic Rolling Forecast is made by the business units. This forecast is made for those key financial and nonfinancial indicators that are also used in the budgeting process (see Chapter 6). The Strategic Rolling Forecast is a prediction of the next four to six quarters and always includes a year-end result prediction. Bases for the forecast are the quarter-end actuals, last-year trends, the sensitivity analysis from the strategic planning pro-cess, and an analysis of environmental circumstances.

The Strategic Rolling Forecast is made three times per year, at the end of the first, second, and third quarters (Q1, Q2, and Q3).

The forecast in Q4 is replaced by the new budget. The Strategic Rolling Forecast is a steering mechanism for the business units and divisions, meant to formulate and to execute preventive actions aimed at achieving the year-end results and at safeguarding future profitability (after the year-end).

When determining the rolling forecast, the business unit first has to look at a worst-case forecast, meaning the results to be expected when no preventive actions are undertaken (*Worst* in Exhibit 3.3). Secondly, the business unit has to look at a best-case forecast, which gives the expected result when all preventive actions have been successfully executed (*Best* in Exhibit 3.3). Based on these two forecasts, the business unit determines a realistic forecast, which lies between the worst-case and the best-case forecasts (*Realistic* in Exhibit 3.3) and is based on an appraisal of the

Exhibit 3.3   Determining a Realistic Forecast from the Best-Case and Worst-Case Scenarios

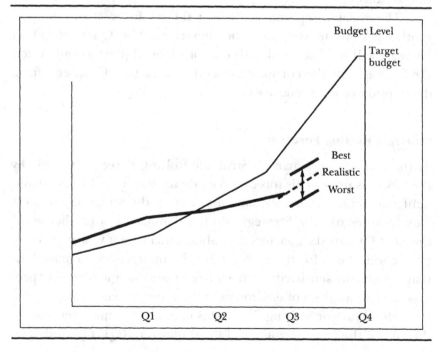

number of actions anticipated to be successful and of their impact on the expected result. In this way, the business unit obtains information for the analysis about the forecast, required in the quarterly report, and higher management levels can get a sense of the realism of the forecast.

When the forecast does not equal one or more of the next four to six quarter-end budgets (both for the financial and the nonfinancials), the business units have to formulate long-term preventive actions aimed at still achieving the quarter-end budgets. The analysis of the forecast needs to decide which factors can be totally or partly influenced by the business unit, giving a root cause analysis of the lagging forecast (based on value-based management and the sensitivity analysis made during the strategic planning process) and describing how the factors can be improved. Every Strategic Rolling Forecast is accompanied by an explanation of the difference between the rolling forecast made last quarter for this quarter and the actuals of this quarter.

The division totals the forecasts of all business units and adds division-specific items to arrive at the divisional Strategic Rolling Forecast. If this forecast does not equal one or more of the next four to six quarter-end budgets, the division has to formulate long-term preventive actions aimed at still achieving these quarter-end budgets. These actions can be consolidated from the business units' actions or they can be separate actions.

The division reports the divisional Strategic Rolling Forecast and the preventive actions in the regular quarterly forecast report to corporate headquarters. The year-end prediction in this forecast is used for external purposes (e.g., during the quarterly meeting with analysts). The forecast is discussed with corporate headquarters when the forecast hits the corporate intervene area (see Chapter 6 for a description of intervene areas).

Splitting the forecast into two types, short-term and long-term, forces the right amount of attention on long-term strategic forecasting. Also, the effort of forecasting is spread because the Quarterly Flash Forecast is performed before (and separate of) the Strategic Rolling Forecast. The forecasting itself takes less

time because it is based on a limited number of key financials (for
both types of forecasts) and key nonfinancials (for the rolling forecast); and input from the strategic planning process (the value-
based management and sensitivity analysis) helps to make the root
cause analysis.

The focus of forecasting is no longer on the absolute accuracy
of the forecast, because as long as a business unit or division stays
within its contingency area, it is not that important that every detail
is right. If the forecast is outside the contingency area or if the forecasted trend is downward in the direction of the intervene areas,
the focus is again not on the forecast accuracy but on the formulation and execution of preventive actions.

BEHAVIORAL IMPLICATIONS

Underlying the split strategic plan and split forecast lies the requirement for an action-oriented attitude. Focus is no longer on
the accuracy of the numbers neither in the strategic plan nor in the
forecast, and not even in the budget. Focus is on how an organization is going to achieve the projected targets on the key value drivers. This requires an attitude shift from being a "bean counter" to
being an action taker.

Detailed financial projections are out, and high level projections for financial and nonfinancial indicators are in. Each action
plan is captured in a Δ value, and management focus is aimed at realizing this value. If the total target is not achieved, analysis is made
of which Δ value, and thereby which action, has not been executed
properly or did not have the desired effect. This is done not only
for financial indicators, but also for nonfinancial indicators. Managing with nonfinancials requires trust. As a manager recently said
to us: "We manage the financials with nonfinancials; this is how
much trust we put in them." In the monthly reports of this manager's organization, the nonfinancials in the balanced scorecard
are regarded as key in managing the business.

Working with clear action plans and Δ values creates openness. Managers can no longer hide in detailed numbers, and the
hockey stick effect has also disappeared. The strategy development

process and the subsequent budgeting and forecasting processes have become business functions where the rubber really hits the road!

CASE: SPLITTING THE STRATEGIC FOCUS AT EMERSON ELECTRIC CO.'S COPELAND CORPORATION

Introduction

This case study describes elements of a management process that is at the heart of Emerson Electric Co.'s consistently high-level performance. This highly disciplined management process is ingrained in the company's culture and enforces performance driven behavior throughout the organization. We visited Copeland Corporation, one of the largest divisions of Emerson, and looked at how Emerson's management process works and how it drives performance in a specific business unit, Copeland Corporation. The purpose of this benchmark visit was to identify strong management practices which we then could tailor into a framework which is beneficial to other organizations.

Company Description

Emerson Electric Co. was founded in St. Louis, Missouri, in 1890. Today, Emerson is a global manufacturer with operations in more than 150 countries and a strong and consistent record for market and technology leadership across five business segments: Heating, Ventilating, and Air Conditioning; Electronics and Telecommunications; Process Control; Industrial Automation; and Appliance and Tools. The company's financial performance shows sales of US $14.3 billion in 1999. The company is widely recognized for its management excellence, and its history of strong financial performance and shareholder return. Its record of continuous growth is highlighted by 42 consecutive years of increased earnings per share, and 43 consecutive years of increased dividends per share. Emerson achieves its impressive performance through a carefully developed and deployed management process among the business segments, and strategic planning to position the company for emerging market opportunities. For instance, the company has recently repositioned itself through mergers and acquisitions to supply many electronics and telecommunications products necessary in today's networked economy.

The success of Emerson's management process is exemplified by Copeland Corporation, a wholly owned division since 1986 and part of the growing Heating, Ventilating, and Air Conditioning business segment. Copeland Corporation is the world leader in the design and manufacturing of compressors and condensing units, supplying virtually every well-known maker of commercial and residential air conditioning equipment, as well as the major names in refrigeration. Copeland Corporation is the largest company in Emerson's Heating, Ventilating, and Air Conditioning business segment, which experienced an 11 percent growth in sales in 1999 to US $2.4 billion. The market for Copeland Corporation products is international and the company services it through 23 plants and 18 sales locations (Exhibit 3.4).

Exhibit 3.4   Simplified Organizational Chart of Emerson Electric and Copeland Corporation

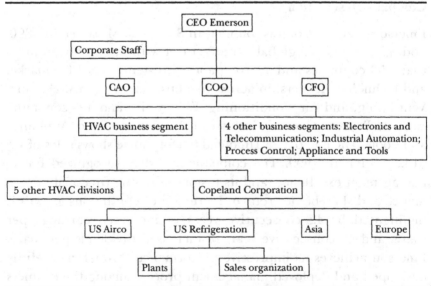

Establish a Clear Responsibility Structure: Emerson Guides Copeland

The executive team at Emerson headquarters formulates strict strategic guidelines and targets for key financial performance indicators for all its divisions. The targets set for these indicators are specific to each business and are established by Emerson after consultation with the divisions. Examples of these indicators and targets include operating profit and inventory turnover which should improve by more than x percent over the next x years. The targets are very challenging and cannot be achieved by simply improving current business compared to last year. Therefore, divisions and businesses are forced to generate new ideas and actions, aimed at both cost improvement and revenue growth.

The company is frequently able to set the same set of indicators for a division for a number of years. This consistency keeps the organization focused on the same value drivers and improves comparability of performance over the years.

These strategic guidelines make expected strategic performance explicit beforehand and divisions and businesses can therefore use them as input for their own strategic planning. The divisions and businesses can spend all their time on formulating strategic actions that should help achieve the strategic targets, instead of trying to renegotiate targets with the executive team of headquarters. This focus increases the quality of the strategic action plans and initiatives.

With the expected performance established, the divisions set to the task of planning how to reach the targets. First each division presents its plan and the corporate headquarter managers' role is to challenge assumptions within the plans. Throughout the process, the executive team truly wants to understand the plans and underlying actions so they devote considerable attention to reviewing and testing the logic and feasibility of each plan. Once the plans have been approved, the executive team limits the review of the operations to four formal control moments per year. Besides these regular reviews, special reviews are held for capital investments or for changes in strategic direction. The divisions have their own responsibility in executing the strategic plans. On a monthly basis, each division reports financial and operational information to the executive team. Emerson's parenting style can be characterized as strategic control, which is applied consistently throughout the company (see Exhibit 3.5).

Balance the Long-Term with the Short-Term: Split the Strategic Plan

Strategic plans normally focus simultaneously on new growth opportunities and on running business improvement opportunities. *Running business* relates to the current operations of a company. However, strategic actions to achieve these different types of opportunities are different in nature, have different time spans, and require different resources. Emerson, therefore, splits the strategic planning process into two different, separate processes. This allows the company to better focus on each type of opportunity and to improve the overall quality of the strategic plans.

The strategic *profitability* planning process is focused on actions that improve the running business. The process focuses on cost reductions and on sales growth with current products and existing market channels. This process leads to incremental improvement. The strategic *growth* planning process is focused on actions that create breakthrough growth opportunities. The process focuses on new markets, on new distribution channels, and on new or revised products. This process results in new sources of revenue for a company in the next five years.

Splitting the strategic planning process into two subprocesses means there are two distinct, separate processes with different timing of the resulting strategic plans, even though many of the same division executives are involved in both planning processes. It also means involvement of different people in each subprocess and results in two separate strategic action plans.

Profitability Planning Process. The business, in close cooperation with division management, prepares action plans and supporting financial data aimed at realizing the strict targets set by the executive

Exhibit 3.5   Emerson's Parenting Style

Definition	Strategic Planning	Strategic Control	Financial Control
Type of industry	Rapidly changing, fast growing, or fiercely competitive industries.	✓ Mature industries and stable competitive situations.	Wide variety of industries.
Parent role	Closely involved with business unit in formulation of plans and decisions. Clear sense of direction.	Planning decentralized to business ✓ units. Parent role is checking, assessing, and sponsoring.	Insists that all decisions are "owned" by the business units themselves.
Business role	Seeks consensus with headquarters and other units for business initiatives (in line with strategic targets).	Own responsibility for strategies, plans, ✓ and proposals.	Independent entities, sometimes working together to achieve mutual benefits.
Organizational structure	Large or powerful functional staffs at center. Shared service departments (marketing, R&D, etc.).	Decentralized with ✓ focus on individual business unit's performance. Headquarters operates as strategic controller.	Minimal staff at the headquarter level, focused on headquarters' support and financial control.
Planning process	Resource allocation driven by requirements of long-term strategies. Planning influence of headquarters is high.	Negotiation of financial and strate- ✓ gic performance targets. Planning influence of headquarters is medium.	No formal strategic planning, process focuses on business unit annual budget and financial targets. Planning influence of headquarters is low.
Control process	Low priority on monitoring monthly financial results. Control by headquarters is flexible.	Regular monitoring of actuals against ✓ planned, on financial and nonfinancial targets. Control by headquarters is strategic.	Concentrates on financial targets and results (contracting). Control by headquarters is strictly financial.
Value creation focus	Creation of new business units for long-term business development.	Long-term strategies and goals of ✓ the business units (facilitating + coordinating).	Operating improvements and financial control.

team. The manufacturing department spends 75 percent and Marketing and Sales spends 25 percent of its planning time on the profitability planning process.

The input from all businesses is combined into a profitability plan for the division. The plan's layout is highly standardized by using a mandatory set of forms. This enables easy consolidation of the business plans and also makes it possible for the executive team to compare the divisional plans (Exhibit 3.6). The profitability plan has a horizon of 11 years: looking back 5 years, looking at the current year, and looking forward 5 years. In this way, Emerson can keep track of past and future performance. Differences in the results forecasted last year have to be explained, building a historical trail of key performance indicators, obtaining in-depth knowledge of the quality of the plans, and learning the reasons behind these deviations. People at Emerson call this "an amazing display of data hanging together." An added advantage of this constantly looking backward and forward is the reduction of the hockey stick effect because managers always have to explain deviations to the executive team.

Then, the divisional profitability plan is submitted to headquarters where it is analyzed by corporate analysts. Based on this analysis, early warning signs (such as issues and questions) are communicated to the divisions so they can prepare themselves for the upcoming review by the executive team. This profitability meeting takes place three to four weeks after submission of the profitability plan. The meeting takes place at the divisional location and lasts two days. The chief operating officer (COO), other members of the executive team, and analysts represent headquarters. Divisional management and functional managers from the

Exhibit 3.6   Steps in the Profitability Planning Process

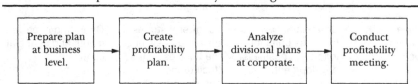

businesses (mainly manufacturing) are present to explain the divisional plans.

During the meeting, the division gives an overview of the strategy, major initiatives, and key issues it is currently facing. Marketing information underlying the plans, such as sales quantities and pricing assumptions, is discussed, and the plans of the engineering, purchasing, manufacturing, and human resources departments are reviewed. Finally, the financial summary is examined.

The executive team tests and challenges the plans based on its knowledge of the division and industry, as well as on the results of the corporate analysis. The purpose of this testing is to ensure that the actions defined by the division are sufficiently rigorous to achieve the targets set by the executive team. The financial numbers are conservative because they represent the minimum performance expected from the division and its businesses. At this stage in the process, the plans usually contain in principle too many actions. Division and business managers present and defend the parts of the profitability plan for which they are responsible. This process results in a final list of action items and also builds a strong ownership of the plans. Emerson's culture is aimed at creating this ownership: "You have to stand up to talk about how to fix things. You might not be the cause of the problem, but you are still expected to fix it." When the plan is approved, a manager has gained the trust and the ownership of the project. However, as one manager put it: "If you waiver, they will grill you." This leads to redoing or improving the plan. The deep and thorough understanding of the business by the executive team is critical to the acceptance of its advice by the divisions and business units.

Growth Planning Process.   Divisional marketing managers start the growth planning process by collecting information from the Strategic Business Review. This review consists of a series of strategic brainstorming sessions conducted between Emerson's chief executive officer (CEO) and each division. Key issues facing the division and its business units are addressed and out-of-the-box ideas are generated. Topics include new markets, synergies between divisions, and potential acquisitions. At the end of these sessions, key actions are identified to be further pursued. Another source of information is the Corporate Planning Conference which is conducted once a year. This conference looks at the overall Emerson strategy, examining the past five years and the next five years. Approximately 400 operating executives, representing all divisions, attend the conference, which is lead by the CEO. The overall strategic direction resulting from this meeting is input for the divisional planning process.

With the collected information, market intelligence storylines are built. These explore new ways to create double-digit revenue growth. The storylines result in specific action plans, aimed at achieving each identified revenue opportunity. The action plans are collected in the Growth Plan, which must show that sales volumes can increase aggressively. It takes approximately four to six weeks with 10 team members to create the plan. The plan has standardized, obligatory financial exhibits that form a basis for benchmarking and analysis. The time span of the growth plan is 11 years, including the current year and looking back five years and forward five years.

Corporate headquarters then conducts a Growth Conference with each division to discuss the Growth Plan in detail. This meeting is attended by the executive team including the CEO, divisional management, and a representation of business management (mainly marketing and sales). The conference consists of presentations and dynamic discussions. The meeting begins with a brief overview of the business, its environment, and its strategy. Then five to seven Growth Plans are presented.

During the conference, the atmosphere is rather challenging because the CEO questions the plans and the underlying assumptions quite aggressively. The division and the businesses have to withstand this without wavering. As one manager explained: "Emerson is not about asking questions but about issuing challenges." The meeting results in a list of funded Growth Plans and related actions, such as further investigations of ideas or programs.

Integrating the Profitability Plan, the Growth Plan, and the Budget. The two plans set the boundaries of the business. The Profitability Plan focuses on the minimum performance required and feasible for running the business. The Growth Plan gives the realm of possibility.

These different outlooks cause a natural tension—the Profitability Plan has to be conservative, whereas the Growth Plan has to stretch and be aggressive. Balancing the two is a challenge.

Growth initiatives that have been tested in the market place and have been judged to be ready for implementation become part of running the business. The expected results of these growth actions are incorporated in the next profitability action plan and become real targets at that time.

The first year of the Profitability Plan is the basis for the budget. The Growth Plan is not part of the budget and is managed separately. Thus, the budget only represents the actual business, making budget targets firm. These targets represent the minimum performance level and do not include new, unproven plans for which results are unsure. All divisions explicitly build in margins to deal with deviations from the budget. All parties understand that the budget cannot be forecasted with exact accuracy, encouraging Emerson to accept deviations to a certain extent. The margin is expressed in a percentage and is negotiated with the executive team.

Because the budgeting process occurs in the last quarter of the year and the Profitability Meeting is held at some time during the first three quarters of the year, the division faces a time delay between the two events. During this time, changes in both external and internal factors can occur. If these changes result in deviations between the Profitability Plan and the budget, the executive team requires a detailed explanation from the division. Emerson calls itself an analytical company that "manages by numbers, not by anecdote." The company values its ability to compare the budgets to the predictions.

Enforce Performance Driven Behavior: "Stern but Fair"

Emerson pays a lot of attention to embedding performance driven behavior into its culture. Through its very rigorous, integrated, and disciplined management process, the company has established a culture that is characterized by challenges, coaching, accountability, ownership, and action.

Performance Reviews.   Emerson spreads performance reviews over time. Because the different meetings do not take place concurrently, divisional and business unit management has more time to prepare and to analyze the information ahead of schedule. The main performance review is called the President's Council (see Exhibit 3.7). This meeting takes place between each division and the COO midquarter, three times a year, and is mainly focused on a short-term financial review of the operations, sales, and other key financial measures. Attention is also paid to the status of activities that come from the Growth Plan. The fourth and last midquarter meeting, the Financial Review, is focused on strategic planning and target setting, and produces the budget for the next fiscal year.

During the months when no President's Council or Financial Review takes place, divisions conduct performance reviews with their businesses called Board Meetings where each business presents its performance results to divisional management. During the same months, the executive team conducts a monthly review called the President's Operation Review. This review is based on detailed monthly reports that are prepared and sent in by the divisions.

Exhibit 3.7   One Coherent Planning and Control Process

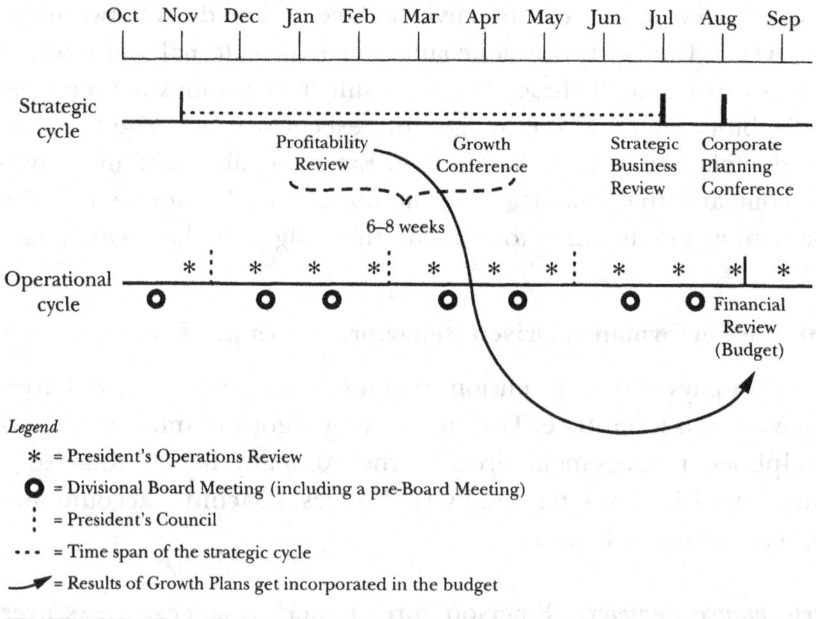

Legend

   * = President's Operations Review

   O = Divisional Board Meeting (including a pre-Board Meeting)

   ⋮ = President's Council

   - - - = Time span of the strategic cycle

   ⟶ = Results of Growth Plans get incorporated in the budget

During the performance reviews, Emerson uses so-called waterfall charts. These are matrices for key value drivers and show actual and forecasted results against the budget over a period of several months. Actuals in a certain period are compared with the forecasted results made earlier for that same period. Managers not only have to explain deviations between actuals and the budget, but also why actuals did not meet forecasted results. In this way, the executive team obtains insight into the quality of the forecasts. The company is very good at tracking variations in performance. Each performance review begins with the manager stating that this is what was agreed upon last time, this is what has changed, and this is the reason why. In case gaps exist, the manager has to explain how the gaps are to be bridged and how this will happen.

A Challenging Culture.   During the various conferences, councils, and meetings, people are challenged about the logic of their plans, actions, and assumptions. The CEO always focuses on the logic that lead managers to their conclusions, thereby forcing managers to look at all of the options. In this process, the company makes sure to "attack problems, not people." In practicality, this means that the company attracts a certain type of person, who fits in this culture.

If a manager misses a plan, higher management levels act like coaches and intervene. This coaching method is considered to be a learning process for the manager, while allowing shortfalls to be discussed openly and nonpolitically. However, divisions and businesses prefer to maintain their independence. As a manager at Copeland explains it: "You get more coaching than you want from corporate headquarters throughout the year."

One of the examples of establishing accountability is the involvement of managers in the planning process. Managers from different functions and levels not only are involved in the preparation of the plans, but also have to present and defend their part of the plan to Emerson's CEO. Another example shows that victim behavior is not easily found within Copeland and Emerson. Even when they cannot be held fully responsible for certain results, managers feel accountable and take action. There is hardly any pointing of the finger and waiting to see what will happen. For example, if a sales manager promises a client a particular delivery time that is unrealistic for the plant manager to meet, the plant manager often accepts some level of responsibility by trying to meet the expectation. This is a team responsible as much to each other as it is to its clients.

The performance management process, the accompanying culture, and the dedicated commitment to it at all levels of the organization force managers to accept responsibility and to help grow the business. Managers are encouraged to have a great understanding of their own business unit and its processes, to think aggressively in the short term, and to think strategically in the long term, all the while understanding trends, tracking differences, and bridging gaps. Some of the benefits for managers at Copeland Corporation include very clear expectations resulting in few surprises. There is also very little ad-hoc reporting, an empowering environment, and predictable performance. The drawback might be that Copeland's management process is rather time-consuming across all management levels. It also requires upper management

---

KEY POINTS

☑ Translating long-term strategic plans into short-term action plans and dealing with the "hockey stick" effect seem to be the main difficulties for organizations.

☑ The strategic planning process is split into two different processes. The strategic growth planning process is focused on actions that create breakthrough growth opportunities. The strategic operational planning process is focused on actions that improve the running business.

☑ Forecasts are only made for a limited set of key financial indicators. The forecast is split into two types: a short-term Quarterly Flash Forecast and a long-term Strategic Rolling Forecast.

☑ An action-oriented attitude is needed to focus no longer on the accuracy of the numbers but on the achievement of the projected targets on the key value drivers.

to develop a deep understanding and knowledge of the businesses. Managers typically have a long-standing record with the company. Lastly, this process might be well suited for more stable business environments as it makes incremental improvements and a rather risk-averse approach to business a success.

NOTES

1. Kaplan, R.S., De Financieel Economische Tijd, 1999.
2. Collins, J.C., and J.I. Parras, "Built to Last," HarperCollins, 1997.
3. Goldsmith, W., and D. Clutterbuck, The winning streak mark II, how the world's most successful companies stay on top through today's turbulent times, Orion Business, 1997/1998.
4. Charan, R., and G. Calvin, Why CEOs fail, *Fortune* Magazine, June 21, 1999.
5. Renaissance Solution Limited, Translating strategy into action, research rapport, 1996; Redwood, S., C. Goldwasser, S. Street, Action management, practical strategies for making your corporate transformation a success, John Wiley & Sons, 1999; and Drucker, P.F., Management challenges for the 21st century, Harper Business, 1999.
6. Kaplan, R.S., Planning Review, September/October 1994.

4

Make Value-Based
Strategies Operational

CHALLENGE OF VALUE THINKING

> Leading companies have invested time in linking strategy
> with operational performance.
>
> *H. Evans and G. Ashworth*[1]

> The Balanced Scorecard is the leading strategic performance
> management solution for aligning strategy and more effec-
> tively measuring and managing a business.
>
> *A. Arbor*[2]

In the New Economy, sources of value no longer consist only of tangible assets like financial capital and physical facilities, but increasingly of intangible assets like brand names and human
capital. In a recent research project conducted by Arthur Andersen
in cooperation with DYG, Inc., and Heathcare Forum,[3] a majority
of the managers polled said that much of the value being created in
their organizations fell outside their formal reporting systems. The
respondents indicated that their reporting systems should be
adapted to capture especially a number of sources of value creation
that are currently not or not sufficiently tracked (see Exhibit 4.1).

81

Exhibit 4.1   Results of a Survey Indicating Relative Importance of
Indicated Sources of Value Creation

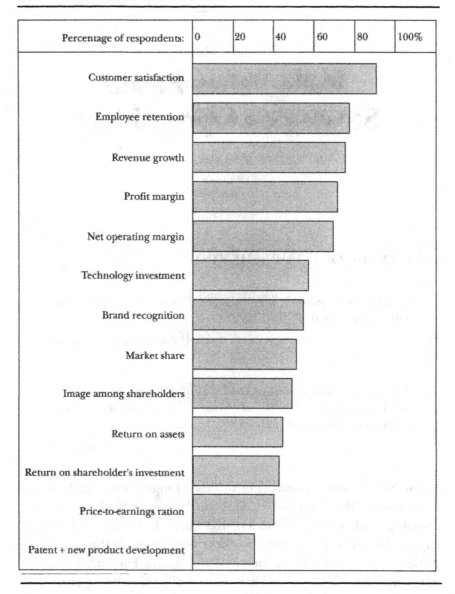

This view is reinforced by research performed by Schiemann and Linge.[4] They questioned executives on how extensively their measurement systems tracked value drivers in various types of performance areas, how often these value drivers were updated to reflect changing circumstances, and the extent to which the value drivers were used in the organization's performance management process (Exhibit 4.2). The results show a strong bias toward financial measurements.

Since 1996, Arthur Andersen has been analyzing the quality of the management information process of a number of organizations by using the so-called Management Information and Reporting Analysis (MIRA).[5] The MIRA offers a structured approach for assessing an organization's internal reporting system as used by its managers. External reporting, such as is used to inform shareholders, banks, and so forth, is not addressed. During such a review, the management reporting system under study is analyzed on the following aspects:

○ *Internal financials.* Internal financial information should provide insight into the financial state of affairs of an organization. The MIRA looks at *content* (which financial data are available and what ends up in the internal reports) and at *users* (who receives this financial information and whether it is clear and relevant for the user).

○ *Nonfinancials.* Nonfinancial information should consist of data, collected in a structured manner, on strategy deployment and on the organization's critical activities. The MIRA looks at *content* (which nonfinancial data are available and whether the data have been linked to the organization's strategy and critical activities) and at *approach* (whether nonfinancial information has been developed in a structured manner).

○ *Dynamics.* Management reporting should be the basis for a number of activities: analyzing the organization's results, decision making, action taking, and evaluating the results of the actions. The MIRA looks at *structure* (whether the reporting layout can be used for dynamic reporting) and at *use* (how managers use reporting).

Exhibit 4.2 Results of a Survey Indicating the Quality of Measurement Systems

Percent of Managers Who Believe That:	Financial	Operating Efficiency	Customer Satisfaction	People Performance	Adaptability/ Innovation	Environment/ Community
				Performance Areas		
Measurements are clearly defined.	92%	68%	48%	17%	13%	25%
Measurements are regularly updated.	88	69	48	27	23	23
Measurements are included in performance review.	98	82	76	57	33	44
Measurements are linked to compensation.	94	54	37	20	12	6
Measurements help drive organizational change.	80	62	48	29	23	9

○ *Communication.* Communication should take place in an organization by people regularly sharing information on the results across horizontal and vertical organizational boundaries. The MIRA looks at *content* (which information is shared), at *approach* (if the information is shared regularly and in a structural manner), and at *participants* (who shares information with whom).

○ *Systems support.* Information systems should provide a stable structure for quick data collection and processing, for reporting of financial and nonfinancial information, and for communication. The MIRA looks at *IT (information technology) architecture* (which IT components are being used and what the quality of these components is) and at *investments* (which IT investments have been made and are planned in the management information function).

○ *User-friendliness.* The information function should generate reports and use executive information systems that are comprehensible and user-friendly. The MIRA looks at *user-friendly reporting* (whether the reports are easy to comprehend and have the right volume) and at *user-friendliness of reporting systems* (whether the information systems are easy to understand and use).

○ *Integrity.* The information function should provide timely, reliable, and complete information in a consistent manner. The MIRA looks at *reliability* (whether the information in the reports is accurate and reliable), at *completeness* (whether any information is missing), at *timeliness* (whether information is available when people need it), and at *consistency* (whether there are any conflicting signals in the reporting).

○ *Target-setting.* An organization aims at improvement by continuously adjusting its targets for critical processes. The MIRA looks at *approach* (which methods are being used to set financial and nonfinancial targets, and have comparable—benchmark—figures of other organizations been included in the reporting) and at *relevance* (have targets been set for the right—relevant—processes).

The results of a MIRA are depicted in a Radar Diagram, in which the eight aspects just described are rated on a scale ranging from A to E (Exhibit 4.3). For each aspect, the organization's performance is compared to criteria derived from best-practice organizations throughout the world. If the organization meets most of these criteria, its score on this aspect is rated an A. The fewer best-practice criteria are met, the lower the score is. An E rating means that the organization's reporting really needs improvement on the aspect in question. A rating of C means that the performance regarding this aspect meets 40 percent to 60 percent of the criteria.

The MIRA has been performed at more than 50 organizations worldwide. They varied in size (small and big), organizational

Exhibit 4.3   MIRA Radar Diagram: Average Scores for the Management Reporting System Analyzed to Date

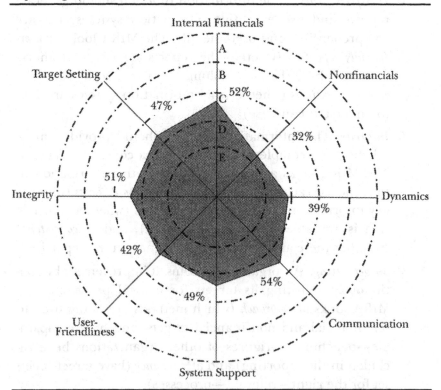

structure (holdings and independent companies), and industry (profit and not-for-profit organizations). The boundary of the filled-in area in Exhibit 4.3 depicts the average score of all the MIRAs performed to date.

Most organizations turn out to be weak on nonfinancials and dynamics, and only a few organizations score better than a C on more than two aspects. Positive points were that financial targets, specified to departments and products, were widely used and were accepted by managers as evaluation tools. The management reports were in general used for making decisions and for defining actions to improve future results. The figures in these reports were considered to be highly reliable. Managers were well informed about the organization's mission and strategy, and a lot of attention was paid to optimizing the use of information technology.

Improvement points were that more nonfinancial information could be included. Also, accountability for the results of key performance indicators could be more clearly defined, and more attention could be paid to the analysis of results and to making reports more action- and future-oriented. A lot could still be gained by linking the reporting system directly to the operational systems that generate the data, thereby decreasing the need for manual handling of the data. The user-friendliness of management reports could be improved, for example, by decreasing the volume and by using more graphics. Finally, more formal approaches could be used to set targets, for example, by using benchmark figures of other organizations. In the Appendix, a more detailed analysis of the MIRA results is given.

A Confused Picture

Taken together the results of the aforementioned research projects paints a confused picture. On the one hand, organizations want to move to more value-based, nonfinancial, leading indicators and better performance management. On the other hand, their measurement systems and performance management process are still mainly focussed on financial, lagging indicators, and organizations do not seem to be action-oriented enough!

Two recent trends that try to address this apparent conflict are the concepts of the balanced scorecard and value-based management. In the balanced scorecard, nonfinancial, leading indicators are combined with financial, lagging indicators to get a balanced overview of the organization's performance and to check whether the organization's strategy execution is still on track. In value-based management, an organization expressly looks at long-term value creation, instead of looking at short-term profit maximization.

Challenges in applying these concepts in an organization are manifold. How can we get all management levels in the organization on one page regarding the strategy? How do we make sure the strategies at the various organizational levels are aligned? Should we also align the balanced scorecards? How do we link the value-based strategy with operations, using the appropriate financial and nonfinancial value drivers? How do we derive concrete action plans, at lower levels of the organization, from the value-based strategy?

IMPLEMENT THE BALANCED SCORECARD

Monitoring financial figures may show that the adopted strategy has worked and that value was created in the past, but they do not show if this also will be the case in the future. Running an organization by monitoring only financial measurements is like driving a car by looking only in the rearview mirror. Financial measurements that show what happened in the past are called *lagging indicators*. To complement these lagging indicators, an organization also needs *leading indicators,* which forecast future results.

The leading indicators are expressed in the form of critical success factors and key performance indicators. A critical success factor (CSF) provides a qualitative description of an element of the strategy in which the organization has to excel in order to be successful. The CSF is quantified (i.e., made measurable) by a key performance indicator (KPI). The use of critical success factors and key performance indicators enables measurement, and thus control, of strategic objectives. If performance indicators that measure the execution of the strategy and the creation of value are not included in the performance management process, it will not be obvious whether strategic objectives and value creation are being achieved. Exhibit 4.4 gives an example of a CSF and KPIs.

Providing good customer service is of critical importance for an organization's success. One of the ways to provide this service is by increasing the focus on the customer throughout the organization and thereby increasing customer satisfaction. Whether customer service is satisfactory is reflected in the number of customers that repeatedly buy products or services ("repeat purchases"). Customer satisfaction can also be measured by proactively asking customers what they think of the services provided ("satisfied customers"). An important activity that helps to keep customers satisfied is responding quickly to complaints ("complaint-processing time").

The balanced scorecard is used to represent the financial and nonfinancial performance indicators in a user-friendly format. Traditionally, a balanced scorecard has four perspectives, or areas: (1) innovation of products/services or people (including learning and growth of people), (2) effectiveness of processes, (3) experience of customers, and (4) financial performance.

1. The *innovation* perspective measures how often an organization introduces new products, services, or production techniques. In this way, the organization makes sure that it

Exhibit 4.4   CSF and Its Corresponding KPIs Example

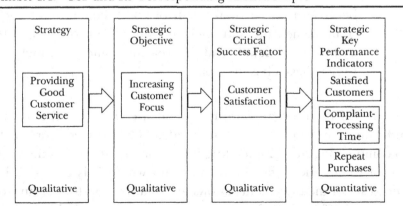

does not become complacent, that it continuously renews itself. Some organizations augment this perspective with *people* aspects. These measure the well-being, commitment, and competence of people in the organization. The people aspects measure cultural qualities like internal partnership, teamwork, and knowledge sharing, as well as aggregate individual qualities like leadership, competency, and use of technology.

2. The *process* perspective measures the effectiveness of the processes by which the organization creates value. It follows the people aspects in the innovation perspective because people impact the ability of the organization to create value by implementing and managing effective processes. The process perspective measures how effectively processes operate. It precedes the customer perspective because efficient processes make it possible for an organization to stay or to become more competitive.

3. The *customer* perspective measures performance in terms of how the customer experiences the value created by the organization. It follows the process perspective because value created by processes is only meaningful when it is perceived by the customer as being valuable.

4. The *financial* perspective measures the bottom line, such as growth, return on investment, and the other traditional measures of business performance. It is the last perspective because it is the final result of good, committed people, of implementing and operating effective processes, of the ability for renewal, and of creating value for which customers have chosen to pay.

In different organizations, the perspectives and the leading indicators can be different, but the idea of a balanced scorecard is to combine lagging and leading indicators, to give an understanding of where the organization was and where it is going. A balanced set of measurements allows an organization to measure the cause-and-effect chain by which customer and shareholder value is created. If value is created by people working on and in processes to satisfy customers and to produce financial results, then managers must be able to measure and monitor all of these perspectives of value creation to effectively manage the business.

Exhibit 4.5 gives an example of the four perspectives of a balanced scorecard, which has been enhanced compared to the traditional format with some extra columns. For each of the four perspectives, it shows the actual performance compared to budget in the center column (using traffic-light coloring); the change compared to history in the left-hand column (indicators: +, −, and

Exhibit 4.5   Balanced Scorecard Example

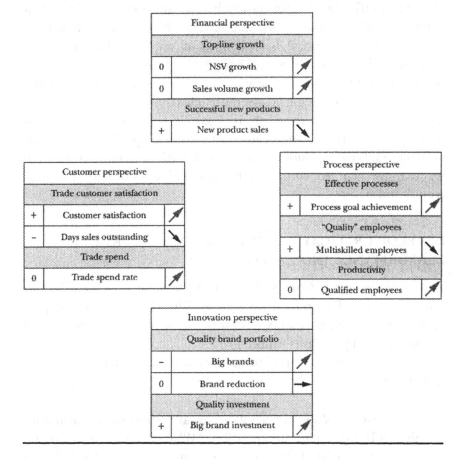

0, with traffic-light coloring); and the expected future performance in the right-hand column (indicators: ↗, →, and ↘, with
traffic-light coloring). For instance, the KPI "multiskilled employees," belonging to the CSF "quality employees" in the process perspective, could be coded blue in the middle column, meaning the
actual result is equal to budget for this period. The left column
could show a green +, meaning the result on this KPI was better this
period than last period: the organization improved. However,
there could be a red arrow pointing downward in the right column,
meaning that the organization expects to do worse next period.
This is a clear signal for the organization to act now to prevent this
from happening!

  The main benefit of managing with a combination of financial and nonfinancial information is that the use of leading, nonfinancial indicators facilitates proactive control and the ability to
take preventive action. A balanced set of key financial and nonfinancial indicators enables management to focus on the really important issues that drive business performance and to monitor the
achievement of strategic goals more closely. Using nonfinancial
information improves the analysis capabilities of managers because
they can identify the root causes of financial performance. The
nonfinancials can include external information, making it possible
for management to compare the internal results with external
trends and drivers.

DEVELOP CRITICAL SUCCESS FACTORS AND KEY PERFORMANCE INDICATORS

The development of CSFs and KPIs is at the center of the effort to
build a balanced scorecard. In this section, the development process of these measurements is described, using the performance
measurement pyramid (Exhibit 4.6).

  The performance measurement pyramid is made up of the
following:

  1. *Mission and strategy.* First, an organization has to formulate
its mission by answering the question, "*What* do we, as an organization, want to accomplish: What is our mission?" To formulate a

Exhibit 4.6   Performance Measurement Pyramid

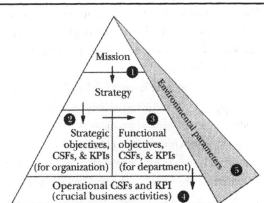

strategy, an organization has to answer the questions, "*How* are we as an organization going to achieve our mission?" and "*How* can we accomplish what we want?"

Suppose an organization has the following mission: To double in size, while retaining a socially conscious image. Possible strategies for achieving such a mission might be: (1) to make the organization focus more on customer satisfaction, (2) to develop new environment-friendly products, and (3) to sponsor local environmental projects.

2. *Strategic objectives, CSFs, and KPIs.* In order to make an organization's strategy tangible, strategic objectives need to be formulated. A strategy is often expressed in abstract terms. By formulating one or more strategic objectives, it becomes clear which activities have to be undertaken in order to implement the organization's strategy. If the organization's strategy is already expressed in specific, measurable terms, the strategy and the strategic objectives will be virtually the same.

Whether strategic objectives are being achieved can be monitored with strategic CSFs and measured with strategic KPIs (see Exhibit 4.4). These strategic measurements are included in the management reports that are used by the organization's board of directors or senior management team. Often, the balanced scorecard of an organization is composed of these strategic measurements.

For an organization with diverse activities, a complete balanced scorecard on the corporate level may not be relevant because the nonfinancial indicators cannot be meaningfully aggregated across subsidiary businesses. In that case, only a limited number of financial indicators are reported.

3. *Functional objectives, CSFs, and KPIs.* A business function or department can support an organization's mission and strategy by translating the strategic objectives into its own functional area by defining functional objectives specifically for that business function or department. The extent to which the functional objectives are achieved is monitored with functional CSF, and measured with functional KPIs (Exhibit 4.7). These functional measurements are used by managers of various functional disciplines or by middle management. The functional measurements are included in a balanced scorecard for the department.

Suppose the research and development (R&D) department of an organization translates the strategic objective "Improve customer focus" into the functional objective "Deliver more innovative research." After all, the more products that are developed that meet the customer's demands, the more satisfied the customer will be. It is critical to the R&D department, therefore, to monitor whether the department succeeds in developing enough

Exhibit 4.7   Functional Critical Success Factors and Key Performance Indicators (for an R&D Department)

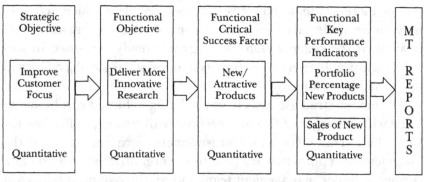

new products that are attractive to customers. Whether customers appreciate these new products can be measured by the sales of new products. Whether the number of new products developed is sufficient can be measured on the basis of their share that these new products have in the product portfolio.

Because every business function or department contributes in its own way to the achievement of strategic objectives, it is essential to determine the functional objectives for each business function or department separately. Management has the responsibility to continuously monitor whether the functional objectives and the strategic objectives are aligned. If this is not (or no longer) the case, the functional objectives need to be reformulated. This is an effective way for the organization to maintain alignment.

4. *Crucial business activities, operational CSFs and KPIs.* In addition to the mission and strategy, every organization has specific crucial business activities. A *crucial business activity* is an activity "that makes the business tick" and, for this reason, must *always* be executed in order for the business to survive, regardless of the chosen mission or strategy. The execution of crucial business activities is *monitored* by means of operational CSFs and *measured* with operational KPIs (Exhibit 4.8). These operational measurements are

Exhibit 4.8   Operational Critical Success Factors and Key Performance Indicators

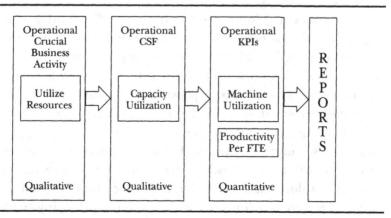

used by managers who are directly involved in the crucial business activities. The operational measurements are included in the balanced scorecard for the department.

An organization has to make optimal use of its assets to prevent product costs from becoming too high. The organization's strategy is "to bring high-quality consumer products to the market at a low price." The organization then has to watch the production costs closely so they do not become too high, resulting in a profit margin that is too small for the organization to be able to continue investing properly. This means one of the organization's crucial business activities is to produce as efficiently as possible, which translates into utilizing resources optimally. The capacity utilization of these resources has to be tracked, by measuring machine capacity and personnel capacity and by calculating the productivity per FTE (full-time equivalent).

5. *Environmental factors and environmental KPIs.* These are measurements that provide information on the environment in which an organization operates and especially on developments that are relevant to the organization. It concerns aspects over which the organization has no or very limited control, but that may have a considerable effect on the results of the organization. This is why, especially during the target-setting process for KPIs, managers have to take into account the influence of environmental factors (Exhibit 4.9). These business environment measurements should therefore be included as an extra perspective in the balanced scorecard of the organization.

Economic developments usually have a direct influence on an organization's business results and, therefore, are critical to the organization's success. Many indicators, such as salary and wage developments, inflation (and interest rates), and the accompanying consumer spending indexes, provide important input for estimating the expected turnover. If the economy grows more slowly than expected, this phenomenon may be accounted for by adjusting the target sales budget downward. If the sales manager does not succeed in realizing the adjusted target, the most obvious explanation ("We had a downward economic trend") cannot be used, and the manager has to look for the *real* causes of not achieving the target.

Exhibit 4.9   Environmental Factors and Environmental Indicators

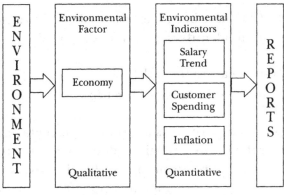

Result and Effort Measurements

The CSFs, important for tracking the results of executing an objective or a crucial business activity (the so-called *result CSFs*) can be determined by answering the following questions:

- O What will be the result when we achieve the objective successfully?
- O What will be the result when we execute the crucial business activity successfully?

The CSFs, important for tracking the efforts that are critical in executing an objective or a crucial business activity (the so-called *effort CSFs*), can be determined by answering the following questions:

- O What do I absolutely need to achieve the objective successfully?
- O What do I absolutely need to execute the crucial business activity successfully?

There are many efforts that may lead to achieving the final result but only those most critical need to be monitored. A *critical effort* is that effort that is most likely to lead to achieving the desired result.

After the CSFs have been identified, we need to answer the following questions to identify the KPIs for each CSF:

○ How do I measure the CSF?
○ How can I see the result of the CSF?

A KPI is usually defined as a ratio or a percentage. After all, a figure of 10 for the KPI "Complaints" does not mean much in itself. We can only value the result properly when it is expressed in percentages, for example: 10 complaints per 1000 customers (1 percent) or 10 complaints per 100 customers (10 percent).

Exhibit 4.10 depicts the strategic objective "Better development and use of personnel." The final result of this objective is to have qualified personnel, which means personnel of a higher quality than before (*result CSF*). Whether the organization's personnel are indeed better qualified can be measured by the number of personnel that is actually capable of achieving the agreed objectives for the current year. The number of personnel that is in the wrong job position can, for example, indicate the absence of well-qualified personnel. Whether personnel quality has improved compared to the previous year can be measured by comparing the results of the aforementioned KPIs of the present and the previous year. One of the main efforts to improve personnel quality is providing training for employees (*effort CSF*). Whether employees get enough training can be measured with the number of training hours per employee and the final education or skill level achieved by an employee.

It is important to distinguish between result CSFs and effort CSFs. If only the efforts are monitored, it may happen that the wrong activities are performed very well. After all, it is not about "doing things right" but about "doing the *right* things right." Therefore, managers should always keep the final result in mind in order to be certain that their efforts lead to the desired result. But the final result is not the only thing they have to think about, as it may take quite some time before the final result is achieved. Managers have to observe if they are still on track to the final goal. They can do this by measuring whether their efforts are having the desired

Exhibit 4.10   Means to Track the Development and Use of Personnel, by Using Result and Effort CSFs and Corresponding KPIs Example

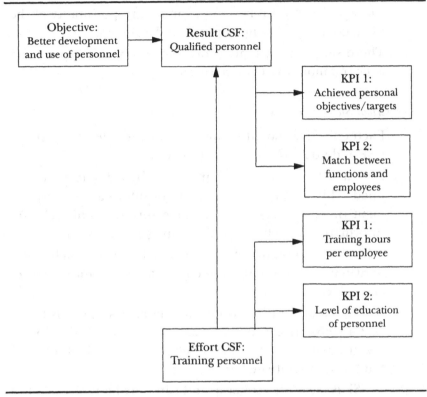

effect. Getting the interim results allows them to adjust their activities, if necessary.

During the development process of objectives, CSFs, KPIs, and targets, there are a number of quality criteria to ensure that the developed objectives, measurements, and targets are specific, measurable, relevant, and time-related. These criteria are:

Objectives

○ An objective has to describe an activity that leads to the desired final result.

○ An objective has to be defined in concrete, not abstract, terms.

- An objective must express action. This is done by using a verb with an active connotation (e.g., "Improve . . .").
- An objective must relate to the area of responsibility of the manager for whom the objective is developed.
- There should be a limited number of objectives per manager (no more than five to seven).

Critical Success Factors

- Each objective should be measured with at least one result CSF and no more than two effort CSFs.
- For each CSF, no more than three KPIs should be developed. This is to limit the amount of information, development time, and costs and to make sure that only relevant information is included in the management reports.
- CSFs should contain not only financial information but also nonfinancial information to ensure a well-balanced view of each objective.
- A CSF is a qualitative notion that describes in words how a certain objective can be measured. Thus a CSF is never quantitative (e.g., not "the number of satisfied customers," but "customer satisfaction").
- A CSF is clear and concise, and can only be interpreted in one way.
- A CSF describes only what has to be measured, not what the direction or the value of the result should be (e.g., not "high personnel quality," but "personnel quality").

Key Performance Indicators

- The definition of a KPI should be concise, easy to understand, and complete (i.e., every term used in the definition is described) and worded so that the definition can only be interpreted in one way.
- A KPI should be measurable in practice. An organization should have the procedures, means, and (some) information systems to make this possible.

○ The definition of a KPI is preferably composed of a numerator and a denominator; percentages provide more valuable information than absolute numbers.

○ The definition of a KPI contains a reporting frequency (monthly, quarterly, yearly).

Targets

○ The target for a KPI should be realistic: a manager should consider the target to be achievable.

○ The target for a KPI contains a certain range. Corrective action should only be taken when the result is not within this range (positive or negative).

○ The target for a KPI is determined together with the manager who is responsible for the result on the indicator in question. This is to enhance support for the target within the organization.

During the development process of KPIs, a distinction should be made between *management* information and *operational* information (Exhibit 4.11).

Operational information gives an overview of the individual activities within the organization. Operational information enables an organization to decide which activities should be redirected or adjusted and which follow-up steps should be taken, showing the consequences in time and money. The process indicators that are used in operational information should not be included in management reporting. Process indicators are usually derived from detailed operational data that generally become available after an activity has been completed. An example of a process indicator is "the delivery time of a *single* order."

Management information, based on CSFs and KPIs, is information that is generated at a higher, more abstract level than operational information. Management information has a signaling function: informing management if a certain process is heading in the right direction, and if performance is in accordance with agreements and targets that have been made previously. The operational KPIs that

Exhibit 4.11 Operational Information as the Basis for Operational CSFs and KPIs

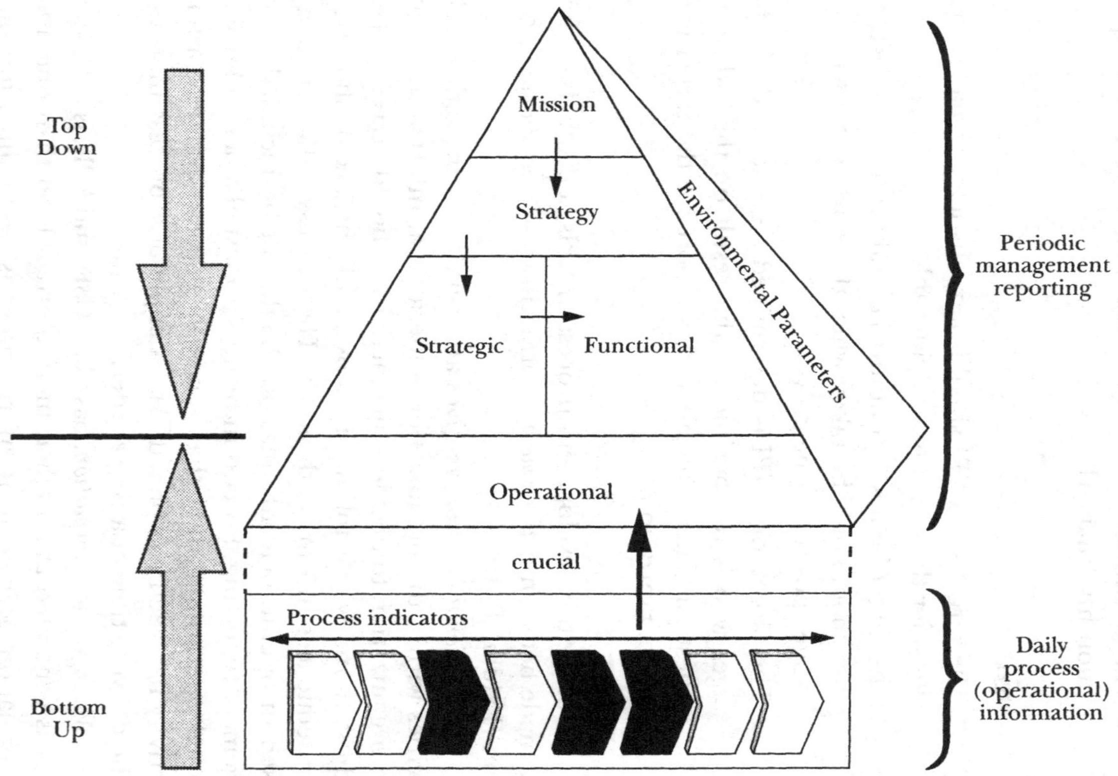

102

are used in management information are often compiled of process indicators. Management information reporting is produced periodically, usually once a month. If managers have not achieved their targets, management generally asks for an analysis of the underlying causes for the failure. For this purpose, the operational data that were mentioned earlier need to be accessed in an ad hoc manner. An example of an operational KPI that consists of process indicator data is "the *average* delivery time of orders."

Performance Measurement in a Corporate Structure

In the previous section, a description was given on how to develop CSFs and KPIs, using the performance measurement pyramid. The pyramid methodology applies to organizations with a relatively uncomplicated organizational structure. In organizations with a corporate headquarters—division—business unit structure, the methodology can also be applied, with some adaptation due to the different accountability setup in a holding structure, for example, a multinational (Exhibit 4.12).

Exhibit 4.12   Relationship between Corporate, Division and Business Unit Measurements

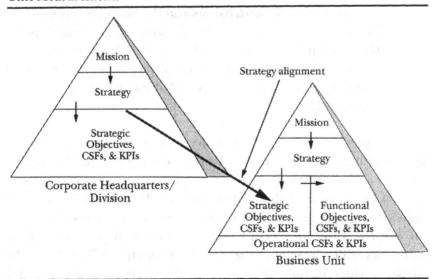

Formulating CSFs and KPIs for organizations with a corporate headquarters—division—business unit structure takes place in almost the same way as for companies with a more simple organizational structure. First, the mission and the strategy are formulated: "What do we want to accomplish as an organization?" Then, the strategic objectives are defined: "How are we going to accomplish our mission?" Defining the strategic measurements, however, follows a more complex methodology:

○ The performance on the strategic objectives is monitored by means of strategic CSFs and measured by means of strategic KPIs. These strategic measurements are developed for and used by corporate headquarters. Because the divisions and the business units often have an autonomous organization, with their own mission and strategic objectives, they will have their own pyramid. Divisions and business units have their own specific strategic CSFs and KPIs, which are used by the management teams of the divisions and the business units. In the case of a corporate structure, like a multinational, there are numerous pyramids: one for corporate headquarters and one for each division and business unit.

○ The strategies of the divisions and the business units should be aligned with the strategy of corporate headquarters. In the same manner, alignment is needed between the measurements developed at the corporate headquarters level and the measurements developed at the divisional and business unit levels.

In summary, the strategic objectives of corporate headquarters determine the direction of the divisional objectives. Between a division and its business units, a similar relationship exists. Objectives of business units should therefore be derived from divisional objectives, which are derived from corporate objectives. In a similar way, the different sets of CSFs and KPIs are aligned: the corporate CSFs/KPIs determine the direction for the CSFs/KPIs of the division, which in turn determine the direction for the CSFs/KPIs of the business units (Exhibit 4.13).

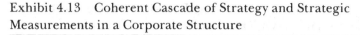
Exhibit 4.13   Coherent Cascade of Strategy and Strategic
Measurements in a Corporate Structure

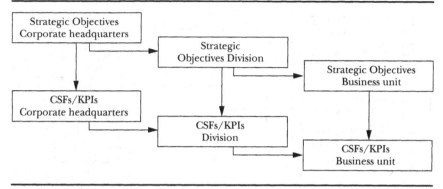

If the just described methodology is used, every division will have its own set of CSFs and KPIs to track its strategy and crucial business processes (1 and 2 in Exhibit 4.14). These measurements are then input for the management report of the division (3) and used by divisional management to steer and control the division (4). In addition to the regular financial reporting of the division to corporate headquarters (5), only the most important indicators— those that give the best insight into the status of the division and that are regularly used by divisional management—are reported on a regular basis to corporate headquarters (6). In this way, corporate headquarters only receives the most important information. Corporate headquarters then uses this information to supervise the division (7). Only when the division does not meet its targets will corporate headquarters step in and start coaching and controlling the division (8). In the same manner, the division can supervise its business units.

Link between Parenting Styles and the Balanced Scorecard

As described in Chapter 2, there are three main parenting styles: financial control, strategic control, and strategic planning. The choice of parenting style dictates the influence that corporate headquarters has on the strategic planning and operational control

Exhibit 4.14   Overview of the Reporting Flow—from Lower to Higher
Management Levels in the Organization

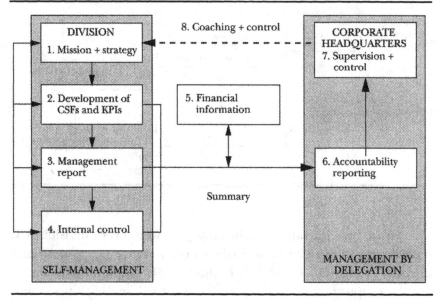

processes of the divisions and the business units. This in turn dictates the content and the level of detail of the information flow
from these divisions and business units to corporate headquarters.
To make a link between a specific parenting style and the shape of
a matching balanced scorecard, we can adapt Weber's model,[6]
which matches types of corporate structures with types of balanced
scorecards, by putting in the types of parenting styles and adapting
the types of control (Exhibit 4.15).

In the strategic planning style, corporate headquarters plays an
active and dominant part in the strategy development process of the
divisions and the business units. It is also heavily involved in deploying and monitoring (the execution of) the strategy. Because corporate headquarters has to stand close to divisions and business units,
it needs the same type of information from all the lower organizational units. The scorecard indicators of divisions, business units,
and corporate headquarters are so similar that these can be consolidated into one balanced scorecard. This consolidated scorecard is

Exhibit 4.15   Influence of Corporate Headquarters on the Content and Use of the Balanced Scorecard, Depending on the Parenting Style

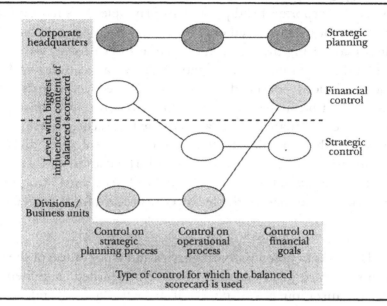

checked in detail by corporate headquarters, a process that makes it possible to intervene on lower levels. In the strategic planning style, corporate headquarters has the dominant influence on development and use of the balanced scorecard.

In the strategic control style, corporate headquarters issues strategic guidelines but divisions and business units make their own strategic plans independently. These plans are evaluated and prioritized by corporate headquarters. Divisions and business units define both short- and longer-term financial and nonfinancial objectives, which are put in "local" balanced scorecards. These indicators are then collected (but not consolidated!) into one scorecard and complemented with indicators that show the added value of corporate headquarters. This scorecard is checked on a high level by corporate headquarters. In the strategic control style, corporate headquarters has the dominant influence on the development of the scorecard. Divisions and business units have the dominant influence on the use of the balanced scorecard.

In the financial control style, the responsibility and authority to develop strategic plans is totally delegated to divisions and business units. Corporate headquarters in principle does not evaluate these plans but is interested only in whether divisions and business units are achieving the financial targets as forecasted in the strategic plans. Corporate headquarters manages a portfolio of businesses and does not need complete balanced scorecards from divisions and business units nor from itself. Corporate headquarters can use the financial indicators in the local scorecards as input to evaluate the portfolio. In the financial control style, divisions and business units have the dominant influence on the strategic and the operational use of the balanced scorecard. Corporate headquarters uses part of the balanced scorecard for financial control purposes.

The links between parenting styles and types of use of the balanced scorecard just described should be regarded as guidelines. Every organization has to decide if a particular link indeed fits with its management style and with the guidelines and the agreements made between the various organizational levels.

LINK QUALITY FRAMEWORKS WITH PERFORMANCE MEASUREMENTS

In the past few years, many organizations have started total quality management projects. The purpose of these projects is to improve the organization's overall quality with respect to operational processes, procedures, standards, and documentation. In many cases, quality frameworks provide, as it were, a manual in which areas are indicated that need to get structural attention to improve the organization's quality permanently. The best-known quality frameworks are the European Foundation for Quality Management model (EFQM) and the Baldrige model. The challenge organizations are facing is how to link these quality frameworks with the CSFs, KPIs, and the balanced scorecard.

The EFQM model (Exhibit 4.16) provides a tool, first, for determining where the organization stands at a certain moment with

Exhibit 4.16   EFQM Model

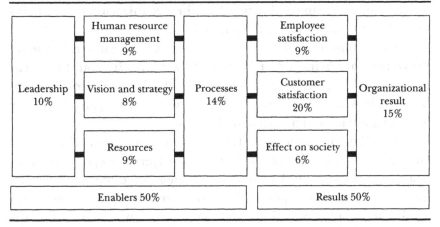

its actual results in comparison to its quality targets and, second, for indicating how these results can be improved. The model has nine components that are divided into two categories. The first category consists of the *results* that the organization has achieved with respect to employee satisfaction, customer satisfaction, the effect on society, and the overall financial results. The second category includes the so-called *enablers*, that is, the activities that have enabled the organization to achieve results. Examples of enablers are: good leadership and good human resource management, a clear vision and strategy, availability of resources (such as financing), and efficient processes. The degree of alignment between the enablers and the results categories determines the success of the organization. The idea behind the EFQM model is that an organization should pay attention in various degrees to the components of the model (shown as percentages in Exhibit 4.16).

The components of the enablers category determine *how* the results are achieved. Leaders should inspire people in the organization to strive for continuous improvement by showing their dedication to establishing an improvement culture. Human resource management strives for making optimal use of employees' knowledge and motivation. The use of other assets (financial, technological, and physical) should also be optimized. All processes should be managed and controlled well and should be continuously improved. As a starting point for this, the organization's vision and strategy have to be clearly formulated.

The components of the results category determine *what* the organization has achieved or is about to achieve. It should be clear what employees, customers, and society think about the organization and how satisfied they are. The results of an organization have both a financial and a nonfinancial aspect.

The Baldrige model (Exhibit 4.17) is composed of seven related areas that influence each other in different ways. Good leadership is followed by development of clear customer and market focuses and strategic plans. Processes are carried out and managed, and people are trained and developed. This entire process is supported by sufficient information and analysis in order to lead to good organizational results. Just as in the EFQM model, the idea behind the Baldrige model is that attention should be paid to all components of the model. If this is not done structurally, an organization cannot consistently achieve good results.

Organizations that have implemented one of these frameworks have an urgent need for good information about each of the components of the framework. They want to have answers to questions like "Do we have good human resource management?" or "Do

Exhibit 4.17   Baldrige Model

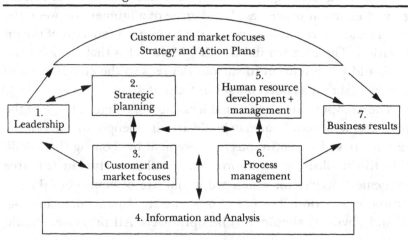

we have the right customer focus?" To answer these questions, many organizations decide to link the development project of CSFs and KPIs to the implementation project of a quality framework. To do this, specific indicators are developed for each component of the model and are subsequently included in the management reports. Only in this way can management be ensured of a good implementation of the quality framework and also, more important, that both organization and employees follow the lines that were set out by the quality framework.

When making the link between a quality framework and a balanced scorecard, it is important to keep in mind the different focuses they have. A quality framework asks for measurements; the balanced scorecard provides the development method for these measurements. A quality framework takes an integral look at an organization and does not have a specific focus; the balanced scorecard focuses specifically on the strategy and can miss other, often operational issues. The areas in the quality framework and the perspectives of the balanced scorecard overlap somewhat but also supplement each other. A quality framework gives high-level relationships between organizational areas; the balanced scorecard looks for specific cause-and-effect relationships. The balanced scorecard follows the execution of the strategy; a quality framework follows the development of an organization to "total quality." Some observers state that quality of leadership will make the big difference between the success and the failure of an organization.[7] Therefore, they are of the opinion that the quality frameworks have to be complementary to the balanced scorecard because these frameworks explicitly focus attention on the category "leadership," which the balanced scorecard does not. This mix of overlap and supplementation makes a joint implementation of a quality framework and the balanced scorecard exceedingly suitable for improving the overall management information function of an organization.

FOCUS ON VALUE CREATION

Managing an organization on the basis of value, or potential for cash generation, is known as *value-based management* (VBM). What counts in value-based management is not periodical profit in terms of accounting, but the value created. The key performance indicator used is economic value added (EVA).[8] EVA is calculated by reducing the so-called NOPAT (net operational profit after taxes) by the amount of the capital costs. If the balance is positive, value has been created; if the balance is negative, value has been destroyed (Exhibit 4.18). NOPAT is found by performing an often considerable number of corrections on the calculated margin, in order to link the margin to the organization's cash flow. The capital costs are the weighted average costs of capital (WACC—equity and debt). The capital amount is found by performing a number of corrections on the corresponding accounting amounts. One can say that value is created (or destroyed) when the return, made with the organization's capital, is higher (or lower) than the costs associated with this capital.

The main benefits of EVA are the introduction of the concept *economic value* and the fact that it makes managers more aware of the costs of capital. EVA can be applied to all activities and investments of an organization. It can be used to evaluate whether the various activities and participations add enough value to the organization or whether the investments should be better done elsewhere. Used at the corporate level, this measure is valuable in portfolio management by identifying the businesses to divest or to invest in. EVA is also used at lower management levels. At these levels, EVA is the key financial value driver for a division or a business unit measuring its own performance and evaluating its own strategic alternatives. When VBM is used at all management levels, the concepts of VBM are truly embedded in the organization. VBM

Exhibit 4.18   Economic Profit Calculation

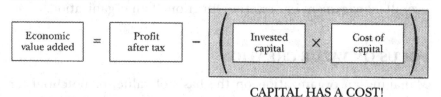

CAPITAL HAS A COST!

concepts can be used to steer changes in behavior and to focus change management.

Value creation is high on the agenda of top management. Financial value creation has been measured, and consequently management's focus and behavior is changing. The next challenge to further extend value-based management is trying to link the financial value tree metrics to the strategic and operational value drivers (Exhibit 4.19). This will make VBM more than just the implementation of a new financial measure; it will then be used to relate strategy and operations at all levels of the organization.

The first step in VBM is the calculation of EVA because this enhances managers' awareness of capital costs. However, it takes more than this to manage an organization on value creation: Managers also have to gain insight into the factors that determine value. These factors are not automatically generated by EVA. It takes a second step: linking EVA to value-creation factors. Exhibit 4.20 shows how this link can be made in a practical way. The trick is to keep

Exhibit 4.19   Financial Value Tree

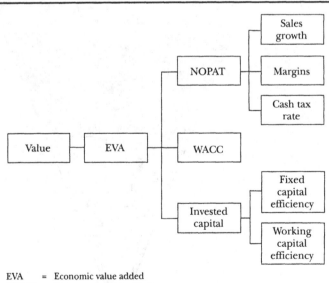

EVA   = Economic value added
NOPAT = Net operational profit after taxes
WACC = Weighted average cost of capital

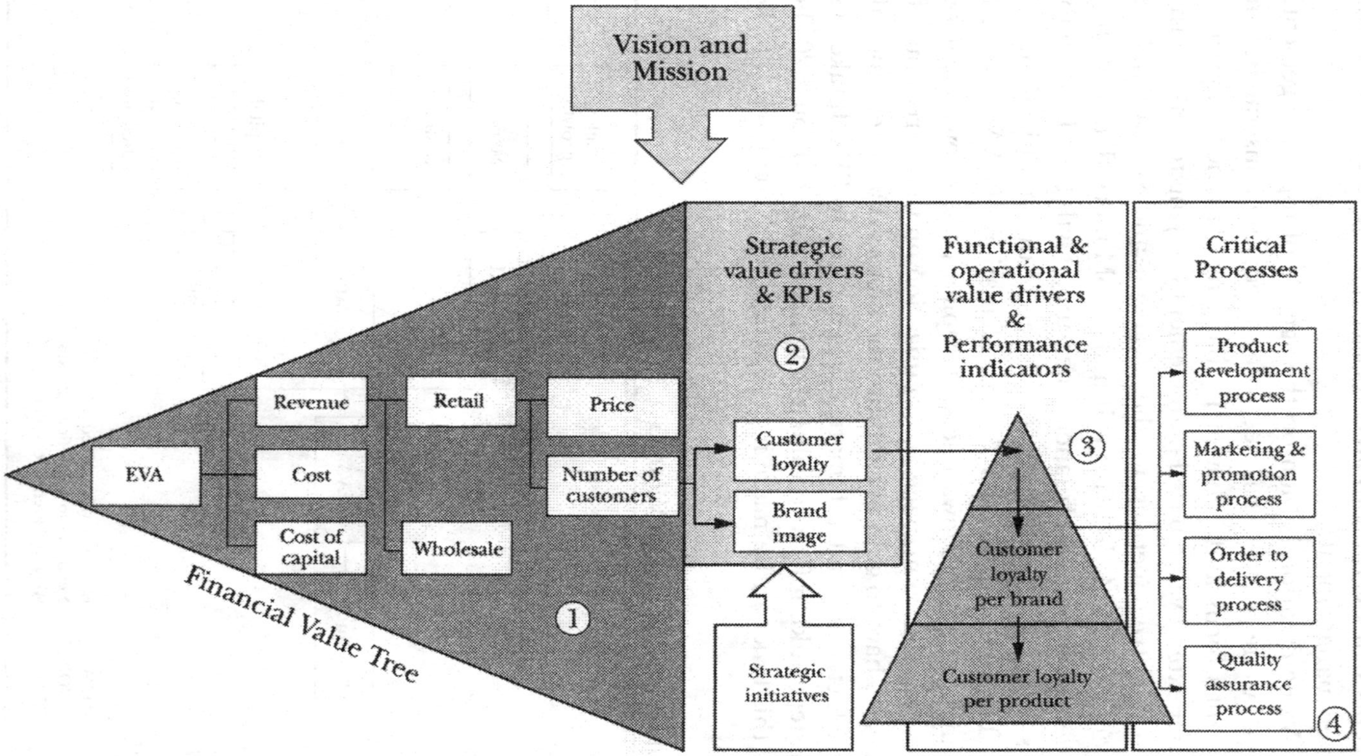

Exhibit 4.20 Linking the Financial Value Tree with CSFs and KPIs

it simple and easy for everyone to understand. Based on its vision and mission, the organization is able to build a financial value tree. This value tree encompasses the key financial value drivers of the organization. The ultimate value driver in the financial value tree, EVA needs to be defined in a way that is easy to understand (① in Exhibit 4.20).

Next, the strategic initiatives and plans are evaluated and prioritized according to their contribution to value creation. The organization then identifies a limited set of key strategic value drivers and KPIs to measure these value-based initiatives (② in Exhibit 4.20). The financial value tree has now been further extended to include nonfinancial value drivers. These nonfinancial drivers are linked to the financial value drivers as much as possible. The causal relationships are often indirect or even systemic in nature (causal loops) and might be difficult to calculate mathematically. The challenge for management is to either quantify or qualify the relationships between leading nonfinancial and lagging financial value drivers, to have confidence in these links, and at the same time to keep these links simple.

The strategic value drivers and KPIs are then translated into the lower organizational levels (③ in Exhibit 4.20). It is important to align the drivers and the indicators with each other at all levels and with the respective strategic plans and initiatives at these levels.

Ultimately, VBM creates a link between financial value and the true drivers of value: business processes (④ in Exhibit 4.20). The strategic, functional, and operational value drivers and performance indicators (both financial and nonfinancial) measure the key value creation processes of the organization. By selecting the appropriate value drivers and performance indicators for each process, these processes can be measured on operational excellence and value creation.

A focus on value creation increases the overall performance and value-creation ability of an organization. This is because everyone in the organization, management as well as employees, sees and understands the link between their activities and their contribution to both the financial results and the strategic objectives of the total organization. Also, value creation becomes measurable at every level of the organization, giving it the focus and attention that it deserves from management at all levels. Value-based management is the glue that binds financial objectives, strategic plans, and operational performance together into an integrated framework focused on value creation.

When the development of KPIs and the determination process of value drivers takes place at the same time, linkages or overlaps may be identified. As a result, the value-based management model can be used during the development process of CSFs and KPIs to determine the possible effects that KPIs may have on EVA. This also works the other way around. During the EVA determination and analysis process, KPIs can explain how the formulated strategies and CSFs have lead to a certain performance.

Information technology can assist organizations in their efforts to create and sustain value. The support for value creation is realized by an integrated set of applications, as well as by using an underlying data warehouse structure that provides the required information. An integrated data warehouse should be fed by enterprise resource planning (ERP) systems and other sources. Based on a consistent set of common data, the ERP system and data warehouses are fully integrated across the organization. The integrated set of applications on top of this structure should provide the information and analysis capabilities that enable value-based management practices. These applications include advanced simulation and scenario modeling tools, risk management applications, a consolidation tool, a corporate performance monitor, and mechanisms for communicating more effectively with stakeholders.

The use of a key financial metric, like EVA, at lower management levels might not result in the expected increase in value creation. The accompanying terminology of the measurement often proves hard to understand and to apply to everyday business by operational managers (e.g., weighted average costs of capital). Another reason EVA might not be used at the business unit level is that the use of shared resources across business units results in allocation efforts and ownership problems because business unit management cannot be held responsible for a lot of these allocations. This may result in business units focusing too much on allocation issues instead of on value creation. In that case, the desired change in management behavior, which has been realized at corporate and division levels, will not occur at business unit levels, thereby discouraging the use of EVA at this level.

BEHAVIORAL IMPLICATIONS OF VALUE THINKING

Focusing on value creation requires a real shift in thinking—no more focusing only on the profit-and-loss account, but looking everywhere all the time for possibilities to add real value to the organization. *Trust* is the key word here: trust in the value drivers, trust in causal relationships between financials and nonfinancials, and trust in each other!

This means you are the owner of a set of value drivers, and are trusted by management and colleagues to determine, define, and revise actions that should create value. There is trust that the actions you define for the nonfinancial value drivers will indeed, through causal relationships, improve the financial value drivers, thereby adding value. After all, not all relations between value drivers can be mathematically calculated. And finally, your set of value drivers really show what you are doing, thereby, making your performance transparent, which requires an open culture and trust in each other that the results on the key value drivers will be used to manage, not to control and punish.

CASE: IMPROVING VALUE THINKING
WORLDWIDE AT SARA LEE/DE

This case study describes how Sara Lee/DE improved its value thinking by implementing key value drivers in the shape of CSFs and KPIs worldwide. Arthur Andersen Business Consulting supported the company during the rollout by providing the methodology and training to the controllers. As part of the project, Sara Lee/DE and Arthur Andersen Business Consulting conducted a pilot at the business unit Kiwi Brands in Australia. The most interesting aspect of this case is the way in which the "train-the-trainer" concept can be used to implement performance management, and thereby value thinking, quickly and efficiently worldwide.

Organization's Background

Sara Lee/DE is a subsidiary of Sara Lee Corporation, which is domiciled in Chicago, Illinois. The main activity of Sara Lee Corporation is developing and selling branded products worldwide. In 1978, the company acquired a 65 percent share in Douwe Egberts, a family-owned coffee-roasting firm from The Netherlands. In 1984, Sara Lee Corporation obtained complete ownership and created the subsidiary Sara Lee/DE (SL/DE). Nowadays, SL/DE is responsible for the divisions of coffee and tea, household and body-care, direct selling, and the region of Asia. Sara Lee Corporation's organizational structure is illustrated in Exhibit 4.21. SL/DE, based in Utrecht, The Netherlands, has sales exceeding US$6.6 billion, with a net profit exceeding US$500 million, and is employing more than 27,000 people.

Exhibit 4.21   Simplified Organizational Chart of Sara Lee Corporation and SL/DE

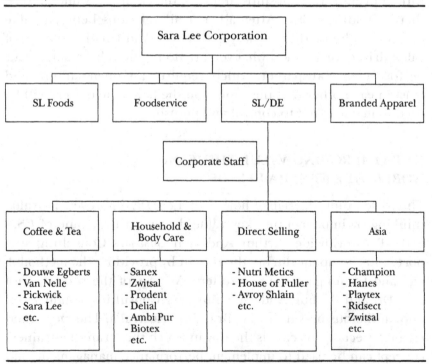

Sara Lee Corporation does not see itself as a manufacturing or distributing company but rather as a collector of brands, with its attention focused on the marketing of finished products. Worldwide, the company has more than a hundred brands, including Douwe Egberts coffee, Kiwi shoe polish, Stegeman meat products, Ambi Pur air freshener, Sanex body care, Hanes clothing, and Coach leather products. Eight of these brands have a worldwide revenue each exceeding US$500 million. The main strategy of the organization is to create and maintain brands with the highest added value and return against the lowest costs. In addition to this, Sara Lee Corporation focuses on optimizing its profits while using a minimal investment. For this reason, the company has divested in recent years by selling off production plants and outsourcing transportation. It is expected that this will continue in the near future as the company strives for a return on investment of 20 percent, up from the current 16 percent.

Establish a Clear Responsibility Structure:
A Decentralized Management Style

SL/DE competes in a wide range of industries. The coffee and tea division operates in a stable, mature industry with a limited number of strong competitors. The household and body care division and the region of Asia have to cope with fierce competition from several, strong multinational companies. The direct selling division operates in a relatively young industry with, until now, a limited number of major international players. Therefore, corporate headquarters employs a decentralized managing style so that management of the various divisions can deal freely with the different industry characteristics they encounter (Exhibit 4.22). In an interview, SL/DE's chief executive officer (CEO) described this managing style in the following way: "Our brand managers do not have to execute directive number 225 from headquarters when they are launching a new product. We, the board of management, give them a framework. We manage the process a little by saying: 'This flavor or trend is in hot demand in the market this year.' But as long as sales are up 12 percent every year and value is consistently added,

Exhibit 4.22　SL/DE's Parenting Style

Definition	Strategic Planning	Strategic Control	Financial Control
Type of industry	Rapidly changing, fast growing, or ✓ fiercely competitive industries.	Mature industries and stable competi- ✓ tive situations.	Wide variety of industries. ✓
Parent role	Closely involved with business unit in formulation of plans and deci- sions. Clear sense of direction.	Planning decentral- ized to business ✓ units. Parent role is checking, assess- ing, and sponsoring.	Insists that all deci- sions are "owned" by the business units themselves.
Business role	Seeks consensus with headquarters and other units for business initiatives (in line with strate- gic targets).	Own responsibility for strategies, plans, ✓ and proposals.	Independent enti- ties, sometimes working together to achieve mutual benefits.
Organizational structure	Large or powerful functional staffs at center. Shared ser- vice departments (marketing, R&D, etc.).	Decentralized with focus on individual ✓ business unit's per- formance. Head- quarters operates as strategic controller.	Minimal staff at the headquarter level, focused on head- quarters' support and financial control.
Planning process	Resource allocation driven by require- ments of long-term strategies. Planning influence of head- quarters is high.	Negotiation of financial and strate- ✓ gic performance targets. Planning influence of head- quarters is medium.	No formal strategic planning, process focuses on business unit annual budget and financial tar- gets. Planning influence of head- quarters is low.
Control process	Low priority on monitoring monthly financial results. Control by head- quarters is flexible.	Regular monitoring of actuals against ✓ planned, on finan- cial and nonfinan- cial targets. Control by headquarters is strategic.	Concentrates on financial targets ✓ and results (con- tracting). Control by headquarters is strictly financial.
Value creation focus	Creation of new business units for long-term business development.	Long-term strate- gies and goals of ✓ the business units (facilitating + coordinating).	Operating improve- ments and financial ✓ control.

every manager has complete freedom. A significant part of their reward is based on incentives, in bonuses and share options."

This means that the dominant management style in SL/DE is that of strategic controller. The board of management (BoM) has decentralized the strategic planning process to the divisions but delivers strategic guidelines to which divisions have to adhere. The monthly and quarterly reviews by the BoM focus on the financial performance of the business units, although nonfinancial performance is becoming more important. The divisions and the business units are responsible for the content and the execution of the strategic plans. Large investments by business units have to be submitted to the BoM, by way of a capital expenditure request. Approved investments are often aimed at improvements in the operational processes but can also be used for long-term strategic investments.

Focus on What Is Truly Important: Global Rollout of Performance Management

Management at SL/DE in general is quite satisfied with the management information function at the company. The corporate reporting set, called the *corporate headquarters' barrel report,* is delivered to the board members according to strict due dates in a predefined format with all the needed financials. The report set is discussed with the divisions during regular meetings, called *barrel meetings.* However, management recently feels there is important management information missing. The reports contain mainly financial status information on a detailed level. They do not contain enough information about the execution of SL/DE's five growth strategies, which are:

1. To build brands in new channels and in new ways.
2. To achieve and maintain low-cost production worldwide.
3. To make acquisitions that are strategic and complementary.
4. To concentrate investments behind high-margin, value-added products.
5. To increase business internationally by focusing on growing economies.

Also, general managers from divisions and business units are asking for more information about customer profitability, product profitability, operational and process bottlenecks, KPIs, and future-oriented information. This gave the chief financial officer (CFO) of SL/DE enough reason to start an improvement project. This project consisted of three parts that would be (partially) executed concurrently (Exhibit 4.23).

In part one of the improvement project, the key financials that every division and business unit have to report to corporate headquarters are reviewed on relevance. A summary of these financials, augmented with key ratios like treasury information and cash flow ratios, is put in a new corporate barrel report. In a dedicated narrative part of the report, the general manager from the division or the business unit must describe important analyses and actions. The financial details of the business unit are put in an appendix.

In part two of the project, every business unit has to identify and consequently report to corporate headquarters three financial and nine nonfinancial CSFs in a balanced scorecard format. The business unit has to make sure that the accompanying KPIs, two per CSF, measure how the business unit supports the achievement of SL/DE's growth strategies.

Exhibit 4.23   Overview of the Parts in SL/DE's Management Information Improvement Project

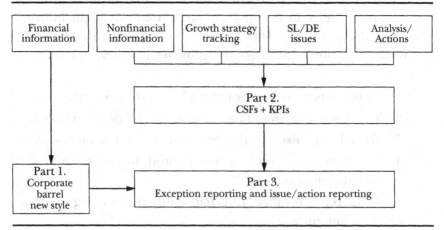

Finally, in part three, the layout and content of the management reports are further refined. A critical budget range is set for each KPI. If the actuals are outside this range, the business unit needs to include an analysis, a description of the proposed actions, and expected results in its report to headquarters. Special issues that affect more than one division are then included in the barrel report. The financial information from part one and the nonfinancial information from part two are now integrated into one barrel report.

This case study concentrates on parts two and three of the project. A four-stage approach was taken to these parts. In stage one, a pilot was performed at one of the business units to test the viability and enthusiasm for the concept of CSFs and KPIs. During stage two, a workshop was conducted with all of the members of the BoM to discuss the findings of the pilot, to test their enthusiasm for the concept, and to agree on the rollout approach. Stage three focused on a "train-the-trainer" session with the CFOs of the 50 largest business units so they could develop and implement CSFs and KPIs with their own management teams. Finally, in stage four, all of the CSFs and KPIs developed at the business-unit level were collected to perform a quality check on them and to standardize them for the complete organization.

Stage One: The Pilot at Kiwi Brands Australia

Kiwi Brands Australia is part of the household and bodycare division of SL/DE. The division's main products are air fresheners, shoe polish, foot care products, and toiletries. It employs 350 people and has good revenue and margin. Kiwi Brands is based in Melbourne.

The reason Kiwi Australia volunteered as a pilot site is that the company had just developed a new mission and strategy. The new mission, "To achieve sustainable profitable growth," was translated into four new strategies:

1. To obtain top-line growth.
2. To focus on customer and end consumer.
3. To consolidate Kiwi's portfolio of brands.
4. To strive for organizational effectiveness.

Exhibit 4.24 Matching SL/DE's Growth Strategies with the Strategies of Kiwi Brands Australia, Using the Strategy Alignment Matrix

Kiwi Brands Australia Strategy	SL/DE Growth Strategy				
	Build Brands in New Channels and in New Ways	Achieve and Maintain Low-Cost Production Worldwide	Make Strategic and Complementary Acquisitions	Concentrate Investment Behind High-Margin Products	Increase Business Internationally
Obtain top-line growth	✓				
Focus on customer	✓				
Consolidate Kiwi's brand portfolio		✓		✓	
Strive for organization effectiveness					

As a next step, the management team wanted to improve the management information so that it would better reflect the new mission and strategy. The pilot, conducted in one week by a team of SL/DE and Arthur Andersen Business Consulting consultants, consisted of interviews with all management team members, covering quality and content aspects of internal reporting (within Kiwi Australia) and external reporting (to corporate headquarters). After the interviews, a workshop was conducted with the entire management team about the current quality of reporting at Kiwi Australia, the concept and development of CSFs and KPIs, the development of action-oriented reporting, and the *dos* and *don'ts* in relation to the implementation of CSFs and KPIs. Finally, the facilitators processed the workshop results, and feedback was given to the CEO and CFO.

The first activity during the workshop was to evaluate which of SL/DE's growth strategies were aligned with and, thus, supported by Kiwi Australia's strategies. Possible mismatches between the strategies were resolved either by rewording or by (slightly) changing the business unit's strategy (Exhibit 4.24). If this was not possible, the management team discussed whether Kiwi Brands Australia should support the growth strategy in question. Subsequently, CSFs and KPIs were developed for these strategies. For example, the "Concentrate investment behind high-margin, value-added products" growth strategy is translated into specific CSFs and KPIs for Kiwi Australia, as shown in Exhibit 4.25. The growth strategy stipulates that Kiwi Australia should only invest in those products in its portfolio that have a high margin and that add value to the business. This means that Kiwi Australia first has to remove low-margin products,

Exhibit 4.25   Translating a SL/DE Growth Strategy, Via a Business Unit Strategy, into Business Unit Measurements

which do not add enough value, from its brand portfolio. The business unit's portfolio has to be trimmed down and consolidated.

If Kiwi Australia wants to offer a portfolio of strong brands, the quality of this portfolio is very important and needs to be monitored continuously. This important CSF for the company can be tracked with the KPI "Brand reduction," which measures how well the company is able to remove low-margin brands from its portfolio so that only the high-margin brands remain. Another KPI that can be used is "Brand leadership," which measures how many of the brands in the portfolio have a strong position in the market. After all, the more brands that have a first or a second position in the market, the stronger Kiwi Australia's portfolio becomes.

Some of Kiwi Australia's strategies do not directly support SL/DE's growth strategies. However, these internal strategies are important for the company to improve its position in the market or to become more effective and efficient. For example, Kiwi Australia's strategy "Organizational effectiveness" is translated into CSFs and KPIs (Exhibit 4.26).

At the time of the pilot, Kiwi Australia experienced some difficulties due to a series of reorganizations. Therefore, an important objective was to strive for an effective organization. A precondition for this was a high-quality workforce. From a long-term perspective, happy employees are better employees. Thus, creating a satisfied workforce was critical to Kiwi Australia.

Exhibit 4.27 shows a selection of the CSFs and KPIs developed during the workshop. During the evaluation of the workshop, the management team agreed that it was possible to develop CSFs and KPIs that not only are relevant to Kiwi Australia but also

Exhibit 4.26   Translating a Business Unit's Internal Strategy into Measurements

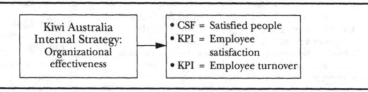

Exhibit 4.27   A Selection of Kiwi Brands Australia's Measurements

Strategies	CSF	KPI	Definition of KPI
Obtain top-line growth	Sales growth	Net sales volume (NSV) growth	Difference between NSV this period and NSV last period
		Market share trend	Change in market share versus last period
	New products	New product sales	New product sales versus total sales
		Successful new products	Number of successful new products versus total new products
Focus on customers and end consumers	Trade customer satisfaction	Customer satisfaction	Number of satisfied trade customers versus total trade customers surveyed
		Days with sales outstanding	Total debtors divided by annual sales, multiplied by number of sales days
	Products ranged	Timely new product acceptance	Number of product acceptances in less then x weeks versus total new product acceptances
	Satisfied end consumers	End-consumer satisfaction	Number of satisfied end consumers versus total number of end consumers surveyed
		Complaints	Number of serious complaints
		Repeat sales	Number of "loyal" consumers versus total consumers surveyed
Consolidation of brand portfolios	Quality of brand portfolio	Big brands	Number of big brands (US$10m earnings or more) versus total number of brands in portfolio
		Brand reduction	Number of brands currently versus number of brands last year

(continued)

Exhibit 4.27   Continued

Strategies	CSF	KPI	Definition of KPI
		Brand leadership	Number of "Top 3" brands versus total number of brands
	Quality investments	Big-brand investments	Investments in big brands versus total investments
Strive for organizational effectiveness	Satisfied people	Employee satisfaction	Number of satisfied employee versus total number of employees
		Employee turnover	Number of employees leaving versus total number of employees
		Absenteeism	Average number of days absent per employee
	Effective processes	Process goals achievement	Number of process improvement goals achieved versus total number of goals set
	Quality workforce	Multiskilled employees	Number of multiskilled (proven to be capable of more than one job) employees versus total number of employees
		Employee promotional capacity	Number of job vacancies filled internally versus total number of job vacancies

give both the household and body care division and corporate headquarters enough information to supervise this business unit. There also existed great enthusiasm in the management team to roll out the CSF/KPI methodology to lower management levels in their organization.

Stage 2: Board of Management Workshop

Not all SL/DE growth strategies can be influenced and supported by an individual business. For instance the growth strategy "Increase business internationally, focusing on growth in strongly developing economies," is a strategy that is directed by corporate headquarters, not by a single division or business unit. During the workshop with all the board members of SL/DE, CSFs and KPIs were developed for these growth strategies as shown in Exhibit 4.28. In this case, the number of growing economies in which SL/DE has business units is measured.

During the workshop, a discussion took place about the manner in which the BoM wants to receive KPI information from a division and a business unit. An option was to only use exception reporting. This means that the BoM would receive consolidated information from the division and only detailed information from a business unit when the results of a business unit's indicator were below target. In the fictitious example given in Exhibit 4.29, Kiwi Australia's indicator "Brand leadership" was below the target of 75 percent. This is important information that will appear not only in Kiwi's management report, but also in the divisional report in the barrel report of the BoM.

Stage 3: Train-the-Trainer Sessions

After the pilot and the workshop, the 30 largest business units started developing CSFs and KPIs to improve both their internal reporting and reporting to corporate headquarters. To support the business units, SL/DE and Arthur Andersen Business Consulting consultants organized "train-the-trainer" sessions. In these sessions the business unit CFOs were trained in the development technique of CSFs and KPIs and were given support tools (a training manual and a list with examples of CSFs and KPIs). After the sessions, the

Exhibit 4.28 Translating a SL/DE Growth Strategy into Corporate Measurements

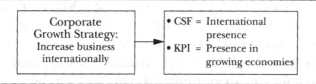

Exhibit 4.29   Consolidation of Business Units' Measurements for Corporate Headquarters Use (e.g., 40% means 2 out of 5 brands have a top 3 position)

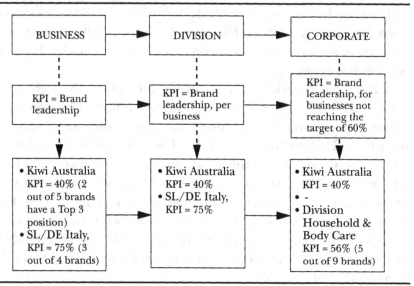

CFOs together with the local management team then developed their own set of measurements. Thus, all business units could deliver the required set of CSFs/KPIs to corporate headquarters.

In preparation for the sessions, several newsletters were sent out. Their purpose was to make the controllers more familiar with the CSFs, KPIs, and the balanced scorecard. One of the newsletters contained a case study, which prepared the CFOs for the kind of project that awaited them after the sessions (Exhibit 4.30).

Stage 4: Quality Check

During the rollout of the CSF/KPI development project across the SL/DE divisions and business units, a CSF/KPI implementation team (CIT), consisting of SL/DE and Arthur Andersen Business Consulting consultants, was set up. This team supported divisions and business units by answering functional questions and by reviewing and aligning the KPI definitions. This was done by collecting all

Exhibit 4.30   Newsletter Example

In the June newsletter we informed you about the status, progress, and planned activities with respect to the improvement of the reports used at SL/DE. In this newsletter, as part of the preparation for the Advanced CFO Training in September, we will focus on a case study of a CSF/KPI project. The objective of this case is to give you a feeling of what actually takes place during such a project. The case is partially based on the Kiwi Australia pilot. The evaluation at the end of the case was obtained from the Kiwi Brands Australia management team.

Newsletter

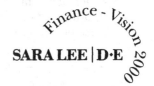

SARA LEE | D·E

"What gets measured gets done!"   August

Introduction

Fred Data, CFO of Household Improvement Ltd (H.I.), an operating company within the Household & Body Care division, returned from the Advanced CFO Training in Utrecht, where he had been further trained in the CSF/ KPI development method and in dealing with possible issues that might come up during the development process. He had also received the assignment of the Board of Management to develop and present, during the LRP-meeting in December, critical success factors (CSFs) and key performance indicators (KPIs) that would give the Board a good insight into his company.

Phase 1. Project preparation

Fred started with drafting an activity plan for the project. The plan contained eight phases:

1. *Project preparation*—setting up a project team and informing the organization about the project.

2. *Strategy alignment*—articulating the strategic objectives of the company and aligning them with divisional and SL/DE's growth strategies.

3. *Development of strategic CSFs/KPIs*—identifying, in a workshop with the management team, indicators that measure the company's strategic objectives.

4. *Development of functional and operational CSFs/KPIs*—identifying, in a workshop with the functions, indicators that measure the function's objectives and critical business activities.

5. *Prioritization of CSFs/KPIs*—reducing the developed indicators into a manageable set, to be used in the first year.

(continued)

Exhibit 4.30   Continued

6. *Development of CSF/KPI defini-tions*—drafting detailed defini-tions and delivery procedures and targets for the chosen indicators.
7. *Development of report formats*—devising layouts in which to report the indicators.
8. *Implementation*—start measuring and reporting indicators, and taking action on these.

Remembering the importance of good and timely communication, to obtain commitment from the people involved, Fred immediately dis-patched an information memo, which described the project's goals.

Phase 2. Strategy alignment

The first activity of the activity plan was to describe H.I.'s strategic objectives. The information Fred used for this was the strategic busi-ness plan and the annual operating plans of the past two years.

Because during the most recent year the strategy had hardly been discussed, Fred also conducted several short interviews with the management team. From these, he gathered from the managers the lat-est viewpoints regarding the strate-gic direction of H.I. Putting all the mentioned objectives in categories, Fred was able to condense these into one strategic objective per category.

He decided to put these strategic objectives to the test in a strategy alignment meeting with the man-agement team. John Jones, CEO of H.I., opened the meeting as Fred had asked him to.

John explained to the group: "Man-agement reports are a major instru-ment in managing our company. One of the main purposes of these reports is to provide managers with feedback on the fulfillment of H.I.'s strategic objectives and the way in which critical business activities are performed."

To this Fred added: "The reports should contain not only financial but also nonfinancial information and should be future and action ori-ented. In any way, the strategic objectives of H.I. are the starting point. Let's discuss the material I have prepared."

The management team discussed each of the strategic objectives, which Fred had put on a chart. The group concentrated on what each objective meant for the future direc-tion of H.I. and whether or not it was in line with the SL/DE growth strate-gies. They finally wound up with four strategic objectives that they all fully understood and had reached consensus on:

1. Top-Line Growth
2. Customer & End-Consumer Focus
3. Cost Focus
4. Personnel Effectiveness

The first three were in line with the SL/DE growth strategies. The fourth was special to H.I. because they experienced last year increasing difficulties in attracting and retain-ing good quality personnel. The group decided to have a separate meeting to discuss one of the growth strategies, which was not

Exhibit 4.30   Continued

currently covered by one of H.I.'s objectives.

Phase 3. Development of strategic CSFs/KPIs

A week later the group met again. Fred Data started the workshop with explaining the advantages of applying CSFs and KPIs in management reports:

"First, they translate strategic objectives into qualitative and quantifiable units throughout the entire organization and management structure. Second, they signal at an early stage, even before the results appear in financial reports, areas and business activities that may be heading for trouble. Third, they provide a univocal and common ground for cross-departmental discussion within the company. Fourth, they direct employees' behavior in the desired direction. And finally, they enable a company to improve its performance continuously."

"Let's start with the first objective: Top-Line Growth," Fred continued. "We first have to decide what the result of this objective is. In other words, with which desired result do we end up if we were successful in fulfilling the objective?"

"Well, of course, with sales growth," Brian Jones, COO of H.I., answered.

"Excellent," Fred praised him. "We call this a result-CSF. And what do we need to do to achieve this result?"

"There are so many things we can do, what do you mean exactly?" Mick Fontaine asked.

"I mean that we have to select the most critical efforts we put in to achieve the desired result. It is true that we can do many things, but we, as a management team, cannot focus on everything. We need to focus on the most critical items," Fred replied.

John spoke up: "It should be the number of new products we introduce every year, and this should be at least 20 percent of our product portfolio."

Fred formulated his answer carefully: "I think you are on the right track, John. However, there are some quality criteria you should keep in mind. I think you already formulated a KPI, the unit of measurement. Critical should be 'new products,' which you can measure with more than one KPI."

"Yes," Brian chipped in. "Next to 'number of new products,' we should also measure 'new product sales' to see if the new products were really successful. And we should also know the number of trade customers, which put the new products on the shelf: 'the customer listing.'"

"Shouldn't then the effort-CSF be better formulated as 'successful new products,'" Mick asked.

On this, the complete group agreed.

"Another thing you have to keep in mind," Fred resumed, "Is that the target should not be formulated in either the CSF or the KPI. Because the target can change every year, it should be separate. Finally, I want to stress that you always have to keep track of the result. You might do all the things right, but if you did

(continued)

Exhibit 4.30 Continued

not do the right things, you still do not fulfil the objective!"

After four hours of brainstorming and discussion, the group had identified result- and effort-CSFs and KPIs for each objective. They also formulated draft definitions and reporting frequencies for the KPIs. They parted with a satisfied feeling. After the workshop Fred Data went back to his office, where he worked out the flip-chart sheets. He sent the results back to the management team for comments:

Strategic Objective: Top Line Growth

CSF: Sales Growth (R)

KPI	Definition	Freq
NSV growth	Difference NSV this period vs. last period	month
Market share trend	Change in market share	quart.
Sales volume growth	Difference in SV this period vs. last period	month

CSF: Successful new products (E)

KPI	Definition	Freq
New products	Number of introduced products	quart.
New product sales	New product sales vs. total sales	month
Successful new products	Number of successful new products vs. total new products	year
Customer listing	Number of new product customer listings achieved vs. total new listings sought	quart.

It was decided to first finish the remaining phases for the strategic CSFs/KPIs before starting phase 4—development of functional and operational CSFs/KPIs.

Phase 5. Prioritization of CSFs/KPIs

The next activity was to select the CSFs/ KPIs that best measured H.I.'s strategic objectives. For this, Fred asked each management team member to rate the CSFs/KPIs developed during last week's workshop, on a scale of 1 (high) to 5 (low). Fred collected the average score per CSF and KPI in a table, which he sent to the management team as input for the meeting.

During the prioritization meeting, the managers discussed only those CSFs/KPIs with a score of 3 or 4. Indicators with a score of 2 or higher were accepted right away; those with scores less than 4 were rejected. They had to make sure that each objective was measured by at least one result-CSF and no more than two effort-CSFs. Also, the managers could chose a maximum of two KPIs per CSF.

If someone had a strong feeling about a particular indicator, he could try to convince the others that this indicator should be included. In this way, the management team was able to reach consensus on a manageable set of indicators. This set was going to be measured and reported during the first year.

Phase 6. Development of CSF/KPI definitions

The prioritization meeting went very well. However, Fred knew the most time-consuming activity of the project still lay ahead: the development of detailed definitions for the prioritized KPIs. He also knew this was a very important activity. If good and accurate definitions were not developed, H.I. would never be able to obtain the sought after common ground for discussion and would not be able to accurately and efficiently measure the indicators with information systems. He decided to organize another one-day workshop in which pairs of managers worked on KPIs assigned to them. For each KPI, they developed a detailed definition, a delivery procedure (the way in which to measure the KPI), and a

Exhibit 4.30   Continued

graph (the way in which to depict the KPI in the report); set a target; and assigned a person to be held accountable for the result of the KPI.

During the workshop, regular discussion took place among the group about the developed material. An argument erupted between Brian and Mick about the definition of *employee*. Brian wanted to count only contractors while Mick had always thought temporary workers were also included. Fred settled the argument and pointed out that the two men had in the past always interpreted the figures differently. This is a partial example of the definition document they made:

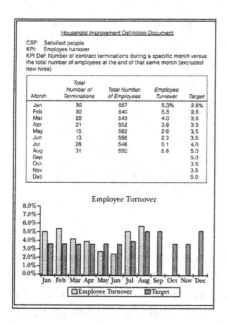

Phase 7. Development of report formats

Three weeks later Fred Data presented the complete CSF/KPI definition document. He also showed the group examples of the layouts in which the indicators were going to be reported. The layout consisted of two parts:

1. A CSF/KPI summary, giving a quick overview of the results.
2. An exception and action report, giving analysis and actions for KPIs with results below target.

The management team reacted enthusiastically and decided to use the same layout for its own internal reporting.

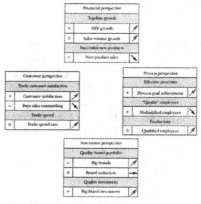

Phase 8. Implementation

Fred asked Jennifer Lee, information manager for H.I., to review the current systems to see if they contained the information needed to calculate the KPIs. After a few days Jennifer came back with answers.

(continued)

Exhibit 4.30   Continued

Many KPIs could be measured with the current systems, although some modification was needed in certain programs. The KPIs that had to do with personnel could be generated by the system of the Human Resource department. For the remaining KPIs, the management team had to decide if new systems were going to be implemented.

Now everything was ready to start using the new reports with CSFs and KPIs. The management team chose a full rollout with a phased approach. First familiarize managers with the new reports (without projections and actions), and later incorporate projections and necessary actions. The management team also conducted an evaluation of the project, with the following results:

- The process provided a useful forum for indirectly revisiting strategy for the business and for reflecting on whether modifications were required. The management team soon discovered the process was an important building block to ensure strategy was up-to-date, understood, and accepted by the entire team.

- The management team saw that it would give them the ability to focus on a number of important nonfinancial performance measurements, which in most cases were a measure of the quality of key processes.

- There was also a strong feeling that KPIs would achieve all the accepted benefits of "what gets measured gets done."

- The strategy alignment process gave them an opportunity to ensure that H.I. was focusing on things that corporate also felt were important, and it gave visibility to CSFs that were unique to H.I.'s local situation.

- The management team also saw this as a tool to achieve a more integrated business plan within H.I. and for managers/staff at all levels to see the linkages from mission all the way to action plans.

- Trying to establish CSFs made the team think very hard about things that were truly vital (critical) to the success of the business. This would certainly help move businesses toward doing "first things first."

the CSFs/KPIs developed by business units, divisions, and the BoM. Then a consistency check of the indicator definitions was made; identical indicators needed to have identical definitions. The CIT subsequently gave feedback to the CFOs on the alignment check and, if necessary, proposed changes to certain KPI definitions. Initially, the CIT received well over 800 different KPIs. After the alignment and quality check, approximately 400 indicators re-mained. These indicators are now incorporated into the different long-term plans of the divisions and the business units, which are sent to corporate headquarters. The CIT also collected informa-tion on the reporting capacity of current information systems of corporate headquarters, divisions, and business units to make sure that the developed indicators could indeed be measured, collected, and reported.

Finally, the CIT made layouts for the CSFs/KPIs summary in the balanced scorecard format and for the exception/action report. These layouts and the final CSFs/KPIs sets were then ap-proved by the BoM. From then on, the CSFs and KPIs from the business units were discussed during the barrel reviews.

Learning Experiences

After a year of developing and using CSFs and KPIs, several inter-esting learning experiences were identified.

○ The train-the-trainer approach turned out to be a cost-effective method of disseminating the knowledge of devel-oping CSFs, KPIs, and the balanced scorecard to a large group of people simultaneously. However, guarding the quality of the developed indicators as well as limiting their number proved rather difficult. Having business units de-velop their own measurements decentrally fits right in with the culture at SL/DE. This culture is driven by entrepre-neurs, who first have to be convinced of the value of a new concept before they will commit to it. Trying to force a new concept on business units from headquarters almost always fails due to the units lack of commitment. So using the train-the-trainer approach meant, on the one hand, a longer development project; but on the other hand, the ap-proach led to greater acceptance of the new measurements. Still, it might have been better to centrally manage the re-sults of this project from the start. The quality of the CSFs/KPIs would then not have differed so much over the business units, and the number of developed indicators could have been limited right from the start.

○ During the long-range strategic planning sessions, the BoM initially did not pay very much attention to the new measurements incorporated into the strategic plans of the business units. This resulted in business unit management becoming disenchanted with the new measurements. The business units failed to realize that the CSFs/KPIs were not meant to be a control instrument for the BoM. Instead, they were intended as a steering mechanism for business unit management itself. SL/DE learned that visible support of the BoM is crucial for the successful use of the new measurements. Therefore, it was decided to start every quarterly performance review of divisions and business units by the BoM with a discussion of the results on the performance indicators. This method drew better attention to the new measurements. It has also resulted in a stronger focus on strategic trends and developments of the business unit. Attention to strategy is no longer an annual exercise. The extent to which the business units use the new measurements depends on the interest and the commitment of the board member responsible for the division. Eventually, in some divisions the indicators are again reported and reviewed monthly; in other divisions they are also reported monthly but less frequently (officially) discussed.

○ Another learning experience of the project is that it takes quite a long time to embed the concept of CSFs, KPIs, and the balanced scorecard in a multinational environment. Although the development process itself took less than a year, it required two complete planning cycles, or two years, to really get the business unit management teams and the BoM to start working with the new measurements. Also, the development project was executed in English, which sometimes turned out to be difficult for people from different backgrounds, nationalities, education levels, and languages. A more regional approach with local examples in the local language might have helped.

○ An added advantage of introducing CSFs and KPIs turned out to be the warning signs that the divisions receive about the future profitability problems of a business unit. Business units could increase their operating margin by cutting back on advertising and promotion expenses. This is fairly easy to identify. However, delaying maintenance expenditures to raise profitability is easy to hide. These techniques are now much more visible with the nonfinancial indicators. Divisional management can react more swiftly and can steer the business unit back to the right track. It can also better discuss with business unit management the long-term problems that are caused by going for short-term profit.

○ The BoM itself is better able to track whether SL/DE growth strategies are executed properly and successfully. Important indications in this respect, like "Branded share" and "New management recruits" are regularly reviewed and discussed by senior management.

KEY POINTS

☑ More and more, sources of value no longer consist only of tangible assets but increasingly also of intangible assets. Both types of value drivers should be tracked by the information system.

☑ In the balanced scorecard, nonfinancial, leading indicators are combined with financial, lagging indicators to get a balanced overview of the organization's performance and to check whether the organization's strategy execution is still on track.

☑ The development of critical success factors and key performance indicators is at the center of the effort to build a balanced scorecard. It is important to distinguish between result and effort measurements.

(continued)

☑   In value-based management, an organization expressly looks at long-term value creation, instead of looking at short-term profit maximization.

☑   Value-based management is the glue that binds financial objectives, strategic plans, and operational performance together into an integrated framework focused on value creation. This is achieved by linking the financial value tree metrics with the strategic and operational value drivers and processes of the organization.

☑   To make value thinking a success, trust is needed: trust in the value drivers, trust in causal relationships between financials and nonfinancials, and trust in an open culture.

NOTES

1. Evans, H., and G. Ashworth, Management Accounting, December 1996.
2. Arbor, A., Business Wire, 36291.
3. Boulton, R.E.S., B.D. Libert, and S.M. Samek, Cracking the value code, how successful businesses are creating wealth in the New Economy, HarperBusiness, 2000.
4. Schiemann, W.A., and J.H. Lingle, Bullseye! Hitting your strategic targets through high-impact measurement, The Free Press, 1999.
5. Waal, A.A. de, J.H.J.M. Mijland-Bessems, H. Bulthuis, Meten Moet! [transl. 'Measurement is a must'], Kluwer BedrijfsInformatie, 1998; and Waal, A.A. de, and M. Fourman, Managing in the New Economy, Arthur Andersen/Show Business, 2000.
6. Weber, J., and U. Schaffer, Fuhrung im konzern mit der balanced scorecard, Kostenrechnungspraxis, 43e jrg., H.3, 1999.
7. American Productivity & Quality Center, Strategic planning: what works . . . and what doesn't, presentations from APQC's third knowledge management symposium, www.apqc.org/free/whitepapers/spwp/, 1998.
8. ™ Stern Steward & Co.

5

Embrace Information Transparency

CHALLENGE OF TRANSPARENCY

> Many organizations spend more time collecting and reporting information than in the high-value activities of planning and analysis. But, the real issues confronting management are often obscured by the sheer volume of information, hidden like a needle in a haystack.
>
> *A. Arbor*[1]

> Top managers are becoming aware that information technology is not just a means of boosting efficiency and profits. Information technology will have to be used as a strategic tool to improve the adaptation skills of the organization and [to] create value.
>
> *Giarte Media*[2]

Information transparency is key to making your organization a world-class performance management organization. Making information transparent means that everyone in the organization can see the information they need and are entitled to when they want and in the format that best suits them. In this way, everyone is at all times informed about the status and developments of the organization. As a

141

consequence, everyone can react quickly and efficiently on warning signals.

But, in reality, managers are currently drowning in data but thirsty for information. The effort it takes to collect, report, process, and digest information has to be reduced. An organization has to strive for efficient data collection and reporting processes. This entails fast collection of data from different sources and the ability to efficiently generate reports that contain relevant information compiled from that data. There should also be a reduction in the time-consuming ad hoc reporting.

The main implication of information transparency lies in the area of systems development. Sufficient information technology (IT) support is needed for reporting, measurement, and analysis. More and more, IT support is playing a crucial role in enabling users to easily access information on a "when needed" basis. This increased importance puts a new kind of demand on IT architectures and IT departments.

The main benefit for organizations, when dealing with this challenge properly, is the time they create for added-value activities. Because it will take users less time to hunt for and to collect needed data, they will have more time to actually process the information. Users will get more time to analyze the information and to take action, thereby increasing the quality of those analyses and actions. When information becomes transparent, users will have a better idea of where they can find certain pieces of information, thereby decreasing the need for time-consuming ad hoc questioning.

Information that is readily and transparently available is information that is there when needed, is easy to use, and is visible for responsible management. This increases the overall added value of information to the users.

PUSH-AND-PULL INFORMATION:
MANAGEMENT BY SURFING AROUND

Information transparency can be accomplished through the use of one, centralized, corporate data warehouse, which collects and stores management information from all organizational levels.

However, one central warehouse is often not considered to be a cost-effective and viable option for large, global companies mainly because of the significant effort needed (in time and resources) to obtain the high level of data standardization and commonality that is required to establish and to maintain such a warehouse.

Consequently, each management level has to find a balance between the information collected and stored structurally and regularly on its own level (the so-called "information push") and the information that has to be available on lower management levels and that can be accessed on an ad hoc basis by higher management levels (the so-called "information pull"). The concept of information transparency means that a minimum of information goes to the top of the corporation, but information is retrievable at lower levels of the corporation so top levels can get the information themselves if they want to (Exhibit 5.1).

The numbers in Exhibit 5.1 depict the concept of information push and information pull, which entails the following:

1. Each management level determines its own set of standardized management information. This is data that this

Exhibit 5.1   Information Push and Pull

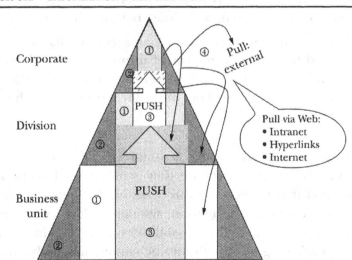

management level wants to receive from all lower-level organizational units that report to this level, for example, key financial ratios and balanced scorecards (if feasible).

2. The remainder of the management information is not standardized. This means the lower-level organizational units can define information items that are specific to them, for example, adding certain performance indicators to the required, standardized balanced scorecard to make it more relevant for them, and adding specific accounts to the standardized chart of accounts to be able to capture extra, unit-specific information.

3. Each management level requests from lower management levels a certain amount of data and information that is needed on a regular basis. This data is common for all these lower levels and is pushed upward. The higher the management level, the less information is needed. The information is collected and consolidated in an efficient and timely manner. This is possible when strict agreements have been made concerning the data items to be pushed upward and the data definitions that have to be standardized across the organizations for these specific data items. One precondition for this is a standard chart of accounts, which should not be too detailed (i.e., not too many accounts).

4. Each management level is able to access, on its own and on an ad hoc basis, management information as well as non-standard data from lower-level organizational units. This information is pulled out of the local systems, which reside at these lower levels.

Information transparency is obtained by storing pushed information in a data warehouse that is maintained at the management level that collects the information. Business intelligence tools (e.g. executive information systems) allow user-friendly, drill-down, and slice-and-dice capabilities on the data in the warehouse, thus allowing information to be viewed and analyzed from different perspectives.

Management information is made transparently available via the Intranet. A standard Web browser provides access to management information at each organizational level. The Web browser provides access to every division's and business's standard homepages, which contain periodic management information such as balanced scorecards, financial (traffic light) reporting, forecasts, analysis, action reporting, and strategic plans. These homepages can be standardized across the organization to create a common, consistent, and thereby user-friendly view of periodic management information. Data warehouses and other management information systems across the organization enable additional analysis and access to more detailed information. Hyperlinks can be added to the homepages to provide links to other web pages on to the Intranet and the Internet, thereby connecting related data and enhancing the overall value of the information.

We call this "management by surfing around." This style of management is based on the premise that management levels get only what is required by organization standard. Other, extra information can only be retrieved by surfing the management web. The information architecture needed for management by surfing around consists of a corporate data warehouse that stores the required standardized common data. These data are limited and mainly financial because data standardization for all relevant data (including nonfinancial) is not considered feasible for a large, diverse organization—it will take too much effort and time to achieve and to maintain the desired level of standardization.

Consequently, this implies a shift from databases toward "linkages." Instead of building a hierarchy of data warehouses, the Web links all stand-alone information systems together, including internal linkages as well as linkages with external stakeholders, such as customers and suppliers. Data is stored in one, local place only. Management is freer to design management information that meets their specific needs, and it is able to access this information via the Web and by surfing around.

When an information architecture has been installed that supports information transparency, managers have the possibility to access management information on a when-needed basis. Their analysis capabilities are improved by the easy access they have to underlying management information systems and data warehouses. Information can be shared among managers and updated online in the systems, thereby keeping track of changes and having more timely, up-to-date information available. Organization-wide, user-friendly, and consistent views of information are presented, based on standardization of parts of the Intranet. The time spent on information gathering and searching for information is significantly reduced. Security is an important issue and needs appropriate attention during the implementation and use of management information on the Intranet and Internet.

CREATE A PERFORMANCE MANAGEMENT PORTAL[3]

Many organizations may already have a strong foundation for performance management, with an existing architecture of layered information systems. The executive or management information systems (EIS/MIS) are fed from decision support systems (DSS) and online analytical processing (OLAP) databases to allow slicing and dicing of summary information. These databases are fed from a data warehouse that provides a single store of data and a single consistent "version of the truth" about different aspects of the business, with data drawn from different sources. This data warehouse in turn is fed from operational systems, including, for example, enterprise resource planning (ERP) systems.

Each of these toolkits and layers has value and supports or provides some part of the total management information and reporting requirement of the organization. ERP vendors are recognizing that they can add significant value for their customers by extending the ERP system, from automating the operation of the business to supporting performance management. Providing a data warehouse or OLAP database capability is one step, but the warehouse in itself does not support performance management. ERP vendors now see enabling performance management as the next value-adding step for their customers. Early indicators suggest that this extension of the ERP system will be an important contributor to organizational effectiveness.

The traditional architecture for performance measurement (Exhibit 5.2) has a number of limitations in relation to effectively supporting a world-class performance management process. There is not necessarily a relationship between the information supplied and the information needed by employees. The cost of delivering secure focused information to every employee is often too high to be economical, so only a subset of people get the information they need to be fully empowered. And often much resource has gone into developing the middle two layers (data warehouse + DSS/OLAP), which from a management information point of view is not necessarily sufficient because there is no support for the needs of the majority of business users.

The following approach is one way to improve the traditional architecture so that information transparency for performance management is provided cost-effectively, across the organization (Exhibit 5.2). Information and reports are related to the strategy by specifying the critical success factors (CSFs) and key performance indicators (KPIs) that they support and by entering these in special data warehouses. This strategic information is combined

Exhibit 5.2   Portal Architecture Is Replacing the Traditional, Hierarchical Architecture

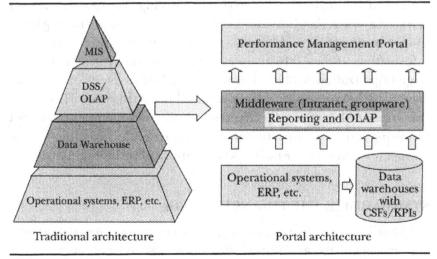

Traditional architecture   Portal architecture

with operational systems and ERP systems. Through Intranet and groupware tools, this information is made available to the user. The cost of distributing the information is dramatically reduced by using a portal, based on groupware and Intranet tools. These enable the functionality required for secure transparency by providing a foundation for an open, secure, scaleable portal for performance management. More tasks can now be decomposed so they can be performed at different locations and at different times. The effectiveness and the information needed for these tasks are ensured through the deployment of integrated systems (like ERP) supported by groupware.[4]

Information is filtered, traffic lighted, and selected to provide and highlight only what is strategically and personally relevant (see Chapter 6 on traffic lighting). There is simple workflow support for action management (see also Chapter 6). Existing information sources and reporting tools are leveraged by using a performance management portal to provide management information for a large number of users.

When taking a performance management portal approach, an organization should use the same portal framework (though with different content) for different organization units. Even where different organizational units may use different operational and ERP systems, the performance management portal provides a standard template for information transparency. Taking the portal approach gives every organizational unit the ability to manage and organize its own information and knowledge and to control the access to this information. It is an effective way to create standardization across a large organization, without having to standardize every operational system, ERP system, data warehouse, and reporting tool. This allows the organization to work effectively in the New Economy, without requiring a massive investment for replacement of existing systems (which work as they are) with new organization-wide standards.

STANDARDIZE THE FINANCIAL DATA

Not surprisingly, most companies readily admit they should manage data as business resources, just as they manage human and financial resources. They just as readily admit that they do not so. Few companies even know what data they have; people cannot gain access to needed data; the quality of data is low; and data are not used effectively.

A. V. Levitin and T.C. Redman[5]

Industry statistics show that the volume of stored data doubles every five years and that less than 10 percent of this data is used for analysis purposes. Simple access to information is currently the number one priority for almost half of the IT managers polled. Many organizations, therefore, turn to standardization of data to ensure that the set of data necessary to run the organization is consistently defined and used across the organization and is easily accessible. A common set of data supports efficient data collection, reporting, and analysis and forms the basis for reliable and consistent information.

Often, parts of the financial data are standardized. This level of standardization has to be expanded so that a common chart of accounts can be created, accompanied by the underlying data definitions, such as definitions of *product, revenue, organization, sale,* and *customer.* The common chart of accounts and data definitions are implemented at all levels and not only enhance the reliability of the financial information but also improve the consolidation process with respect to speed and ease of use. The set of corporate common data can be expanded, based on corporate headquarters' needs. This set can include further standardization of data definitions, for example, *common product* and *customer coding.*

Another option is to implement the so-called "one database concept." This concept consists of a corporate data warehouse containing the organization-wide standardized financial data. The data warehouse facilitates internal and external reporting and extensive (drill-down) analysis capabilities. Access to this data warehouse varies. Sometimes this is limited to corporate headquarters, whereas in other cases it is used as the sole source for periodic financial information across the organization for corporate headquarters and for division and business levels.

Common data definitions increase the reliability of financial information and speed up the consolidation and closing processes. They also create a common language across the organization and make information easier to interpret. Finally, they facilitate analysis and benchmarking of data. The level of standardization can be limited to allow for an adequate level of flexibility for divisions and business units. Each organization has to find a balance between the need for flexibility and the required level of standardization.

CONDUCT MANAGEMENT TEAM MEETINGS IN A DECISION ROOM

To facilitate the discussion and decision-making process, organizations set up dedicated rooms that are specially designed for the conduct of management team meetings. The rooms provide access to and display management information in a user-friendly way. During the management team meeting, information is consulted online, which facilitates the meeting and makes the decision-making process more effective. In this room, each management team member has access to a monitor that displays the presentation materials during the meetings. Furthermore, the monitors can be linked to the EIS so information can be analyzed during the meeting. The executives typically use this system on an individual basis to view and to analyze management information.

If the organization does not yet have the technical means, a paper version of a decision room can also be created. In that case, the monthly management reporting, including a balanced scorecard and graphs with financial and nonfinancial trend information, is displayed on the walls in poster-size format. Another example is a decision room that includes a Management Cockpit. This is a specially designed meeting room in which the key value drivers and strategic performance data are displayed graphically on monitors mounted on the walls of the room. Each wall represents a different type of information.

The main purpose of the decision room is to have a dedicated place to share information and to create a common understanding of the strategic direction throughout the organization. This is established by giving employees access to the decision room and by discussing periodic performance and actions with them in this room.

A special decision room improves the quality and the speed of the performance review and decision-making processes by online access to management information. The room facilitates information and knowledge sharing with managers and (if applicable) with employees. The setup of a decision room for executive management can be a costly investment, especially when the room is equipped with the latest technology. However, if the decision room is not linked to management information systems and displays hard copy information, it is less flexible and harder to maintain.

BEHAVIORAL IMPLICATIONS OF INFORMATION TRANSPARENCY

A mindset that is able to deal with information transparency is needed. Managers have to be able to deal with "management by exception": they will get less information (both in volume and in detail level) automatically delivered to them. And they need to find additional information *only* when this is needed to do their job (see also Chapter 6 on management by exception). The role of technology is also becoming bigger in this respect. Less paper will be used. Managers need to acquire the skills to be able to manage by surfing around on their Intranet and on the Internet.

Managers also need to get used to less standardization. Traditionally, many efforts have been made in organizations to create more standardization of data. However, the focus becomes different with information transparency. The standard information that has to be reported to the different management levels should be standardized across the organization. Effort has to be directed at agreeing on the level of standardization that is desired or required for the organizations. All the data that does not fall under this agreement will be free. Every organizational unit can decide on its own what to do with this data; there will not be any central guidelines or edicts anymore.

An important consequence of creating transparency of information is that information is no longer power because information becomes a commodity in the organization. Also, the performances of managers becomes more visible. After all, information transparency allows information to move up and down the organization. This openness can create serious pitfalls where managers are not able or willing to trust one another and to share their information. Therefore, clear ground rules are needed. Some of these are:

o The information, consisting among other things of CSFs, KPIs, and balanced scorecards, are owned where the strategy is created—at the business level.

o The highest level in the organization, the corporate headquarters, defines the content of the data and the information that is needed on a regular basis and in a standardized format (③ in Exhibit 5.1). The business level then chooses what other information can be seen by higher levels in the organization.

o KPI information and related actions will not be used against a manager, but only to support him or her. The information is used by higher management as a tool for support and coaching, rather than as a tool for identifying fault and apportioning blame. This combats a culture of "punishment by fact." Instead, a culture of coaching is created.

With these ground rules adopted, information transparency can save labor and cost for the individual organizational unit in respect to collecting and reporting information. Without the ground rules, organizational units may resist implementation of information transparency, not because it is a bad thing for the business but because they fear loss of control and independence.

CASE: CREATING A PERFORMANCE MANAGEMENT PORTAL AT WAKEFIELD MDC

This case study describes how a local authority is developing a performance management portal, provided by Arthur Andersen and Show Business, to support the Modernizing Government program currently taking place in the United Kingdom (U.K.) The portal will give the City of Wakefield Metropolitan District Council (MDC) all the information it needs to satisfy the requirements of the Best Value legislation. This program has been imposed by the British goverment on all local authorities from April 1, 2000.

Best Value is about measuring, managing, and improving the operation of U.K. local authorities. These improvements should include social and environmental outcomes as well as cost and efficiency factors. The goal of Best Value is to meet the commitments of the Modernizing Government Agenda in the United Kingdom and to deliver high-quality and efficient services that are responsive to citizens' needs. The government is also promoting joint strategic-policy making by encouraging collaboration with other service providers and stakeholders, in both the public and private sectors. The Best Value regime aims to make a real and positive difference to the services that local people receive.

The Best Value program places a number of requirements on local councils. They have to publish an annual performance plan and review all their services at least every five years. These reviews have to challenge why and how a service is provided; compare their performance with others (not just in the public sector); increase competition to secure efficient and effective service provision; consult with local taxpayers, customers, and the wider business community; and finally achieve and demonstrate continuous improvement in service delivery. These requirements are known as the 4 Cs: Challenge, Compare, Compete, Consult.

The Best Value regime, as well as the wider public-sector modernization challenge, demands continuous improvement in services through cultural change, outcomes-centered management, and the identification and the implementation of best-practice methods.

Organization's Background

The City of Wakefield MDC is a local authority in West Yorkshire, in the North of England. It covers the townships of Wakefield, Pontefract, Castleford, Normanton, Knottingley, and Hemsworth. The Council serves around 300,000 residents and directly employs some 13,500 staff. It delivers a full range of local authority services, except police, fire, and public transportation.

Wakefield's corporate strategy is aimed at delivering significant service improvements via the Best Value review process. The strategy focuses on increasing organizational competencies, achieving continuous improvement, setting a corporate standard for service reviews, implementing the EFQM Excellence model and the balanced scorecard across the organization, implementing a new performance management information system, and looking at networking opportunities with other service providers.

The Council is audited annually on its compliance with Best Value and on the outcomes of the Best Value reviews by the U.K. Audit Commission (Exhibit 5.3). This audit includes detailed information on organizational performance. Making information available for audit online through a performance management information portal will significantly simplify and enhance this process.

Embrace Information Transparency: Installing a Portal

Demonstrating Best Value, as well as meeting the challenge posed by public sector modernization, demands continuous improvement in citizen services. This improvement has to come through both

Exhibit 5.3   Best Value Audit Process

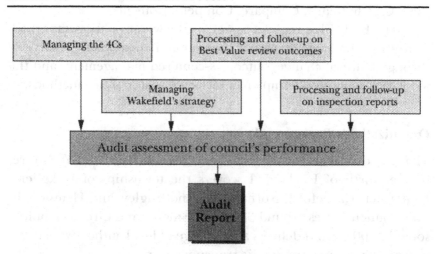

outcomes-centered management and the identification and the implementation of best-practice methods. The challenge is how to deliver timely and relevant performance information and manage subsequent performance improvements without a significant budgetary overhead.

It was Wakefield's contention that these objectives could be achieved via a networked and, in the long term, cross-organizational performance management system. The Council therefore identified the need for a technical solution to support its service development and Best Value strategies. Wakefield's criteria for this performance management system included:

○ Full support of the Council's use of the European Foundation for Quality Management (EFQM) Excellence model and the balanced scorecard, both service- and theme-based, across the organization.

○ Support for management at both operational and strategic levels, managing not just measures around cost and efficiency. Measures were also required for strategic objectives, service delivery, quality, and fair access to services for all citizens.

○ Integrated explanatory reports of results and trends, as well as action plans to managers, complemented with business intelligence information.

○ Capability to support collaborative decision making and working by enabling users to share best practice and to learn from outcomes.

○ Easy and straightforward use for staff.

○ Utilization of industry-standard technology and data formats.

○ Capability for linkage to existing information sources, and accessibility across the organization via the corporate intranet using a Web browser.

The Pilot

The Council decided to pilot the strategy within its Housing Services. For the pilot the Action Driven Balanced Scorecard (ADBS) system, running on Lotus Notes and developed jointly by Arthur Andersen and Show Business, was chosen. The Council had looked at other potential MIS systems, in collaboration with Leeds University Business School and Stratica Ltd (the Business School's consulting arm). They recommended ADBS as a scaleable system, incorporating both numerical performance data and supporting textual action reports and strategic plans.

The goal of the project is to encourage and to develop a performance management (as opposed to performance monitoring) culture within the Council. Performance data, which could be analyzed and drilled down, is published to managers and accessible to elected Councillors, via the Council's intranet.

The approach of the pilot is depicted in Exhibit 5.4. Critical success factors and key performance indicators were identified by a consultation exercise utilizing the Strategic Value Chain Methodology. The resulting 38 key value drivers provided the basis for the Housing Services scorecard. The Council also prepared 10 further

Exhibit 5.4   Pilot Project Approach

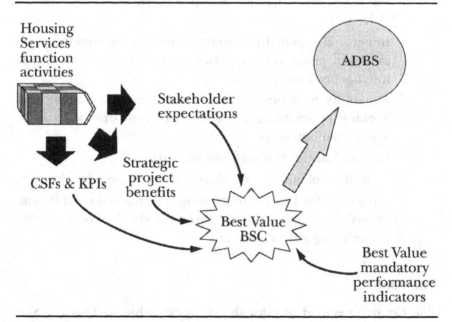

scorecards for management of the statutory Best Value indicators. These corporate scorecards are models to be further developed over the initial five-year Best Value review cycle. Also local indicators of service performance can be added.

Individual managers possess their own ADBS on their desktop PC (see Exhibit 5.5). A variety of ADBS systems, both service- and theme-based, will exist across service departments and the wider organization. Other scorecards cover crosscutting themes, such as Community Safety and Social Inclusion, where input and data are received from a variety of Council Departments and outside agencies.

Technical Architecture

Data is entered either at local level, into the central corporate performance management server, or directly from the council's existing

Exhibit 5.5   ADBS Front Screen for Best Value Corporate Health Measures: May 2000

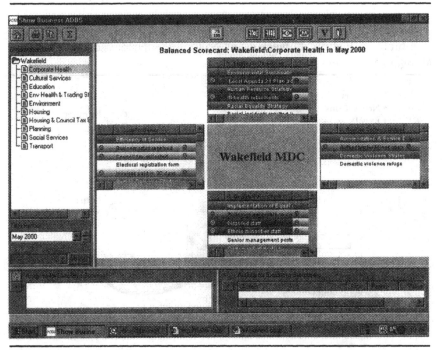

IT systems, using automated links. The system is supported by extensive intranet-based material on Q-Net, the online Wakefield Quality Network. Q-net includes background material on purpose, methodology and technique, and user assistance and technical support (see Exhibit 5.6). Q-Net also provides best-practice information to support performance improvement and innovation.

The portal is designed to provide information on an organization-wide basis and across departments and services. ADBS provides the information required for the evolution of the Council toward a modern, responsive, and outcomes-driven organization. The portal also significantly facilitates the collation and the provision of statutory data returns, capturing data in a central system that can be used as "real" management information. This is a major improvement on the historical supply of annual data, produced by Councils purely to satisfy central government requirements and seldom used in support of organizational objectives.

Exhibit 5.6   Technical Overview of Wakefield's Performance Mangement System

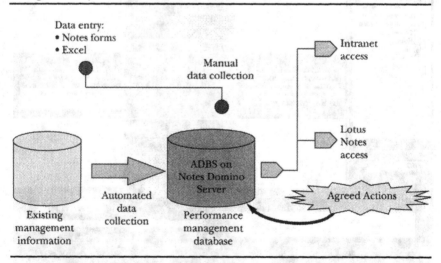

Support for Cross-Agency Working

The Council sees significant opportunities for cross-agency partnerships by utilizing the new performance management portal. The possibilities currently under review or being implemented include the following (see Exhibit 5.7):

○ Managing the performance of joint-service delivery, via the Government Secure Intranet and Local Government Secure Intranet, allowing a common data standard both to transfer data and to build interorganizational scorecards across the U.K. public sector.

○ Internet-based collaboration with government departments, local authorities, partner organizations, the voluntary sector, business partners, and other public bodies.

Exhibit 5.7   Cross-Agency Cooperation, Using Portals

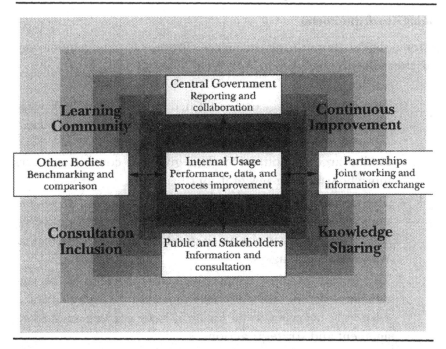

○ Data sharing with external partners to facilitate benchmarking, process improvement, and best-practice information.

○ Facilitating electronic service delivery. Developing electronically available performance information is a significant step toward fulfilling the U.K. governmental target that all public services should be accessible electronically by 2005.

These links encompass strategic planning and policy, as well as operational management and direct service provision. The targeted ideal scenario is that of a seamless collaboration/performance management system operating across the public sector and its current or future partners via Internet technology. Wakefield's Best Value team has already received numerous inquiries and requests to view the completed system from across the public sector. This is just the beginning!

Benefits of the Portal

After a period of operating the new performance management portal, the following benefits to Wakefield became clear:

○ The balanced scorecard, contained in the portal, deals with a wide series of performance issues, not just financial ones. Internal processes, organizational skills, and customer satisfaction are also addressed. This gives the council a better, more holistic overview of its performance.

○ The portal prompts users for both explanations of performance results and action plans to address performance issues. This encourages a much greater action orientation of Wakefield's managers.

○ The portal enables performance management to be undertaken at all levels of the organization and enables a corporate overview to be taken of both performance management and strategic actions.

○ The balanced scorecard data, made available via networked technology, significantly supports elected members, both executive and nonexecutive, in their corporate governance and scrutiny roles.

○ The collection of statutory data returns for Best Value and other (often cross-service) requirements at a corporate level is greatly facilitated.

CASE: EFFICIENT CONSOLIDATION AT PHILIPS

During the past decade, Philips Electronics, the Dutch electronics company, has been working steadily toward improving its reporting and consolidation processes. Several programs have been undertaken to improve information dissemination in the company. As part of a larger project in the area of performance management, Arthur Andersen reviewed Philips's technique in the area of consolidation and financial reporting. Through its efficient and reliable reporting process, Philips is able to provide meaningful information in a timely way to its managers, making them able to react quickly on developments inside and outside of the company.

Organization's Background

The foundations for Royal Philips Electronics were laid in 1891, when Dutch engineer Gerard Philips established a company in the city of Eindhoven, The Netherlands, with the aim of manufacturing incandescent lamps and other electrical products. Today, Philips Electronics N.V. is one of the world's largest electronics companies, featured as number eight on *Fortune* magazine's list of global top 30 electronics corporations. Sales are in the range of US$34 billion. The company employs approximately 230,000 people in over 60 countries. Philips is active in about 80 business segments, varying from consumer electronics and domestic appliances to security systems and semiconductors.

Philips Electronics is considered the world leader in digital technologies for television and displays, wireless communications, speech recognition, video compression, and storage and optical products, as well as the underlying semiconductor technology that makes these breakthroughs possible. The company has world-class solutions in lighting, medical systems (particularly scanning and other diagnostic systems), and personal and domestic appliances.

To give an indication of its capacity, Philips produces over 2.4 billion incandescent lamps per year, about 30 million picture tubes per year, and more than 50 million integrated circuits each day. Around 2.5 million heart procedures (scans and intervention procedures) on X-ray equipment are completed each year using Philips technology. One in every seven television sets worldwide contains a Philips picture tube, and 60 percent of all telephones contain Philips components. Thirty percent of offices around the world are lit by Philips Lighting, which also illuminates 65 percent of the world's busiest airports, 55 percent of soccer stadiums, and 30 percent of hospitals worldwide. This company truly has a global and cross-industry reach.

Philips is organized in seven divisions, each containing several businesses. The businesses consist of logically grouped product-market combinations and are the primary points of accountability in Philips. The company is headed by a Board of Management (BoM) that is supported by the corporate center, which consists of several supporting departments.

Embrace Information Transparency: An Efficient Consolidation and Reporting Process

Philips uses the "one database concept" to collect the monthly, quarterly, and annual figures. Periodically, 1,200 reporting organizations (factories, sales offices, and research centers) send their data directly into a single database called COMAR, which stands for COnsolidation and MAnagement Reporting. The data streams are strictly defined, documented, and standardized across the organization. These standards must be adhered to by all reporting units, a policy that results in a consistent collection of the same data each reporting period. COMAR is a database system intended for the storage of financial as well as limited nonfinancial (e.g., personnel) data for the purposes of consolidation and management reporting.

Each of the 1,200 reporting organizations has to complete a set of standard reporting forms (SRF). These prescribed forms request all information that is required by the BoM, the product division, and the business unit from a particular reporting organization. There are, for example, SRFs for P&L information, for balance sheet information, and for specifications of cost categories. The SRFs are based on the standard chart of accounts, which was implemented throughout Philips. The chart of accounts is mandatory for enterprisewide reporting purposes. Divisions and business units can also use their own accounts, which are added to the chart of accounts. These accounts often contain more-detailed, local information.

Using the SRFs ensures standardized input of consolidation data throughout Philips. Completing a SRF can be done online with a direct link to the COMAR system or via an automatic interface with the local general ledger system of the reporting organization. More than 70 percent of the input already takes place via the automatic interface, and this percentage will increase even more in the next few years.

Even though Philips starts its financial year on January 1 and closes on December 31, they use their own Philips calendar to perform the monthly closings. In weeks, this calendar follows a 4–4–5 schedule each quarter. Each month is always closed on the last Sunday in the month. From that day onward, the reporting organizations have three working days to close their books and submit their SRFs to feed the accounting data into COMAR. Then COMAR reviews the SRFs against a master file to check for consistency, accuracy, and reliability of the data (Exhibit 5.8). Data that does not pass the check are entered in the repair file. After the master file check, COMAR calculates automatically several financial ratios. All data is stored in the history file, which contains data from the current and previous reporting periods. The control file indicates who has to perform what activity when in the consolidation process. If the timetable in the control file is not adhered to, the control file will give a warning signal to corporate control.

Exhibit 5.8   Technical Drawing of the Data Streams through the COMAR Data Warehouse and CAPS System

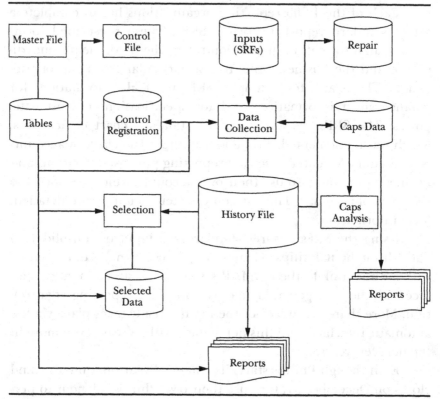

On the following Thursday at 6 A.M., the accounting information of all reporting entities has to be present in COMAR. Because all data is entered in the standardized format, consolidation of the figures can be done automatically in COMAR. This Thursday is dedicated to checking the data, by corporate control, for inconsistencies. For this analysis the CAPS system, a centrally developed management reporting application, is used. CAPS uses the COMAR data warehouse as an information source and is able to slice and dice information in every possible way. This means that a single source is used for extracting management reports as well as for providing management and staff members with the right information they need for analyses and action plans. A selection of data from the history file can be added to the reports for trend analysis and other purposes.

The Businesses and Product divisions use COMAR and CAPS, among other systems, for information purposes so they can write an analysis for the BoM reports. Divisions and business units are allowed to request any necessary final changes or corrections after consulting with corporate control. These changes can be corrections to errors, but they also can be updates to figures that have a major impact on performance (mergers, takeovers, major sales deals, etc.).

By the first Friday of the following month, Corporate Control analysts finalize their commentaries using the final data for the BoM and, in the case of quarterly and annual reports, also for external investors and financial analysts. On Friday evening at 6 P.M., the monthly report is delivered to the BoM.

The time it takes Philips to close the books and generate the management reports (five working days) is quite short for a company of its size. According to studies, industry averages for closing the books are around two to three weeks. The main reason that Philips does this so quickly is that time-consuming subconsolidations are done automatically by the COMAR system. Having COMAR in place also means that everybody in the company is using the same data, thereby preventing the lengthy discussion about the reliability of the data (which traditionally comes out of the use of many different systems).

The standard classification of the accounts and the standardized reporting forms ensure that all standard information can be aggregated quickly and efficiently. The use of reporting organizations and SRFs also enable a slice-and-dice analysis of the management information, which means it can be approached from different dimensions at the same time (sales per region for a product division).

Finally, the COMAR one database concept facilitates the process by providing powerful information-processing technology. COMAR puts the primary responsibility of recording the basic data and guarding the quality of this data (correctness, timeliness, and completeness) at the level where the data is generated. Also, there is no more redundancy in data storage because every piece of data is sent to one unique source, enabling fast reporting. Technical and functional system management for management reporting can be concentrated in one location (central help desk function). Standardization and uniformity lead to more transparent data management.

The monthly enterprisewide report details the performance of each business unit based on a standard format used across the business units. The business and product division formats consist of one page, giving the key financials for each business (such as cash flow, income from operations, economic profit realized) and projecting actuals versus budget. Due to this relatively simple and uniform layout, board members can see quickly where potential deviancies occur.

KEY POINTS

☑ The challenge of embracing information transparency lies in reducing the effort it takes to collect, report, process, and digest information. This creates time for managers to perform added-value activities.

☑ Sufficient information technology (IT) support is needed for reporting, measurement, and analysis. IT support plays a crucial role in enabling users to easily access information on a when-needed basis.

☑ Each management level has to find a balance between the information that is collected and stored structurally and regularly by itself (the "information push") and the information that has to be available on lower management levels and that is accessed on an ad hoc basis ("information pull").

☑ A mindset that is able to deal with information transparency is needed. Managers have to be able to deal with the fact that they will get less information automatically. And they need to find additional information themselves *only* when it is needed to do their job.

Within the business units, different reporting styles can be found. The business units are free to decide on the content and the layout of their own management reports as long as the required financial data is entered in COMAR. Many business units within Philips today are using the balanced scorecard and traffic light reporting to highlight deviations from plan. The use of a consolidated balanced scorecard at the BoM level is not deemed relevant because it is of no use to consolidate the nonfinancials. A board member explains: "What does customer satisfaction with Philips mean? Nothing, because a customer can only be happy with the services of a particular business unit." The balanced scorecards from the business units are used by the BoM and division management to obtain a better insight into the state of affairs of these businesses.

NOTES

1. Arbor, A., Business Wire, 36291.
2. Giarte Media, Het Financieële Dagblad, 23-05-1999.
3. This idea was described earlier in *Managing in the New Economy,* A. de Waal, and M. Fourman, Arthur Andersen/Show Business, 2000.
4. Venkatraman, N., and J.C. Henderson, Real strategies for virtual organizing, Sloan Management Review, volume 40, number 1, Fall 1998.
5. Levitin, A.V., and T.C. Redman, Data as a resource: properties, implications, and prescriptions, Sloan Management Review, volume 40, number 1, Fall 1998.

6

Focus on What Is
Truly Important

CHALLENGE OF INFORMATION OVERLOAD

Why is it, many managers wonder, that such a large percentage of the most reasonable, analysis-driven, implementable strategies never make it from concept to reality?

R. Simons and A. Davila[1]

The difficulty is not a matter of knowing how to measure. The difficulty, rather, is knowing what requires attention and what does not.

M.W. Meyer[2]

The objective is not simply to take action, but to take meaningful action.

F. Kröger, M. Träm, and M. Vandenbosch[3]

You have to be able to keep your distance; don't try to track every small detail.

H. Rootliep[4]

Recent developments in management information systems (MIS) enable management to gain better insight into their business. The challenge therefore is an overload of management information, rather than a lack of it. This overload needs to be reduced.

Management today is dealing with many different information needs. New management theories that have been developed over the past 10 years in the area of performance management, such as balanced scorecard reporting, value-based management, critical success factors (CSFs) and key performance indicators (KPIs), web-based reporting, and the like, have changed the information needs dramatically. Until now, the traditional way of dealing with these changing information needs was by adding new information to the old stack. This resulted in reports getting more voluminous, many reports still being delivered on paper, and information systems that did not yet comply with the new information needs. Storing unnecessary data is expensive, not because it wastes the storage medium, but because it diverts management attention and makes needed data more difficult to find.[5]

It is a challenge to not try to know every detail. The art of management is not to know everything that is happening in an organization, but to know what the key issues of the business are—to focus on the most critical business issues and to take action on these. Reports should function as an enabler for action taking. Focusing on what is truly important entails focusing on key value drivers that are crucial to the business, on exceptional events or figures, on analyzing financial and nonfinancial results, on corrective action plans, and on the impact of those action plans. For many managers, this is an arduous task.

When dealing with this challenge properly, organizations will get two major benefits: (1) more transparency and (2) more focused decision making and action taking. Transparency is a key requirement for focusing on what is important for an organization. And by focusing on truly important issues, management can make decisions that are focused on solving crucial business issues, thus improving the quality of decisions. Decisions are based no longer on piles of paper, but on those key value drivers that matter to the organization. As a prominent chief executive officer put it: "You have to be able to keep your distance." When, at the same time, proactivity of managers and employees is fostered, a major step is taken toward focusing and improving what is important. In the ideal situation, managers and employees know exactly what to do and what not to do, thus facilitating the organization's focusing on truly important issues.

APPLY BUDGET CONTINGENCIES

Organizations may decide to use contingencies in the budgeting process. Because budgets are a "snapshot in time," management can never fully guarantee that budgets will be achieved exactly as planned. Contingencies can be defined (① in Exhibit 6.1), that constitute performance ranges representing acceptable deviations from the budget. Only if business performance is outside the agreed contingency area will corporate headquarters or divisions intervene and

Exhibit 6.1   Budget Set Out over the Year with the Contingency Area and the Two Intervene Areas

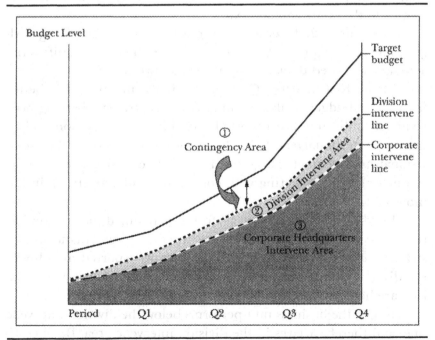

take on a more active (coaching) role. This active role includes more-frequent performance reviews and more-detailed reporting.

In order to implement this type of "management by exception," target budgets are agreed at the business level for a limited set of key financial performance indicators. Examples of such key indicators are economic value added, net operating profit, return on capital employed, and contribution margin. For each of the key indicators, contingencies are set between each business unit and corporate headquarters, as well as between the business unit and the division. The contingencies are based on sensitivity analyses performed during the strategy development process. Management reports include traffic lights that visualize if actual or forecasted performances on the key financial indicators need divisional intervention (e.g., by using yellow to indicate they are in the divisional area, ② in Exhibit 6.1) or corporate headquarters intervention (e.g., by using red to indicate the results are in the corporate headquarters intervene area, ③ in Exhibit 6.1). Performance reviews take place on an exception basis—corporate headquarters or division management only intervenes if performance is outside the contingency area.

In Exhibit 6.2, different situations that can occur during budget control are depicted and described. The thick line signifies the actuals; the dotted thick line signifies the forecast.

In the first quarter (Q1), the business unit performs better than target budget. Only key financials and strategic leading nonfinancial indicators are reported monthly to the division and to corporate headquarters. Monthly review meetings are held with divisional management. Large business units conduct a once-a-year (strategic) review meeting with corporate headquarters (① in Exhibit 6.2).

In Q2, the business unit performs as planned, not as good as the target but still in the contingency area. Only key financials and strategic leading nonfinancial indicators are reported monthly to the division and to corporate headquarters. Monthly review meetings are held with divisional management (② in Exhibit 6.2).

In Q3, the business unit performs below the division intervene line, and thereby arrives in the division intervene area. Detailed financials and strategic leading nonfinancial indicators are reported

Exhibit 6.2   Examples of Budget Control Situations

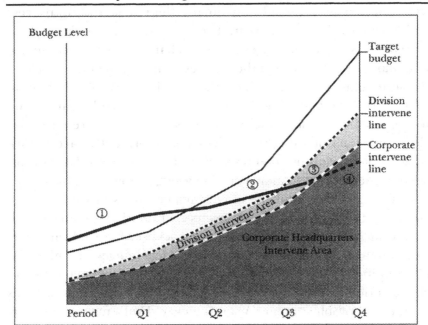

at least monthly, and maybe more frequently, to the division. Still, only key financials and strategic leading nonfinancial indicators are reported monthly to corporate headquarters. Longer monthly review meetings are held with divisional management. The division now acts as custodian of the business unit (③ in Exhibit 6.2).

The strategic rolling forecast predicts that the business unit performance will end up in the corporate intervene area in Q4. Detailed financials and strategic leading nonfinancial indicators are reported at least monthly, and maybe more frequently, to the division and to corporate headquarters. Monthly review meetings are held with corporate headquarters. Corporate headquarters now acts as custodian of both the business unit and the division (④ in Exhibit 6.2).

The budget-setting process takes less time because it is performed only with key financials and because there are clear targets and contingency areas with which lower levels can work. Defining the contingency areas requires business unit management to know its industry and market very well. Discussions about the achievability of the budget are held only during the budget-setting process and no longer during the year. There is no need to talk about or to renegotiate the budget every time changes occur because the boundaries between which the business unit can operate are clear. Because contingency areas have been defined, the absolute accuracy of the forecast is no longer relevant. Control is aimed no longer at the forecast accuracy, but at the drafting of preventive actions aimed at obtaining the budget. These preventive actions are based on a rigorous analysis of cause-and-effect relationships, thereby increasing the managers' knowledge about their business.

The definition and use of contingency areas provides a clear structure for corporate headquarters and divisional management regarding the timing of interventions. Ownership and entrepreneurship are stimulated because there is less danger of higher levels stepping in too soon. Budget contingencies enable management by exception, thus allowing management sufficient time to focus on the real problem areas. When integrated with management reporting, contingencies can be translated to traffic lights (see the following section), thereby enhancing management's focus. Contingencies allow for reasonable deviations from budget, based on a sensitivity or a risk analysis. Because there is real exception reporting, less time is required for the performance review. There are direct and clear consequences (e.g., custodians) when actuals or forecasts go wrong, which increases accountability.

The level of detail of the budget impacts the concept of contingencies. Setting contingencies for every budget line item is rather time-consuming and can become unmanageable. Consequently, a limited set of key financial performance indicators has to be used in the budgeting process.

A variation on using budget contingencies is applying the concept of *flex*. An organization can build in flex, which represents the potential deviation in percentages of certain KPIs from the budget. Each division determines the flex, based on the expected effect of external risk factors. This flex is negotiated between the division and corporate and becomes part of the management reports.

Another alternative is to set minimum and maximum budget targets. The area between the minimum and the maximum targets is mainly used for management compensation purposes. Incentive compensation varies based on actual performance within or outside this area. Only the minimum targets are part of the periodic management reporting and performance review process.

FOCUS ON EXCEPTIONS

In this concept, the organization has defined and subsequently tracks a limited set of key value drivers (as described in Chapter 4). Exception reporting is used to report on these key value drivers. These reports give the actual results of *all* key drivers, but they highlight performances that are outside a certain range (negative *or* positive) from the expected target. For the key value drivers that are inside the range, no additional information is needed. For every key value driver outside the range, the organization obliges the manager responsible for this value driver to provide additional reporting that analyzes the causes of the deviation and describes corrective actions.

"Traffic light" reporting is a way to quickly focus on exceptions (Exhibit 6.3). The first page of the report gives a summary that depicts deviations from the plan, by highlighting the deviations. Specific colors are used to express the percentage deviation from target. For example, the color red for more than 10 percent under target, yellow for 5 to 10 percent under target, green for on target, and blue for above target. The colors in the exception reports can also represent the management intervene areas defined in the budgeting process, where actual performance is outside the budget contingency area (see the previous section). The red "traffic light" then indicates for example the corporate intervene area.

Exception reporting enables management to steer the business more efficiently and effectively by quickly focusing on deviations. Problems in the business are immediately noticed, fostering swift analysis and action taking without spending too much time on matters that do not need immediate attention.

Some companies may find that exception reporting does not fit in their culture. Their culture may be such that management always wants to have a complete and detailed view of performance,

Exhibit 6.3 Example of an Exception Report

Division X	EVA		Sales		Margin		IFO		Volume		CAPEX		Cash Flow	
	Actual	Budget	Actual	Budget	Actual	Budget	Actual	Budget	Actual	Budget	Actual	Budget	Actual	Budget
Product 1	200	180	4,200	4,000	3,200	3,130	1,120	1,100	2,500	2,480	230	235	760	758
Product 2	45	43	1,540	1,540	900	880	512	500	270	286	60	80	98	95
Product 3	57	51	430	448	410	400	60	58	430	300	35	60	115	103
Product 4	156	148	1,700	1,680	768	750	234	230	601	589	40	40	280	270
Product 5	6	16	280	220	95	94	30	90	100	90	2	21	23	23
Others	15	14	130	125	280	150	20	20	40	35	30	31	-12	-9
Total	483	446	8,300	8,013	5,533	5,404	1,976	1,968	3,941	3,780	397	449	1,264	1,241

which means that all data must be available. The overload of information will not be reduced in such a culture.

FOCUS ON ACTION MANAGEMENT

The main aim of measurement is management—action taking. Therefore, organizations have to include action reports in their management reporting set. These action reports describe the corrective actions that are planned to remedy a situation.

Preventive action reporting is another possibility. In that case, not the actual results but the forecasts are the basis for action taking. If the forecasted result for the next period and the target for that same period deviate outside a predefined range, preventive actions are formulated to make sure that the target still can and will be achieved. Included in the corrective and preventive action plans are the projected results of the actions because their effects may not show up in the results until later quarters.

Exhibit 6.4 gives a preventive action report for a key value driver. It displays an unfavorable deviation between forecast and target, the underlying root cause analysis, the description of preventive actions, and the expected results for the value driver in the coming periods.

The implementation of preventive action reporting, based on forecasts, instills proactive behavior. The responsible manager is forced to think about the future and to plan and execute preventive actions if the forecasts deviate from the targets. The effects of the preventive actions and environmental changes are described, providing a good estimate of future performance. The quality of the performance reviews increases because the reviews are more future oriented and because preventive actions and their effects have already been incorporated in the projected results.

CONCEPT OF RETURN ON MANAGEMENT

This section does not describe a benchmark idea, but an interesting concept nonetheless. It concerns the concept of *return on management,* which is promoted by Robert Simons, professor at Harvard

Exhibit 6.4 Example of an Action Report for a CSF and Its Corresponding KPI, Describing the Forecast, Budget, Analysis, Corrective Actions, and Expected Impact of These Actions

Period: Q2
Date: 3-4-00

CSF	KPI	Forecast Q2	Budget Q2	Analyses and Feedback	Action Description	Due Date	Responsible Person	Projected Result Q2	Q3	Q4
Time to market	Average lead time	15	12	Lead time will increase because several experienced people will leave shortly after one another.	1. Increase expertise through recruiting.	Q2	1.X	14	14	12
					2. Build multidisciplinary teams to increase synergy.	Q3	2.Y			
					3. Invest in new manufacturing software.	Q4	3.Z			

Business School.[6] This concept stipulates that managerial energy is the most important and most scarce resource of an organization and should therefore be deployed carefully. The organization has to make sure that managers are putting their time and energy into the right projects and issues: They have to focus on what is really important. Return on management (ROM) is a ratio that is defined as "productive organizational energy released divided by management time and attention invested." The higher the ROM, the more successful the organization is.

The concept of ROM sounds easy, but in daily life there are many obstacles that prevent an organization from obtaining a high ROM. Frequently encountered obstacles are the wealth of business opportunities with which managers are faced nowadays, which makes choosing the right ones difficult. Managers tend to address those issues that are closest to their hearts or with which they are most comfortable, though these might not necessarily be considered the most urgent ones. Often, there are many well-intended procedures that are supposed to help managers focus but that actually grow bureaucratic and overly complex in time. Finally, the vigilance required to keep up the focus on issues often turns out to be too much for managers.

So how can an organization help its managers to improve the ROM? By looking at the following five *acid tests* put forward by Professor Simons:

1. Has the organization made clear which opportunities are out of bounds (i.e., managers cannot spend time on them)? This prevents managers running after each and every opportunity.

2. Does the organization's critical performance measurements evaluate managers and employees on their ability to execute the strategy? Often "politically correct" measurements have been installed that take into account sensitivities that exist in the organization. High-ROM-driven managers do not care about these measurements. They only want to look at the really critical performance measurements, those that make the difference between success and failure, however painful that may be.

3. Are managers bogged down by too many measurements? As a rule of thumb, managers should have the number of measurements that they can memorize.

4. Does the organization spends its managers' time wisely? Managers will spend their limited time on a new process (or concept) only when it truly adds value. High-ROM organizations therefore operate exception based, alerting their managers to real issues.

5. Is everyone watching what the boss is watching? In this way, the energy of everybody is directed toward the same issues, the things that really matter.

ROM is a function of managerial focus and communication. Through communication, everyone in the organization should get a clear understanding of the strategic objectives and should know what they should be doing to achieve these objectives. And also about what they should not be doing!

VARY THE TIMING AND THE CONTENT OF PERFORMANCE REVIEW MEETINGS

In general, performance review meetings take place on a monthly or a quarterly basis. Based on different motives, organizations have adjusted the timing and also the content of these meetings. If performance review meetings take place at various management levels (corporate headquarters, divisions, and business units), these meetings need to be coordinated so they are not planned for the same time period. Managers are then able to spread their attention and to equalize the workload that comes with these meetings.

A good match between the timing of performance reviews at divisional and corporate headquarters levels enables divisional management to better focus on each of these performance reviews. Combining performance reviews with reviews of the strategic plan and the budget saves time and effort for both corporate headquarters and divisions. Furthermore, senior management's attention remains focused on that particular business.

Another idea with respect to the timing of performance reviews is to plan review meetings not immediately after the actuals become available. Instead, management is given a limited period of time to analyze the results and to initiate actions. This results in a more positive setting for the performance review meetings. Managers whose actual results are below target then have the opportunity during the meeting to present the actions that they have initiated to correct problems. In this way, management is motivated to take action immediately, if the actual results turn out not to meet the targets, in order to avoid losing face in the meeting with their peers.

Instead of a fixed schedule for performance review meetings, it is also possible to install exception-based performance reviews, where only performances are reviewed of a division or a business unit that did not meet its targets. This means that corporate headquarters mainly spends time on divisions and business units that really need attention. No time needs to be spent on preparing and executing performance reviews as long as the business unit performs on target. If management is given time to come up with actions plans before deviating results are reviewed or communicated, managers are forced to take action immediately if the actuals do not meet the targets, fostering proactive behavior.

In many organizations, management wants to discuss nonfinancial performance during performance reviews. However, in practice there is hardly enough time to talk about financial indicators, let alone nonfinancial ones. One possibility is to split the performance review between the division and its business units into a meeting specifically about the financial performance and a meeting specifically about the nonfinancial performance. These two meetings should be held within two weeks of each other. This enables management to spend sufficient time discussing performance, especially relating to the nonfinancial indicators.

If corporate headquarters only meets with the divisions when their results do not meet the targets, divisions might lose motivation if they perform very well for a longer time. Divisional management that is doing well can perceive this lack of attention from corporate headquarters as a sign that they are not important. A combination of exception-based performance reviews with regular performance reviews (with equal management participation) might overcome this drawback.

RAISE THE FREQUENCY OF BUDGETING

Most organizations formulate a budget once a year. As product life cycles shorten and the business environment becomes more volatile, the reliability of once-a-year budgets decreases. Increasing the frequency of the budgeting process and simultaneously shortening the time span of the budget enhances the reliability and thereby the value of the budgets. In order to maintain a longer-term focus, the budgets should be accompanied by forecasts, thereby stretching the time period of operational management attention.

The introduction of more frequent budgeting, for example, biannually, makes the budget process more reliable, mainly because the planning horizon is shortened. This higher frequency enables management to reassess the business regularly and to set new targets (if needed) during the year. Because the shorter planning horizon makes the future more predictable, the achievability of the targets increases, and thus the control over results and accountability also increases. The latest insights from the budgeting process can be used to increase the quality of the strategic plans. Combining a biannual budgeting process with forecasts supports both a short-term focus and a longer-term focus on performance. In this event, the entire budgeting process would require more time. It should therefore be considered, especially in mature industries, whether this extra effort is outweighed by the expected benefit.

LINK FORECASTING TO SPECIAL EVENTS

In general, forecasting takes place monthly or quarterly. However, when the timing of forecasting is linked to certain events, instead of just being a periodic activity, the forecast provides information that is valuable during or before that event. Such events include the annual shareholder meeting, the quarterly press releases, and the budgeting process.

In the case of only two forecasts a year, the first forecast could be prepared before the annual shareholder meeting. This is a year-end forecast that enables corporate headquarters to inform the shareholders about the latest estimates. The second forecast is prepared just before the start of the budgeting process. This forecast provides input for the budget and consists of the latest year-end estimate and underlying assumptions. The organization saves time by eliminating two of the four (previously quarterly) forecasts.

Forecasts linked to specific events increase their value to managers, who can use the information for those events. Also, the information value of the events is increased by the release of up-to-date information that is important for the participants of those events. However, forecasts can become less relevant for internal use if they are focused too much on the external event and the external stakeholders. Internal stakeholders might need different information (e.g., nature, level of detail) from the forecasts. Also, the number of event forecasts might be insufficient to meet internal management needs for future oriented information.

BEHAVIORAL IMPLICATIONS OF FOCUSING

An important behavioral implication of exception management is that managers have to learn to deal with uncertainty. After all, they will receive fewer details. This can make managers uncomfortable because they feel they do not known everything and therefore are not in full control. However, learning to deal with this feeling will enable managers to focus on the big picture.

One of the issues that keeps cropping up during the performance management process is that of accountability. Managers do not like to be made accountable for processes and results they do not fully control. However, in the New Economy a fast and efficient execution of business processes can only be done in team-based environments, where people are highly dependent on the performance of other people. Therefore, *accountability* gets a new meaning. If you are accountable, you are the *first* to take action! You have to take the initiative for corrective or preventive action. Such an action might be to go to your "neighbor" in the process and ask him or her for help to improve the results. If the neighbor is unwilling, then you could go to the next-higher management level to seek help.

To make management by exception a success, senior management has to be a role model. Senior managers have to "walk the talk." This means they have to restrain themselves from asking for too much (additional) information, and, during review meetings, they should avoid delving too deep into operational issues of the business. If they succeed in adopting this attitude, senior managers will set an example for the rest of the organization and for other management layers by not requesting details but sticking to the bottom line.

CASE: FOCUSING ON PERFORMANCE INDICATORS AT KLM ROYAL DUTCH AIRLINES

This case study describes the bottom-up implementation of CSFs and KPIs in an international environment. Because of specific circumstances, this implementation was driven not by corporate headquarters but by the divisions themselves. The way this impacted the development and the acceptance of the new measurements indicates that there is not necessarily only one right way to implement a balanced scorecard. Rather, every implementation has to be tailored to the company's specific situation and needs.

Organization's Background

KLM Royal Dutch Airlines (KLM) is an international airline, operating worldwide. Its home base is Amsterdam Airport Schiphol in The Netherlands. KLM's three core activities are passenger transport services (KLM Passenger); airfreight transport (KLM Cargo); and the maintenance of airframes, engines, and components (KLM Engineering and Maintenance). The company's goal is "to be the first-choice passenger and cargo airline while consistently enhancing shareholder value, providing a stimulating and dynamic working environment, and participating in mutually beneficial relationships with partners."

In recent years, the economics of the aviation industry have stayed relatively unchanged. The industry is capital and labor intensive, with more fixed than variable costs and small margins.

Global competition has intensified, with new, often low-cost entrants winning important market segments. This puts increased pressure on margins. To stay competitive, partnering between airlines has become more important in the aviation industry. KLM was the first to develop a strong American–European alliance, by choosing to partner with Northwest Airlines in 1989. An alliance can strengthen its market position by optimizing the overall network and capacity, by generating synergy from joint revenue management, and by combining sales and purchasing.

Through its alliances and close cooperation with European and intercontinental network and route partners, KLM offers passengers and airfreight shippers 160,000 city-pair connections worldwide, via several hubs. Measured by international revenue, KLM ranks sixth among the 250-plus members of the International Air Transport Association (IATA). The number of employees is about 30,000. Consolidated operating income for 1998/1999 amounted to US$190 million.

Focus on What Is Important: Implementing the Balanced Scorecard

Due to recent developments in the industry, reorganizations, and the change of management, various organizational units of KLM felt the need for changing their management information process.

KLM Cargo had recently completed a major reorganization, from a functional structure to business units, to better react to the continuously changing needs of its clients. The management of KLM Cargo felt that a new management information function was needed to support the new organization. The deputy executive vice president explained his reasoning: "When reorganizing within a company, you sometimes take shortcuts. You rearrange all the information you have to achieve maximum availability of information, but that is something different from starting with the needs of the managers."

As a first step, the management information function in place was benchmarked, by Arthur Andersen, against those from other companies. Arthur Andersen's Management Information and Reporting Analysis (MIRA) was used for this (see Appendix for a description of the MIRA). The benchmark results revealed the strongest points of KLM Cargo reporting to be the use of targets, the forecasting information, and the timeliness of sales information (done on a weekly basis). Employees were informed quickly about new developments within the division, and communication was very open. Improvement points focused on the content of reporting—management information was too financially oriented, and the link to operational information was not clear enough. The deputy executive vice president commented: "There was insufficient insight into the specific critical success factors of each unit. The benchmark forced the managers to think in terms of processes, input, throughput, and output. Main questions were: In what does your unit need to excel? What do you really need to do well?"

The recommendation from the benchmark was to define a limited set of financial and nonfinancial CSFs and KPIs for each level in the organization so managers could focus on important and relevant aspects. The management reporting could also be made more action oriented, which entails more emphasis on making analyses, action formulation, and action tracking.

Within the KLM Passenger division, the reason for changing the management information function was different from that of KLM Cargo. In aiming for the division's goal, "to deliver an excellent product that customers want and appreciate at a competitive price," KLM Passenger applied its knowledge of customers to continuously tailor services to select market segments. This had both operational and management consequences. For instance, applying e-commerce by selling tickets through the Internet affects KLM's relationship with traditional distribution channels (e.g., travel agents) and the cooperation with alliance, network, and route partners. These changes in products and activities meant that more information (e.g., brand, channel, and partner information) was needed. KLM Passenger management decided that a benchmark of its management reporting function would give the division good insight into potential improvement opportunities.

The most valuable features of Passenger's management information function turned out to be the extensive use of targets, financial ratios, and forecasting information; the timeliness of sales information (weekly), and the use of nonfinancial information based on key result areas (KRAs), which are similar to CSFs. A major improvement opportunity was limiting the amount of generated information by implementing the concept of "different information for different purposes." A growing amount of information about customers, products, channels, network, traffic, and so on, was generated periodically for managers. However, no distinction was made between information for periodic control, information for detailed analysis, and information for supporting daily operations. In short, there was a real danger of information overload. The executive vice president of Passenger received, besides the Passenger Monthly Report, more than 20 other reports, including many KRA reports. Therefore, the main recommendation was to define a limited set of financial and nonfinancial CSFs and KPIs for each level in the organization. Also, exception reporting should be introduced to enable managers to focus only on issues needing immediate attention.

Finally, based on the experience of the two divisions, KLM Corporate also decided to benchmark its own management information function against those of other corporate headquarters of multinationals. The benchmark study, again using Arthur Andersen's MIRA, showed that KLM's corporate headquarters had a fair amount of relevant, nonfinancial information available, for instance, information on personnel, production, productivity, airplanes, quality, and punctuality. Another strength identified was the system support for the reporting process, which was relatively simple and neatly arranged, with limited interfaces. The main area of improvement was the gap in the information between the corporate headquarters' report and the divisional reports, which was caused by applying different accounting procedures. Adding up the financial results or costs of the divisions did not automatically match the results of KLM as a total. Also, there was a need for exception reporting and standardization of the report layouts.

As mentioned before, KLM decided to start improvement projects at corporate headquarters and at various divisions. Normally, the first improvement project should start at KLM Corporate, with

KLM senior management articulating and translating the corporate strategy into clear strategic objectives. Then they would turn these objectives into strategic CSFs and KPIs. The divisions would subsequently start aligning their objectives with the strategic objectives and begin developing CSFs and KPIs for their own businesses. However, KLM's corporate management was heavily involved in many high-impact strategic initiatives at that time and was not ready to start the project at corporate headquarters. Some of these initiatives were the joint venture with Northwest, an important companywide change program, and a Corporate Governance project. As one of the senior managers stated: "If you want to start a management information improvement project at the same time, the question you may ask yourself is: Are we able to do so?"

Though senior management at corporate headquarters was not yet ready to begin the project, the divisional managers had an urgent need for better information to control their business. As one divisional manager responded: "But, we cannot wait." Therefore, the development of CSFs and KPIs at the divisional level began first. Managers accepted the fact that when corporate headquarters had finished its improvement project, a certain amount of alignment or even redevelopment of CSFs and KPIs on divisional level might be needed.

Improving KLM Cargo's Reporting

The improvement project at KLM Cargo started by reviewing the current content of the management reporting system of its four main business units: Operations, Mail, Special Cargo, and Customer Services. The review was done by a project team of Arthur Andersen consultants and KLM Cargo employees. The purpose of the review was to obtain more-detailed insight into the quality of the reports currently in use. For this reason, the current monthly management reports and documents containing information on strategy, objectives, and CSFs/KPIs were collected. Next, key elements of the strategy and objectives of the unit were identified and matched with the current CSFs and KPIs in the reports. In Exhibit 6.5, column 1 lists the objectives. The CSFs related to the

Exhibit 6.5   Business Unit Table, Mapping the Available Measurements with the Business Unit's Objectives

1. Objective	2. CSF	3. KPI	4. Present
1. Sustain margins.	Productivity	Platform transports per man-hour	
	Productivity	Documents per man-hour	
	Productivity	Bags per man-hour with average weight of 8 kg	Yes
	Utilization capacity	Load factor	Yes
	Net margin		
2. Develop new products.		Number of new products	
3. Differentiate basic services and let customer pay accordingly.	Physical product differentiation		
	Cost pricing/Margin selling		
4. Improve quality.	High quality		
	Quality of Operations	Pending and paid claims	
	Quality of Operations	Left behind freight due to capacity shortage	
	Adequate staff/Quality level of staff		
	Reliable bookkeeping		
	Timeliness	On-time provision of reports	
	Correctness		
5. Customer-driven service	Short connections	Delayed short connections	
	External communications		
	Customer satisfaction		

objective were put in column 2. The KPIs related to the CSFs were gathered in column 3. Finally, it was indicated in column 4 if a KPI was already presented in a current management report. Empty spaces in the table meant there were no measurements available. CSFs or KPIs that could not be linked were not included in the table, on the basis that they were not or could not be relevant for the business unit. Although in some cases a CSF could not be linked to an objective, specific CSFs turned out to be very important for the management team after discussion. In that case, a new objective was added to the list (i.e., row 5 in column 1).

In some Cargo business units, a clear link between strategy, objectives, CSFs, and KPIs could be found. In that case, only a limited number of extra nonfinancials were added to the business unit management report to get a complete balanced set. In other business units, as well as on Cargo divisional level, only a few relevant CSFs and KPIs were present. Workshops were then held with the management teams to develop additional CSFs and KPIs. The balanced scorecard layout was chosen as the reporting format and was used as a management summary on the first page of the report (Exhibit 6.6).

To stimulate analysis and action reporting, one page for each KPI was included to show the actuals, to put in an analysis, to formulate actions, and to describe the expected results of these actions (Exhibit 6.7). This format encourages managers to think about actions and to be better prepared for the monthly review meeting with top management.

Improving KLM Passenger's Reporting

The improvement project at KLM Passenger started with reviewing, in a project team of Arthur Andersen and KLM Passenger consultants, the relevance of the existing KRAs in relation to the divisional objectives. Then, to apply the principle of "different information for different purposes," for each management level the relevant KPIs were identified. KPIs needed for daily operations were excluded. For example, sales information for each daily flight was operational information, needed by revenue managers who are responsible for the allocation of capacity (in this case, equal to

Exhibit 6.6   Examples of Balanced Scorecard for the KLM Cargo Division (results are fictitious)

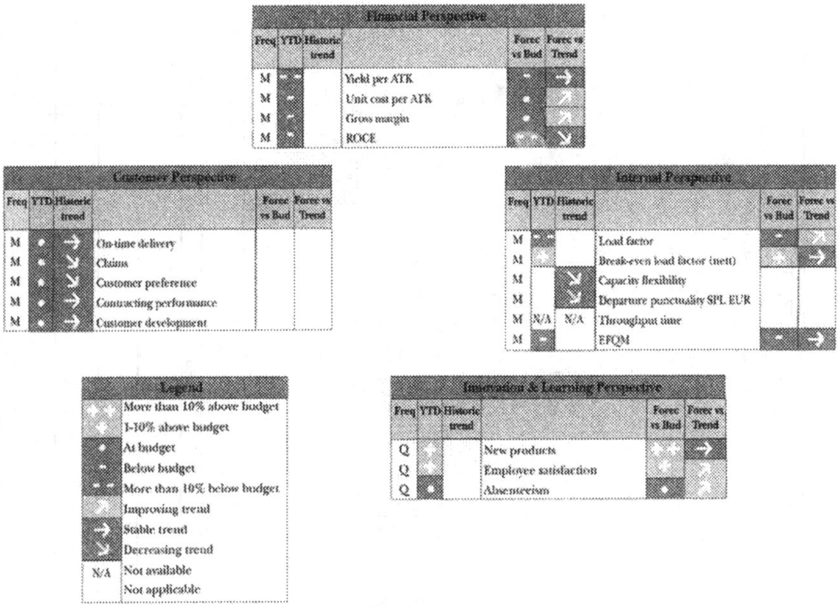

number of seats) to the sales areas. Sales area managers periodically needed information about the total sales in their area. The executive vice president of Passenger needed information on the total sales of KLM Passenger. If a sales area manager then wanted to have more-detailed information about a specific flight, he could ask one of his employees to pull this information from the systems. This employee did not get all the details automatically at his desk. The result was a clear cascading of management reports with a specific set of CSFs/KPIs for each organizational area and level.

A check was made by the project team to ensure that the final set of KPIs for each management level was truly in balance. A set is "balanced" if the measurements covered all of the important functional and operational elements and gave the management team a manageable number of indicators. Another check was made to determine the extent to which the information was readily available on the defined KPIs.

Exhibit 6.7 Reporting Format per KPI (results are fictitious)

Objective or Process	Strengthen position	Data Supplier	AMS/BB
Custodian	Manager	User(s)	EVP/Board of Man. Dir.
Involved units	All	Frequency	Monthly
Definition	Load factor: traffic (ton-kilometers) divided by capacity (available ton-kilometers)	Issue date	January 19, 1998
Target	Target 1997/98: 67.3%	Number	09

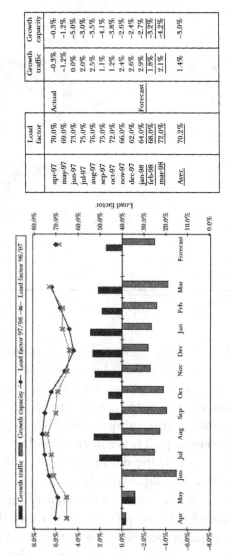

	Load factor		Growth traffic	Growth capacity
apr-97	70.0%	Actual	-0.3%	-0.3%
may-97	69.0%		-1.2%	-1.2%
jun-97	73.0%		0.0%	-5.0%
jul-97	75.0%		2.0%	-3.0%
aug-97	76.0%		2.5%	-3.5%
sep-97	75.0%		1.1%	-4.1%
oct-97	72.0%		1.2%	-3.8%
nov-97	66.0%		2.4%	-2.6%
dec-97	62.0%		2.6%	-2.4%
jan-98	64.0%		2.9%	-2.7%
feb-98	68.0%	Forecast	1.8%	-3.2%
mar-98	72.0%		2.1%	-4.2%
Aver.	70.2%		1.4%	-3.0%

Observations	Actions	Results	Date
Positive It is expected that the load factor will be above target for 97/98.			
Negative			

Improving KLM's Corporate Reporting

The improvement project at KLM's corporate headquarters concentrated on aligning the management information between corporate headquarters and the divisions, the addition of KLM Group and alliances information to the management report, and the improvement of the layout of the information. A project team was formed of Arthur Andersen consultants, the corporate controlling department, and a dedicated employee at corporate controlling to coordinate the team. The project started with individual discussions with the CEO, the COO (chief operations officer), the CFO (chief financial officer), various directors of the divisions, and people in the organization who were involved in the management reporting process.

To align corporate headquarters' and divisional reports, clarity about the accountability structure was needed. The financial items had to be calculated and reported in the same way, enterprisewide. The report content needed to be extended because, although KLM Group and network results (including the alliances) were available in the organization, this information was spread over different reports or consolidated less frequently. To meet the wishes of the CEO, network results were included every month in the corporate report. KLM company information was consolidated and included in the corporate report every quarter.

The layout of the corporate report was enhanced in such a way that KLM's CEO could easily read, in one summary page, the performance of the entire KLM company and the key indicators of the different divisions. By using traffic light coding, the CEO had a quick overview of where corporate attention was really needed. For more details, the CEO could refer to the detailed divisional reports.

As expected at the outset of the various improvement projects, differences appeared in the final layouts of the reports of the different divisions. At the time that KLM Cargo started to define its balanced scorecard layout, KLM Engineering and Maintenance had just finished its improvement project using another layout, symbols, and color coding. When the new corporate report was introduced, senior management expressed the wish to standardize the layout and symbols in the management reports of corporate headquarters and the divisions. The controllers of KLM first made a proposal for this standardization based on commonalties throughout the reports. The proposal was discussed with divisional controllers, updated and finalized, and then presented to the divisional and corporate managers. As a result, all of the divisions changed over to the agreed upon reporting layout. Managers no longer had to spend time reading legends for the scorecards or trying to find out what the color coding or symbol meant in each report. Attention could now be focused on what was important.

KLM's Experiences

KLM has noticed true benefits from the improvement initiatives during its management team meetings. The new management reports restrict the discussions to the essential topics. Additionally, the relationship between strategic and operational objectives has become clear. The management reports are more focused because they do not contain all kinds of different, sometimes less relevant, information anymore. Also, the reporting formats support more analysis and exception reporting and are truly action oriented.

Because all of the business units in a division now use the same reports and KPIs, internal benchmarking has become possible. A good development is that business units use this information for continuous improvement. Business units with low scores leverage information from the business units with high scores to improve the overall operations. At corporate headquarters, the main benefit is that there are no longer discussions during the monthly review meetings about the accuracy of the figures in the divisional or the corporate report. Everyone can focus on the real issues.

As KLM's corporate controller commented: "KLM's planning and control processes have been revised in recent years in many respects. Corporate headquarters' performance management project just started after having redesigned our business planning process. We first redefined our business model to include three core businesses, of which one business is a virtual combination of different divisions. Then, we introduced a tactical planning process for the three businesses, including quarterly rolling forecasts. Finally, we aligned internal reporting between divisions and corporate and introduced new KPIs for the board of managing directors. Last but not least, we speeded up our monthly closing. The balanced scorecard concept, including more action-oriented reporting, is now widely spread in our company. Some KLM Group companies are introducing the concept as well. It is our aim to modernize and update the reports regularly. Current examples are joint venture reporting and reporting on business risks and business controls. It is a constant struggle to keep the reports state-of-the-art in a fast-changing business environment like the airline industry. But at the same time this is a very interesting challenge for modern controllers."

CASE: LIMITING THE AMOUNT OF INFORMATION AT NEC

This case study describes a management process that is focused on limiting the information to truly crucial data, that is, practicing "management by exceptions" by strictly focusing on problem areas. Arthur Andersen took a look at the headquarters of NEC in Tokyo in the NEC Super Tower to discuss this management process.

Organization's Background

NEC Corporation (NEC), founded in 1899 as Nippon Electric Company, is a leading international electronics manufacturer of communications systems and equipment, computers, industrial electronic systems, and electron devices. NEC operates primarily in a single industrial segment that is called C&C, which stands for "the integration of computers and communications." NEC has approximately 152,000 employees in about 50 countries. Revenues are US$37 billion with a net income of US$310 million (1998 figures). NEC is the world's second largest producer of semiconductors.

NEC is organized into 5 marketing groups, 11 operating groups, and the corporate staff (Exhibit 6.8). The marketing groups focus on specific markets: Nippon Telegraph and Telephone Corporation group (NTT), the Japanese government and public organizations group, and the private-sector customers

Exhibit 6.8   Simplified Organizational Chart of NEC Corporation

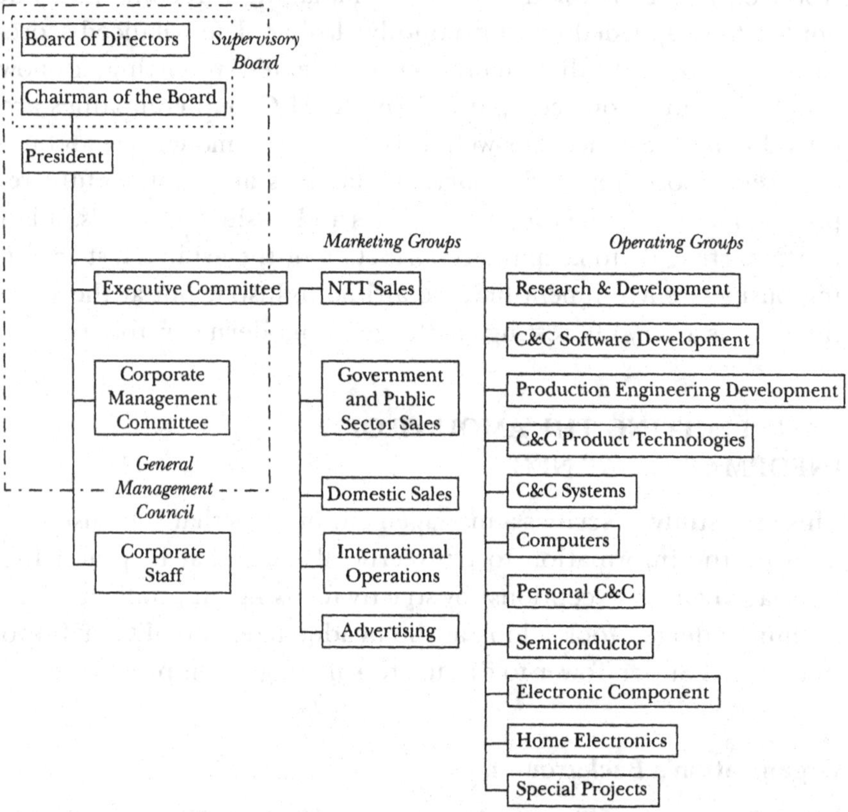

```
┌─────────────────────────────────────────┐
│ ┌───────────────────┐  Supervisory       │
│ │Board of Directors │   Board            │
│ │                   │                    │
│ │┌─────────────────┐│                    │
│ ││Chairman of the Board│                 │
│ │└─────────────────┘│                    │
│ └───────────────────┘                    │
│ ┌─────────┐                              │
│ │President│                              │
│ └─────────┘                              │
```

Marketing Groups   *Operating Groups*

Executive Committee — NTT Sales — Research & Development

— C&C Software Development

Corporate Management Committee — Government and Public Sector Sales — Production Engineering Development

— C&C Product Technologies

General Management Council

— Domestic Sales — C&C Systems

Corporate Staff — International Operations — Computers

— Personal C&C

— Advertising — Semiconductor

— Electronic Component

— Home Electronics

— Special Projects

group. The international operations group is in charge of international marketing activities across all product categories and handles the coordination of overseas manufacturing. The advertising group coordinates NEC's advertising and promotional activities both in Japan and in overseas markets. The operating groups are responsible for research and development (R&D) and for manufacturing of the products. The operating groups consist of 70 units. The role of the corporate staff is to provide professional and technical assistance to top management, to marketing groups, and to operating groups.

NEC's strategy is to give top priority to customer satisfaction. It is constantly looking for ways to improve the quality of its manufacturing, service, and management processes in order to create products and services that deliver greater value to its customers. NEC is concentrating on the multimedia sector while simultaneously leveraging its comprehensive strengths in the fields of communications equipment, computers, and electron devices. Also, new business units are developed in such areas as Internet-related products and services. Additionally, NEC continues to improve its profitability by aggressively reducing production costs through the promotion of its globalization strategy and the introduction of innovative production lines, as well as by cutting fixed costs.

Focus on What Is Truly Important: Exceptions

Every month, eight days after month-end closing, the senior management team of NEC (consisting of the chairman, the president, and three vice presidents) receives a short, concise management report. The first page of this report is a summary of actual versus forecast for several financial indicators that are common to all operating groups. This makes it possible for the senior management team to see in one glance where possible problems are located in the company.

The second page is the new forecast for the same financial indicators. The expected results of corrective actions should show up in this overview. When environmental changes have taken place or are anticipated to take place, NEC's senior management team expects operating groups to have taken these into account when making their actions and forecasts. In this way, it is not easy for operating groups to use the excuse that unforeseen external things happened.

The third page compares the new forecast with the previous forecast to be able to check the quality of the forecasting process. This page will point out when operating groups have not dealt sufficiently with environmental changes.

The report is complemented by various detailed financial overviews for the operating groups (like a profit & loss [P&L] statement and a balance sheet). If the senior management team needs more information about certain issues, it can go into NEC's executive information system (see details in the next section) to look at the financial and nonfinancial details of the operating groups and their underlying units.

Managers of all operating groups and the senior management team meet on a monthly basis to communicate and discuss the results of each operating group. This meeting takes place in the second half of the month to give the operating groups the time to come up with action plans if actual results did not meet the forecast. During the meeting, the results of the operating groups as well as the actions already initiated or completed are shared among the managers. Because action plans are communicated along with the results, long discussions can be avoided and the setting of the meetings is more positive.

This constitutes a form of "proactive after the fact" control. The monthly report can show that some managers have issues in their operating group ("after the fact"). These managers also know that they have to face their peers later in the month during the monthly meeting and that they will have to explain themselves. Therefore, they proactively address their problems before this meeting. In this way, they are able to state in the meeting either that their issues have been solved or, at a minimum, that they are under control.

Besides getting together at the regular monthly meeting, NEC's senior management team practices management by exception—it only meets separately with the management team of an operating group, for a performance review on location, when that particular operating group did not meet its forecast. As long as the group hits the forecast, the senior management team does not interfere. In this way, an extended period of time can elapse before NEC's senior management team actually meets with an operating group's management team.

Before the monthly meeting, managers from the operating groups can schedule an intermediate meeting with the senior management team to discuss specific issues and to get their help to start solving these issues.

Embrace Information Transparency by Using Technology

NEC's financial information is available in two separate data warehouses. One warehouse is for the senior management team and is especially designed and used for corporate-level analysis. The information in this warehouse contains summary overviews from the operating groups and its units and is made available through an executive information system. NEC's senior managers use this system individually to view and to analyze management information in a user-friendly way.

The other data warehouse is used by managers and staff during the execution of business operations. It is designed for detailed analysis of their particular divisions and business units. NEC also uses an intranet to distribute management information throughout the company, especially to foreign subsidiaries.

NEC has designed a decision room for the top management team. In this room, each senior management team member has access to a monitor, which displays the presentation materials during the meetings. Furthermore, the monitors can be linked to the executive information system to analyze information during the meeting. Typically, an analyst will stand by during these meetings to recall specific information when the need arises during the meeting.

KEY POINTS

☑ The challenge nowadays is not a lack but an overload of management information. Managers need to start focusing on what is truly important: on key value drivers that are crucial to the business, on exceptional events or figures, on analyzing financial and nonfinancial results, on corrective action plans, and on the impact of those action plans.

☑ Contingency areas constitute performance ranges representing acceptable deviations from the budget. Only if

(continued)

the performance is outside the agreed contingency area will higher management levels intervene and step in.

☑ The implementation of preventive action reporting, based on forecasts, instills proactive behavior. The responsible manager is forced to think about the future and to plan and execute preventive actions if the forecasts deviate from the targets.

☑ Managers have to learn to deal with uncertainty because they will receive fewer details. Accountability gets a new meaning: if you are accountable, you are the *first* to take action. You have to take the initiative for corrective or preventive actions.

NOTES

1. Simons, R., and A. Davila, How high is your return on management?, Harvard Business Review, January–February 1998.
2. Meyer, M.W., Permanent failure and the failure of organizational performance, in: H.K. Anheier (ed.), When things go wrong, organizational failures and breakdowns, Sage Publications, 1999.
3. Kröger, F., M. Träm, and M. Vandenbosch, Spearheading growth, how Europe's top companies are restructuring to win, Pitman Publishing, 1998.
4. Rootliep, H., in: S.G. Simsek, Met visie aan de top (transl. 'With vision at the top'], Kluwer BedrijfsInformatie, 1998.
5. Levitin, A.V., and T.C. Redman, Data as a resource: properties, implications, and prescriptions, Sloan Management Review, volume 40, number 1, Fall 1998.
6. Simons, R., and A. Davila, How high is your return on management?, Harvard Business Review, January–February 1998; and Simons, R., Performance measurement & control systems for implementing strategy (text & cases), Prentice-Hall, 2000.

7

Enforce Performance-Driven Behavior

CHALLENGE OF THE RIGHT BEHAVIOR FOR IMPLEMENTATION

> The improvements happened because management at these companies had two things in common. They focused on managing what mattered and they made a commitment to walk the talk.
>
> *B. Maguire*[1]

> I think that the most important thing is that people have responsibility. And I don't mean paper responsibility.
>
> *P. Fentener van Vlissingen*[2]

> No matter what you say, others will listen to what you do.
>
> *B. Maguire*[3]

As already mentioned in Chapter 3, the main challenge for chief executive officers (CEOs) today is not just having a good strategy but implementing this strategy. For an organization to thrive, managers must be able to get things done, to deliver on commitments, to follow up on critical assignments, and to support people and hold them accountable to their promises. Managers need to replace passive reporting *performance measurement* with proactive, results-oriented *performance management.*

In order to create an organization that is guided by performance-driven behavior, several things have to happen.

○ Make sure that every individual knows what is important for him or her. What is the required performance expected of him or her, and what actions are required to reach strategic goals?

○ Individual responsibilities, targets, and incentives should be aligned with the strategic objectives of the organization. Then, people should act on what was agreed.

○ Management should set the right example by walking the talk, consistently delivering on what was promised. This walk-the-talk culture should be focused on actions and should follow up on these actions. Did they deliver the results that were expected of them?

○ A culture of trust in people has to be established and fostered. Management gives the employees not only the responsibilities and the tools to achieve agreed upon results, but also enough freedom to achieve these results in the manner that management sees fit—and management trusts that the results will be delivered.

So no more mingling into other persons responsibilities, no more asking questions of ever increasing levels of detail, no more review meetings that change focus and subjects every time, and no more swapping of the parenting style all the time, because these send confusing signals to the organization.

ALIGN INDIVIDUAL OBJECTIVES WITH STRATEGIC OBJECTIVES

In practical terms, strategic human resource management means getting everybody, from the top of the organization to the bottom, doing things to implement the business's strategy effectively. The idea is to use people most wisely with respect to the strategic needs of the organization. That doesn't just happen on its own. An integrated framework that systematically links human resource activities with strategic business needs can help.

W.F. Cascio[4]

Employee performance is the single most important characteristic that stipulates whether an organization is successful.[5] To illustrate the power of employee commitment and performance, consider the following:

○ Highly committed employees work harder and generate higher sales than do employees with low commitment, they are more effective in controlling operational costs, and they receive higher overall performance ratings from supervisors.[6]

○ Employee retention is a key driver of customer retention, which in turn is a key driver of organization growth and profits. A study showed that a 7 percent decrease in employee turnover led to a total increase of more than $27,000 in sales per employee and increases in profits per employee of almost $4,000.[7]

○ Employee loyalty is related to customer satisfaction, which in turn is related to organization growth and profits. Statistical analysis of sales data at Sears, Roebuck & Company showed that employee attitudes drive both customer satisfaction and changes in revenue. A 5 percent improvement in employee attitude results in a 1.3 percent improvement in customer satisfaction, which in turn results in a 0.5 percent increase in store revenue. Independent surveys showed that national retail customer satisfaction had fallen for several years; but in the time period for which the data was analyzed, employee satisfaction at Sears had risen by 4 percent. During the same time, customer satisfaction rose by almost 4 percent, which translated into more than $200 million in additional revenues for that year and increased Sears market capitalization at that time by nearly $250 million.[8]

For an organization to receive full benefit from the efforts of its employees, four preconditions have to be fulfilled:

1. The objectives of all management levels are aligned with the mission and the strategy of the organization.

2. These objectives are translated into clear expectations regarding the performance of employees.

3. Employees know how to fulfill the expectations, and they know what kind of support they can expect from management.

4. The set of human resource instruments (performance review, incentives, training, and development) is attuned to the realization of the organization's objectives.

In Arthur Andersen's Performance Alignment Model (PAM) these preconditions are taken together to arrive at a logical model (Exhibit 7.1). The model consists of four consecutive steps:

Step 1. At the starting point are the mission and the strategic objectives of the organization. These are formulated by answering the questions: "What does the organization want to achieve?" and "How does the organization want to achieve this?" (①"in Exhibit 7.1).

In order to make the strategy as tangible as possible, concrete strategic objectives are formulated. To measure whether these objectives are realized, strategic critical success factors (CSFs) and strategic key performance indicators (KPIs) are identified. A business unit can support the execution of the mission and the strategy of the organization by translating the strategic objectives into objectives for the unit and then working toward achieving these business unit objectives. The degree to which the business unit is successful with this is measured by CSFs and KPIs, which are specific for each business unit (② in Exhibit 7.1).

Finally, the operational objectives are identified, based on the crucial activities of the business unit. A *crucial activity* is a business activity that the organization, no matter which mission and

Exhibit 7.1   Steps in the Performance Alignment Model Needed to Develop Individual Measurements

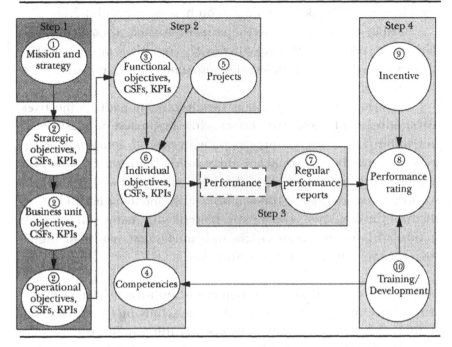

strategy have been chosen, always has to perform well in order to survive and thrive (see also Chapter 4). The achievement of the operational objectives is measured by operational CSFs and operational KPIs.

Step 2. Strategic, business unit, and operational objectives are translated into objectives for the various functions in the business unit. These functional objectives are, in fact, the requirements that an organization places on a certain function so that this function has added value for the organization. The functional objectives are translated into functional CSFs and functional KPIs (③ in Exhibit 7.1). Senior management's functional objectives are directly derived from the strategic objectives of the organization.

For every functional objective, the competencies are identified that the individual needs in order to achieve that objective successfully. *Success* means that the average target set for the functional KPI is achieved. The competencies are expressed in the knowledge and the skills that a person has (④ in Exhibit 7.1).

Often, an employee participates in ad hoc, special projects. Therefore, project objectives also exist. For this type of objective also, average targets and needed competencies are identified (⑤ in Exhibit 7.1).

Functional and project objectives become individual objectives, after individual targets have been set for the person in question (⑥ in Exhibit 7.1). When the targets are being set, the competencies the person currently has are taken into account. For instance, when the employee has just started in this function, the target will probably be set lower than average so the employee has time to adjust and to settle in. If the employee is very experienced, with many working years in this or in similar functions, the individual target may be set higher than the average target for this function.

Step 3.   After the individual objectives and targets have been defined, the employee can start working at achieving them. Through regular, periodic performance reports, the employee gets feedback about whether the achievement of the individual objectives is still on track (⑦ in Exhibit 7.1). If performance is slacking, the employee, together with the superior, can define corrective actions.

Step 4.   During an annual review, the performance of the employee is officially discussed (⑧ in Exhibit 7.1). On the basis of this review, an adjustment of the salary and bonus can be made (⑨ in Exhibit 7.1). The amount of adjustment depends on the incentive structure of the organization. Also during the review, the individual objectives and targets for the next year are discussed and agreed upon by the manager and the employee.

The formal review gives important input for the development plan, which is made for every employee (⑩ in Exhibit 7.1). This plan includes activities to improve the knowledge and skills of the individual, to improve performance in the current function, or to prepare the individual for the next function.

The chance of actually achieving the objectives of the organization are considerably improved by using the performance alignment model. This is because the objectives of all management levels are aligned with each other, so all employees know what is important for the organization and what is expected from them. Everybody works under the same regime with a distinct and clear structure.

The assessment and reward criteria are related with the strategic objectives of the organization, which causes these human resource tools to directly support the achievement of the strategy. Also, the assessment criteria are clearly formulated and are relevant for both the organization and the individual, making them much more acceptable to employees.

Research shows that the motivation of employees to perform well is improved when their goals are clear to them. An employee's ability to see the connection between his or her work and the organization's strategic objectives is a driver of positive behavior.[9] This clarity is achieved by formulating and using individual objectives that are derived from the strategy. Also, uncertainty about the assessment criteria used for review and reward purposes is less because the employee knows beforehand which criteria will be used. The identification of functional and individual objectives and competencies helps improve the quality of the development of function descriptions and competency profiles.

Finally, the implementation of individual objectives, individual targets, and clear assessment criteria, linked with a flexible reward structure, can lead to a culture change. The commitment of employees to achieve the objectives of the organization is higher. Also, norms and values, with respect to "what is good and what is wrong," are clearer and more uniform.

INCENTIVES BASED ON CONTINGENCIES

The incentive compensation structure can be linked to the budget by using the predefined contingency areas (see Chapter 6 for an explanation of contingency areas). When defining the contingency areas for specific key value drivers during the budget process, the bonus level is directly tied to these areas (① in Exhibit 7.2).

Exhibit 7.2   Level of Incentive Is Linked to Contingency and
Intervene Areas

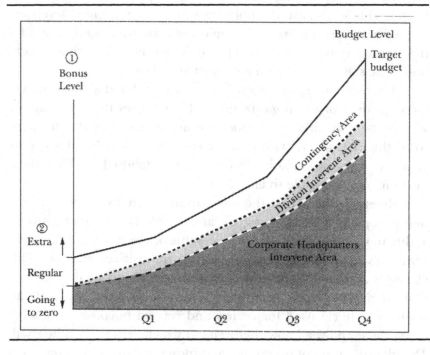

Management compensation is dependent on year-end performance against target (② in Exhibit 7.2). The more the actuals are
below the target budget, the lower the bonus level is. In the corporate intervene area, no bonus is received at all. Outstanding performance above the agreed target budget is rewarded with extra
compensation.

LINK TIME HORIZONS OF FORECASTING
AND COMPENSATION

Many organizations experience difficulties with respect to the
quality and the reliability of forecasts. One of the reasons for this
is a discrepancy between the time horizon on which management
is focused and the time span that is covered in the forecast.

Management is primarily focused on the time horizon that is covered by the management compensation program, which most often is one year. The forecast horizon may well be longer, for example, six quarters ("rolling forecasts"). This results in management not paying enough attention and not putting enough effort into preparing the rolling forecast, thereby decreasing the added value of this process. Aligning the forecasting horizon with the time horizon that is subject to management compensation then improves the quality and reliability of the forecasts.

Instead of adjusting the time horizon of the forecast to the time span covered in management compensation, the opposite can be applied. In that case the management compensation period can be extended to include longer-term strategic achievements.

USE SYNERGY INDICATORS

In every organization, cooperation is one of the most important success factors. If people within an organization do not cooperate, the quality of supplied products and services is severely impacted. Usually there are a number of people, teams, or departments involved in executing business activities and achieving results. All these people should be willing to cooperate in order to attain the organization's strategy and targets. And even when an organization is already successful, it is very likely that its results would have been even better if cooperation among the employees would have been better. This means that cooperation is one of the prerequisites for performance-driven behavior.

It is therefore remarkable that cooperation within an organization generally remains underexposed in management reports. One of the reasons for this is that cooperation is often looked upon as a sociopsychological issue. It is not quantifiable and cannot therefore be measured.

In the 1960s and 1970s the so-called social indicator was being used. This indicator found its origin in sociopsychological specialties, in which people had a need for registering and describing social developments. Governments and trade unions felt very strongly about the laborer's welfare, which was expressed in terms of quality of labor, health, well-being, and employment. Two examples of social indicators are (1) the absentee rate and (2) the ratio of the number of female to male employees.

The social indicator was mainly used by personnel managers to account for their social policies. Unfortunately, no one ever defined social indicators to measure the extent to which cooperation occurred among employees. Managers failed to see the importance of these social indicators because they were not related to strategy. Strategy remained managers' prime concern at all times. For this reason the social indicator did not make it into the 1980s, and presently they are used solely in social annual reports. Nowadays, it appears that little has changed since the 1980s.

Because cooperation is one of the factors that leads an organization to success, it should be incorporated in management reports. By doing so, managers can monitor the degree of cooperation within the organization periodically. In this section, the concept of CSFs and KPIs will be used for tracking cooperation (see Chapter 4 for a description of CSFs and KPIs).

Measuring Cooperation with Synergy Indicators

In the professional literature four aspects are discussed on the topic of cooperation:

1. *The organization should tailor itself to its environment.* The employees of the organization should cooperate in a client-oriented manner. Measurement of product or service quality, as perceived by clients, can provide an indication of the extent to which employees cooperate within an organization. If it turns out that the quality as perceived by clients is unsatisfactory, it may well be a result of poor cooperation.

2. *All employees must understand and preferably agree on the targets at which the organization aims.* In-depth discussions during target setting have a positive effect on the readiness among

employees to work together in attaining the targets that were set.

3. *There should be clear definitions of the organizational structure and the responsibilities and the accountabilities derived from this structure, and all employees should understand and respect these definitions.* If a department has certain responsibilities appointed to it and, at the same time, is regarded as incompetent by other departments, there will be a negative effect on the cooperation between the departments involved. Employees will try to avoid working with people from the incompetent department and will attempt to perform the operations themselves.

4. *Cooperation and communication are inextricably tied together.* Alignment of and feedback on the activities and the responsibilities of individuals and departments take place through communication. The communication can be verbal (e.g., through regular meetings), or it can be written, either manually or electronically (e.g., through written reports and collective usage of information systems).

The four listed aspects can be translated into CSFs for cooperation. These can be of a strategic, functional, or operational nature (Exhibit 7.3). The degree to which there is alignment between an

Exhibit 7.3 Mapping the Aspects of Cooperation with the Level of Critical Success Factors

Aspect	Strategic	Functional	Operational
Alignment of organization and environment	✓		
Consensus on goals and objectives		✓	
Organizational structure		✓	
Communication		✓	✓
Other			✓

organization and its environment is a *strategic* CSF for cooperation because, in general, quality and customer satisfaction are elements of an organization's strategy. Consensus on the goals that are to be achieved is a *functional* CSF for cooperation because it concerns consensus between departments or groups of people on the objectives derived from the strategy. The organizational structure is another functional CSF for cooperation. Every manager and employee must conform to it if an organization is to implement its strategy successfully. Communication can be both a *functional* and an *operational* CSF. It is functional when it concerns communication about the organization's objectives; it is operational when it is used for performing daily operations.

The category "other" includes CSFs that cannot be placed under any of the other four categories, but that are nevertheless of importance to a specific organization. Usually they are of an operational nature.

For each CSF, one or more KPIs can be determined. This serves to make CSFs quantifiable and allows managers to monitor progress over a time period. If two departments cooperate well, there is a good chance this cooperation will lead to synergy, that is "one plus one makes three." Synergy occurs, for example, when different departments share knowledge and, as a consequence, can provide their customers with unambiguous information. We call KPIs that measure cooperation *synergy indicators*. The target of a synergy indicator must be set; and, just as with regular performance indicators, all parties involved in the particular cooperation should receive periodic reports on achievement toward this target. This procedure enables managers to initiate corrective actions, if needed. By using synergy indicators managers have a tool at their disposal for measuring cooperation.

Implementation of Synergy Indicators

CSFs and synergy indicators that deal with cooperation within an organization form a special type of CSFs and KPIs. They can be an important addition to management reports. The development and implementation of synergy indicators has taught us a number of interesting lessons.

- ○ *Involvement creates awareness of cooperation.* Talking about cooperation makes employees in an organization aware of the importance of and the need for cooperation. This has a positive effect on cooperation, even at an early stage of the implementation of synergy indicators.

- ○ *Providing users with good training and information is required before the development of synergy indicators can begin.* Managers are often confronted with employee skepticism toward synergy indicators at the beginning of the development project. "Measuring cooperation" sounds too abstract and intangible. This is why it is essential to explain concepts such as cooperation, critical success factor, and synergy indicator right from the beginning and to illustrate the concept by using plenty of examples. During the project, the employees themselves have to indicate which synergy indicators they consider to be important.

- ○ *Keep data-gathering methods simple.* It often happens that the required data for determining synergy indicators are not available in an organization's information systems. Managers should take into account that the required data gathering can be time-consuming for the employees involved. Possible alternative methods of data gathering may be random checks, questionnaires, or contracting out.

- ○ *The measurement frequency of synergy indicators is usually lower than that of the regular KPIs.* Synergy indicators are usually unsuitable for weekly or monthly measurement because for most of these indicators the required data is not available on a permanent base. Thus, measuring requires an extra effort, which may be relatively too high compared to the amount of extra information that it gives monthly or weekly. In such cases quarterly reports are recommended.

- ○ *Targets for synergy indicators are often not available right from the start.* In these cases a possible solution may be to keep track of the actual values of a synergy indicator for a certain trial period and then to determine a target value on the basis of an analysis. The absolute value however is often irrelevant. More important is to find out whether there is an increase or a decrease of cooperation over a certain period. This can be done by means of a trend analysis.

BEHAVIORAL IMPLICATIONS OF THE PERFORMANCE ORIENTATION

Trust is key in the application of performance alignment. A new mindset of management is required to make "management by trust" possible. This management style entails letting go of strict control measurements and guidelines and starting to trust the ability of lower management levels and employees, including trusting the information one receives from these levels. This means also giving *and* taking accountability. Installing accountability in the organization is a two-way street. Higher management levels have to give accountability. But lower management levels and employees need to accept and take accountability. Creation of a dynamic environment in which everyone feels accountable for what he or she is responsible for and takes action on will be difficult but necessary to make performance alignment a success.

Part of this dynamic environment is an error-friendly culture. Room for error is necessary to take people in the organization through a learning process. You can learn from mistakes and from things that did not work, usually even faster than when everything always goes as planned. Complacency should be avoided at all times.

This error-friendly culture requires a positive and participative management attitude that is not based on punishment. People do not want to take on responsibilities when the risk of being punished for making errors increases. Risk avoidance, and even fear, will impede the culture you want and must create and will not to lead to people who are confident enough to take on responsibilities. In creating this culture, it is important not to accuse people of errors. People know themselves that something went wrong.

Managers' role is to understand what happened and to coach toward a solution, not to point a finger.

CASE: ALIGNING THE ORGANIZATION AT SOCIAL HOUSING ASSOCIATION HET OOSTEN

In recent years, the social housing association Het Oosten, much like the other housing associations in The Netherlands, had to change from being an organization in the public sector to a market-oriented organization. In the old situation, management of an association was based on policies and rules dictated by the government, and the finances of an association consisted of limited grants from that same governmental entity. In the new environment, an association must be managed in accordance with the needs and the developments of the housing market. The association now also controls its own finances without grants.

This change required a new management model for the associations. The need to become more market oriented meant that management information had to meet requirements that were different from those that were previously necessary. This case study examines how the social housing association Het Oosten managed to embrace the change by aligning strategy with functional and individual performance, using Arthur Andersen's performance alignment model. By achieving this alignment, Het Oosten has the right information at its disposal to enforce performance-driven behavior.

Organization's Background

Het Oosten is a prominent organization in the public housing sector and ranks among the 20 largest Dutch public housing associations. Het Oosten rents, manages, and sells houses in every price category throughout Amsterdam. The association also engages in the development of new buildings and the purchase and redevelopment of existing buildings. Large projects are usually executed in cooperation with developers, private investors, and other housing associations.

Het Oosten consists of five business units:

1. *Project development.* This business unit develops new building projects and redevelops houses in the organization's portfolio. Its projects range from urban renewal projects to the construction or reconstruction of entire areas, including shopping centers and artist's studios.

2. *Real estate.* This business unit is responsible for portfolio management. Its main activities are the purchase and selling of properties.

3. *Renting.* This business unit develops and renders services to tenants and is responsible for the association's communication with them. Its tasks are to sign tenant contracts, to maintain communication with tenants, and to recover rent arrears. One of the business unit's departments is called Tenant Affairs.

4. *Maintenance and control.* This business unit takes care of the maintenance of houses and corporate buildings of both the association and third parties. Its activities include emergency repairs, planned maintenance, and the development and collection of technical housing information. One of the departments of this business unit is called Maintenance Advice Agency.

5. *Finance.* This business unit monitors the financial position of the association. Its main activity is to secure low-cost funding as well as solvency in the housing sector, which enables Het Oosten to continue its policy and investments.

The five business units are supported by the department's executive staff, executive secretary, product development, and information technology (IT). Het Oosten's workforce is 225 people.

Enforce Performance-Driven Behavior: Implementing Individual Indicators

In order to be able to make the change described at the beginning of this case study, Het Oosten needed a new information-reporting system that was accessible for all employees in the organization. This system would help the organization to execute its strategy, to initiate corrective actions, and to encourage discussions on performance and quality. As a guide for the development of the new information system, Het Oosten chose the performance alignment model developed by Arthur Andersen Business Consulting.

Measuring Mission and Strategy: Step 1

The first step in the development of a new information-reporting system was to develop the mission statement and the strategy of the association in more detail and to create a framework to measure the execution of the strategy.

The project began with an analysis of all relevant documentation, such as the annual report, discussion memoranda, and management conference reports. After the analysis, interviews were held with the supervisory board, the board of management, the management team, and a municipal representative (at that time, municipal authorities supervised housing associations). The interviews dealt with developments in the housing sector and questioned how Het Oosten was to prepare for these developments. The mission and the strategic objectives were further developed in a workshop and operationalized by means of CSFs and KPIs. Both the management team and the supervisory board participated in this workshop.

The mission of Het Oosten is: "To guarantee good and affordable housing for various groups of people in an attractive and multicultural environment." To achieve its mission, Het Oosten aims at realizing the following objectives:

- To work in a customer-oriented fashion. Customer orientation includes anticipating the housing needs of customers, being accessible to customers, involving tenants in housing policy and management, and facilitating housing choice by offering the possibility of customized housing.
- To provide housing to low- and moderate-income tenants. The association wants to realize this by using real estate profits for social housing purposes, by helping tenants move up the

housing ladder (i.e., move to higher-rent housing), and by creating and preserving affordable houses.

○ *To invest in communities and neighborhoods.* The association wants to play an active part in diminishing urban decline. Het Oosten tries to do this by raising the quality of life in specific communities and neighborhoods. This is important both for retention of property value and for getting tenants involved in preserving the neighborhood.

○ *To build a strong internal organization.* A strong internal organization is essential to operating successfully in the commercial housing market. Such an organization is built by promoting a professional, result-oriented culture; by improving associates' productivity and efficiency; and by striving for synergies between business units and departments.

○ *To aim at a strong market position.* The association wants to achieve this by improving the price-to-quality ratio of its products and services and by entering into strategic alliances. Additionally, Het Oosten wants to improve its corporate identity on the housing market, to attract both tenants and buyers.

○ *To improve the financial position.* In order to continue its operation as a housing association, Het Oosten needs a long-term, stable, financial position.

The aforementioned objectives can be measured, for example, with the indicators that are shown in Exhibit 7.4. The KPI "Degree of popularity with potential tenants" equals the difference in the number of housing requests by potential tenants before and after the association invested in a certain neighborhood. The KPI "Cost price of productive hour per department" is measured by dividing the total salaries and allocated costs of a department by the total number of productive hours of that department. These hours can be gathered from the time reports that every employee of Het Oosten has to complete. The KPI "Demand by potential tenants for a rented unit" is determined by comparing the average number of housing requests by potential tenants for a vacant Het Oosten unit

Exhibit 7.4   Het Oosten's Strategic Objectives and Measurements

Objective	Strategic CSF	Strategic KPI
To work in a customer-oriented fashion.	Increase in range of products.	Turnover from new products.
To provide housing to low- and moderate-income tenants.	Appropriate supply of houses (existing and new).	Share of affordable houses portfolio in Amsterdam.
To invest in communities and neighborhoods.	Increase in value (financial) due to location.	Degree of popularity with potential tenants.
To build a strong internal organization.	Productivity.	Cost price of productive hour per department.
To aim at a strong market position.	Demand for products and services of Het Oosten.	Demand by potential tenants for a rented unit.
To improve the financial position.	Improved financial position.	Solvability.

to the average number of housing requests by potential tenants for
a general vacant unit in Amsterdam.

Developing Business Unit and Operational Objectives and Indicators: Step 2

Strategic objectives apply to Het Oosten as a whole. Each business
unit can contribute to achieving some or all of these objectives. In
this section, the development approach is discussed. Also, examples are given of the link between strategic objectives and business
unit and operational objectives for the maintenance and control
business unit and the renting business unit.

The same approach for developing the objectives and the measurements was used for both business units. First, interviews were
held with all business unit managers. This was followed by a customer survey that examined the demands and expectations of customers with regard to the services provided by each business unit.

An analysis was made of the business unit's reporting set. The business unit and operational objectives were then discussed in a number of workshops and were made measurable by means of business unit and operational CSFs and KPIs. All business unit managers and some employees participated in these workshops.

Due to the nature of the activities of the maintenance and control business unit, this unit could contribute to the strategic objectives "To work in a customer-oriented fashion," "To provide housing to low- and moderate-income tenants," "To build a strong internal organization," and "To aim at a strong market position." Exhibit 7.5 includes some of the business unit and operational objectives and indicators for this business unit.

The renting business unit could contribute to all of the organization's strategic objectives. Exhibit 7.6 shows a number of business unit and operational objectives and indicators that were developed.

Developing Individual Objectives and Indicators: Step 3

The new reporting system for individual performance management was developed in phases, for each business unit and supporting departments. The first phase consisted of drafting the procedures on how to develop individual objectives and indicators. In the second phase, the individual objectives and indicators were developed for managers, followed by those for other employees of the business unit. Finally, after each business unit had been dealt with, the project results were submitted to a quality test in order to ensure mutual alignment.

Within the business units, the first step was an interview with the management team member who was responsible for that specific business unit. Discussion topics were which activities the business unit performed, possible factors for success or failure with respect to the business unit, and the content of the business unit reporting. After the interview, functional objectives were developed in two workshops that were attended by managers from the business unit and the aforementioned management team member.

Exhibit 7.5   Maintenance and Control Business Unit's Objectives
and Measurements

Strategic Objective	Business Unit Objective	Business Unit CSF	Business Unit KPI
To work in a customer-oriented fashion.	House management (maintenance and advice) that meets the demands of internal and external customers.	Customer satisfaction with regard to maintenance and advice.	Maintenance response time.
To provide housing to low- and moderate-income tenants.	Preservation and improvement of housing unit quality.	Unit quality.	Ratio corrective/ planned maintenance.
To aim at a strong market position.	Operate in accordance with the market.	Price/performance ratio (performance = quantity and quality).	Cost price per product.

Strategic Objective	Operational Objective	Operational CSF	Operational KPI
To work in a customer-oriented fashion.	Maintenance planning.	Quality of long-term plan.	Additional costs for corrective maintenance.
To provide housing to low- and moderate-income tenants.	Budgetary control.	Budgetary control.	Number of budgeted jobs.

These functional objectives consisted of a combination of business unit and project objectives. For the business unit managers, the business unit's objectives were usually adopted unaltered.

After managers had formulated their functional objectives, all other employees of the business unit did the same. For this to happen, a short informative session about the project was followed by three workshops (Exhibit 7.7).

Exhibit 7.6   Renting Business Unit's Objectives and Measurements

Strategic Objective	Business Unit Objective	Business Unit CSF	Business Unit KPI
To provide housing to low- and moderate-income tenants.	Allocation of units in accordance with municipal authorities rules.	The right person in the right unit.	Appropriate allocation of units.
To build a strong internal organization.	Professionalization of business unit.	Productivity.	Productive use of time.
To aim at a strong market position.	Efficient monitoring of price/quality ratio.	Early signaling of unbalanced price/quality ratio.	Level of acceptances by potential tenants.

Exhibit 7.7   Approach of Development of Individual Objectives and Indicators for Employees

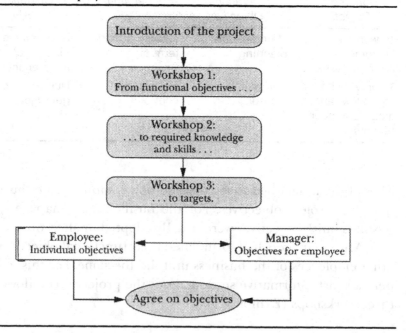

In the first workshop, employees had to formulate the functional objectives themselves. As a starting point, they used the business unit objectives, the functional objectives given by managers, and the job descriptions of the functions or positions within the business unit. Beforehand, the business unit managers were asked to indicate which objectives they considered important for their employees. The employees discussed possible functional objectives and were later given feedback by the consultants from Arthur Andersen, who had been present as objective observers during discussions. In the second workshop, the objectives were developed further into indicators. In the third workshop, the indicator definitions were finalized, the individual objectives were formulated for each individual, and targets were set for the indicators.

In between workshops, associates handed over their forms, which included their functional objectives and measurements, to the consultants who checked whether any of the employees needed extra help. One person per business unit had been appointed to function as the contact person for the unit. The evaluation of all the workshops took place together with this person, and any problems were discussed. The final result of the workshop consisted of sets of functional and individual objectives, functional indicators for each position in the business unit, and individual targets for these indicators, which were then agreed upon by the individual and the manager in question.

Maintenance Advice Agency. The Maintenance Advice Agency of the association consists of construction engineers, installation engineers, project managers, and tenant contact advisers. A project manager is responsible for the quality of houses and buildings, the quality of the maintenance work, and budgetary control of projects. For a construction engineer, work quality is also important. However, the project manager is responsible for the quality of the entire project, whereas the construction engineer is only responsible for activities performed by that particular individual. The project manager has to make sure that work is done within the budget, and other employees have to watch the price-to-quality ratio of materials and services provided by contractors. The tenant contact adviser takes care of communication between tenants and Het Oosten, which includes both providing tenants with information on future work and informing the association about tenant wishes and complaints (Exhibit 7.8).

Tenant Affairs.   Tenant Affairs consists of one senior staff member and a number of junior staff members. Most of the employees of this department have the same objectives because Tenant Affairs operates as a team. Employees often have to step in for each other when handling tenant contacts. This is why objectives are defined that apply to the team as a whole, such as supporting each other and sharing information (Exhibit 7.9).

The individual objectives were derived from the functional objectives. In practice, these two types of objectives were virtually the same. Targets differed when employees had less-than-average experience or worked part-time. In a number of cases, individual project objectives or learning objectives were added. Exhibit 7.10 lists several examples of objectives for various positions.

The individual objectives and targets are discussed once a year in an evaluation meeting between the individual employee and the manager. They discuss whether the achieved results of individual indicators have been below or above target in the past year and possible causes for this. The main aim of reviewing performance using individual indicators is not to judge the person but to improve his or her functioning.

At the end of the meeting, the employee and the manager need to complete a form for the next year. This form includes individual objectives, definitions of indicators, and personal targets for the coming year. Resources or preconditions (e.g., special management information needed from another department, a certain computer program, or extra time and means) needed to achieve the objective are indicated. At the end of the meeting, it should be clear to both employee and manager what performance to expect in the next year. Finally, a similar meeting is held between manager and the management team member responsible for the business unit to discuss the manager's own individual objectives.

Exhibit 7.8   Maintenance Advice Agency's Functional Measurements

Functional Objective	Functional CSF	Functional KPI
Project Manager		
To create and maintain an acceptable technical quality of houses and buildings.	Quality of housing unit.	Examined housing units.
To ensure good planning and supervision.	Good planning and supervision.	Realization within the time planned.
	Complete and reliable documents on costs with regard to contracts.	Discrepancies due to more or less work.
To realize project within budget.	Budgetary control.	Discrepancy compared to budget.
Construction Engineer		
To ensure good planning and supervision.	Good quality of planning and supervision.	Realization of own activities within planning.
To operate in accordance with the demands of the market.	Price/quality ratio in accordance with market.	Cost price of delivered products.
Tenant Contact Adviser		
To inform customers well in advance about maintenance projects.	Customer satisfaction about information service.	Tenant organizations' satisfaction with information service.
To inform employees well in advance and sufficiently about maintenance projects.	Information on time.	Provide advice on time.
To incorporate tenant wishes in maintenance plans.	Implemented tenant wishes.	Implemented tenant wishes.

Exhibit 7.9   Tenant Affairs' Functional Measurements

Objective	Functional CSF	Functional KPI
Senior Staff Member		
To carry out arrangements made with tenant organizations.	Managers who are well informed on arrangements with tenant organizations.	Managers who are satisfied about the information on arrangements with tenant organizations.
Junior Staff Members		
To ensure good management of contacts with tenant organizations.	Good contacts with tenant organizations.	Satisfaction of tenant organizations about contacts.
To be optimally accessible and recognizable for internal and external customers in order to provide information that is timely, correct, and complete.	Customer satisfaction about accessibility. Minimum number of employees on duty.	Customer satisfaction about accessibility. Actual number of employees versus planned number of employees on duty.
To find and contribute to solving problems relating to the quality of life and to propose improvements.	Structural proposals to improve quality of life.	Quality of proposals to improve quality of life.
To promptly deal with objections to rent increases or rent disputes.	Effective processing of rent increases.	Reasonable rent increases.
To cooperate optimally with and to support other employees.	Prevent work backlogs.	Reported backlogs.

Because regular status reports are provided throughout the year, employees can monitor their performance. They can, if necessary, talk to their managers and subsequently take action to improve their performance. Midyear, there is an interim performance review in which progress and possible actions are discussed. These actions are then included in the form.

Exhibit 7.10   Individual Measurements Example

Objective	Individual CSF	Individual KPI
To ensure quick and complete implementation of the new software system.	Test plan.	Timeliness of activities versus test plan.
To encourage commercial operation of Het Oosten versus other housing associations.	Insight into the commercial operation of Het Oosten.	Delivery of a strength-weakness analysis.
To become all-round	Knowledge transfer.	Number of days spent at other projects.

In the evaluation round that takes place several months after the performance review, the result of the performance reviews is one element considered in the evaluation. More important than the final scores on individual indicators is which actions individuals have taken to improve the results on specific indicators.

Experiences with the Performance Alignment Model: Lessons Learned

During the project and especially as a result of the discussions during the workshops, the following lessons learned emerged:

○ *Involvement and support by management is crucial.* Managers played an important role in the success of the project. It turned out that if managers in business units or departments were not committed or were only partially committed to the project, employees showed little commitment as well.

More than once, lack of time was given as a reason why managers and other staff had not completed the objectives—other developments and activities in the organization had absorbed the time and attention of employees.

This is why it is important to determine in advance the priority level of the project compared to other projects.

○ *Be prepared for hidden problems.* The discussion about objectives, desired results, and requirements to achieve those results brought a number of problems to the surface. Some examples are little trust in managers, fear of changing or raising the targets, insufficient time and means to do the work properly, and discontent with having to share responsibility for results with colleagues who possibly perform less efficiently. To gain support for the results of the project, it was important to make these problems debatable.

To encourage employees to discuss problems during workshops, it was decided that managers should not participate in these workshops. In this way, employees felt free to address issues, especially if these concerned one of the managers. The Arthur Andersen consultants who facilitated the workshops fulfilled a fiduciary role and reported, but only with the consent of employees, specific problems to management.

○ *Safeguard the quality of the measurements.* The selection of the final set of KPIs was often done on the basis of ease of measurement. However, this endangers the quality of indicators because the final set does not provide an objective picture of the current status. In such cases, it would have been better to omit less relevant indicators entirely and to choose other less specific indicators.

After the workshops, it was realized that many KPI definitions had not been described in enough detail. It often occurred that if definitions were reviewed at a later stage, the exact meaning was unclear. For example, did "within a week" mean within five working days or within seven days? Or did "as quickly as possible" mean within two weeks or within two months? Definitions with a high level of detail prevent confusion and ambiguity.

Effort indicators (e.g., cooperation, atmosphere, effort, and customer friendliness) often proved to be soft and difficult to measure. However, these indicators are important input for performance reviews because they provide information on the competencies of individuals to operate in the relevant work environment. Remarkable was the number of departments that mentioned team objectives like cooperation and atmosphere at work. In most of the cases, these departments decided not to measure these team objectives and to make these standard discussion points in performance reviews instead.

○ *Clarify and articulate instances of cross-departmental cooperation.* Because the entire organization was involved in the project, several overlaps and interrelations within and between departments came to the surface. This led to better insight into, as well as improvement of, internal processes. This is why it was no surprise that during the workshops people more than once said that failure to achieve certain objectives was caused by other departments that had not kept commitments. To prevent the project from becoming an instrument to blame others for lagging results, it is important to focus on how to improve the cooperation between departments and business units.

○ *Develop a detailed vision of the relation between the new performance management system and the existing reward system.* Employees asked a lot of questions about the link between the new reporting system and the current evaluation and reward system of Het Oosten. During the project, the association had not yet developed a vision on how to link the two. One reason for this was that working with individual objectives was completely new to Het Oosten. So it was difficult to prevent confusion among employees. By formulating a vision on how the new system would fit into an organization's human resource architecture, management could significantly take away uncertainty among employees.

After employees had worked for some time with the new system, they noticed that their responsibilities became clearer and that they could better align their work activities with these responsibilities. The staff departments in particular were positive about the fact that the project had made their work and consequently their contribution to the realization of the association's objectives more visible and tangible. Employees who depended on activities performed by others to meet their objectives suddenly wanted to have meetings to make agreements. Because employees gained insight into each others' responsibilities and dependencies, there was an increase of clarity and consultation.

An important job of managers was to evaluate and complement the individual objectives formulated by their employees. In most cases, the quality of the objectives was sufficient and required little or no adjustment. As for the targets, management only had a monitoring role. One of the initial concerns of employees was that they would be judged on the basis of ever-increasing, unrealistic targets. But in practice, management adjusted the individual targets set by employees to more realistic levels.

Performance alignment made control tasks of managers easier by improving the information supply. At any time of the year, both managers and employees could see and predict whether objectives and targets would be achieved. Additionally, performance measurement functioned as a means to make issues debatable. Employees usually tried to improve their performance themselves first, sometimes after consulting a colleague. Only if they did not succeed would they consult their managers to find the causes of lagging performance and to define actions to achieve better results in future.

After the project was finalized, one of the project managers commented: "Initially we were very skeptical. We thought, 'Another change? What's the use?' But once we participated in the workshops, we noticed that managers and colleagues listened well to what we had to say. We thought we knew exactly what we were doing, but it turned out that it was a good thing to talk and discuss things. For example, when we now have a joint project or need information from others, it allows us to do our work quicker and more effectively. The way we contributed to the objectives set by Het Oosten also became clear. Before the project, I often did not even know these objectives."

In conclusion, despite initial skepticism, individual performance alignment has led to better alignment of employees and departments, better possibilities to adjust activities and to take action, better insight into the objectives of the organization, improved understanding of the processes that are crucial to achieving these objectives, and, above all, greater insight into how employees contribute to the achievement of the objectives.

CASE: INTRODUCING SYNERGY INDICATORS AT POWER SUPPLY INC.[10]

In this case study, we follow the introduction of synergy indicators at Power Supply Inc., a regional power supply organization in The Netherlands. The power supply market is changing continuously. Until recently, protective measures in the Dutch and European markets gave local power supply companies a monopoly position. This monopoly position is rapidly disappearing, and more power suppliers, many of which are foreign, are entering the market. Because of these developments, Power Supply has to go through a cultural change process: from a monopolistic, traditionally organized organization to a dynamic, customer-oriented enterprise. Employees will have to start working in a more businesslike manner in order to stay ahead of competition. During the change process, customer orientation will be the main focus for which effective cooperation between the various departments is essential.

Organization's Background

Power Supply's mission is "to supply power at the lowest possible price and to offer clients a high-quality service." The organization offers two services to its customers: (1) supplying electricity, gas, and heating; and (2) providing connections to the power distribution network. It is not Power Supply itself that generates energy. The organization purchases energy from various producers, such as electricity from the Electricity Board and gas from the Gas Union. Power Supply has three departments (Exhibit 7.11): Customers Services and Technical Services engage in the primary process of supplying power; Operational Services provides support.

Exhibit 7.11   Organizational Chart of Power Supply Inc.

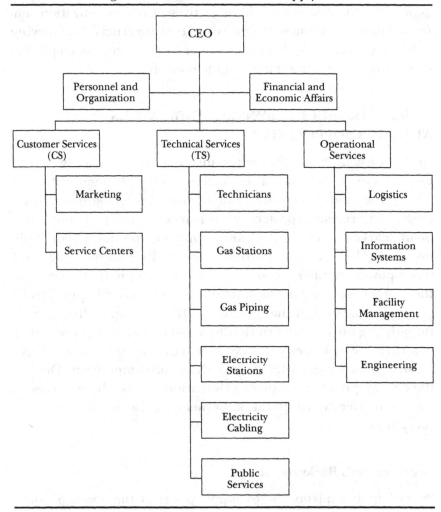

Customer Services has three responsibilities: (1) to answer questions from and to give information to customers; (2) to sell services; and (3) to invoice and monitor timely payment for rendered services. Power Supply adheres to the one-entry principle, which means that the only contact point with Power Supply that customers need is the service center involved. *Technical Services* is in charge of the technical aspects of power supply, such as extension and maintenance of the mains, installation of connections to the mains, and remedy of defects and breakdowns. *Operational Services* provides support for the other two departments and for the employees departments (e.g., information systems, building management, logistics, and engineering).

Why Is There a Need for Measuring Cooperation?

During the installation or reinstallation of a connection to the electricity mains, the activities of Customer Services and Technical Services are strongly interdependent, as can be seen in Exhibit 7.12.

The management of Power Supply was under the strong impression that cooperation between the two departments was far from optimal. They based this impression on the number of client complaints, the backlog of work (installations were often completed too late), and the bad atmosphere between employees from the two departments. The following possible causes were identified:

- ○ There existed different procedures for executing the business activities. As a result, the two departments had different approaches for installing connections to the electricity mains. The fact that different procedures existed meant also that the desired one-entry principle did not work in practice.
- ○ No clear definitions had been made of the departments' roles and responsibilities, which caused employees to point at one another as soon as certain processes progressed less favorably.
- ○ Most of the time, communication between the two departments took place informally by phone without any written documentation of the agreements that were made. This often resulted in misunderstandings, with the client eventually ending up as the victim. This was shown by the results of a recently performed analysis of client complaints.
- ○ Both departments operated in a closed manner. Employees insufficiently took into account the effect that their activities

Exhibit 7.12 Flowchart for Installing a Connection to the Electricity Mains

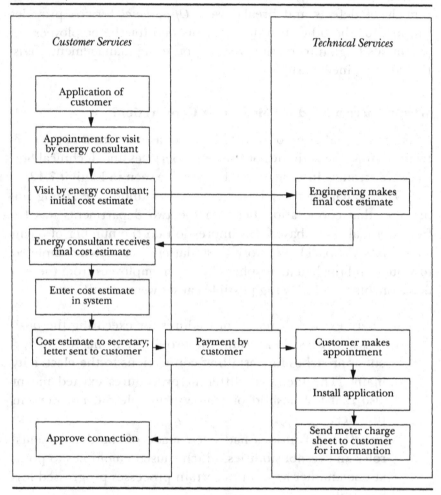

Customer Services
- Application of customer
- Appointment for visit by energy consultant
- Visit by energy consultant; initial cost estimate
- Energy consultant receives final cost estimate
- Enter cost estimate in system
- Cost estimate to secretary; letter sent to customer
- Approve connection

Payment by customer

Technical Services
- Engineering makes final cost estimate
- Customer makes appointment
- Install application
- Send meter charge sheet to customer for informantion

could have on the activities of colleagues from the other department. This became evident when the two department heads met to discuss the cooperation between their departments. It turned out that the departments were mainly concerned with their own performance level. The two departments competed with each other as to who was really engaged in the main process and who was "merely there to support."

○ Neither department had defined performance levels for the activities that had to be performed, such as desired delivery time or maximum waiting time for installation. Because of this, it was difficult to analyze the extent to which people had to cooperate to improve the efficiency of the organization as a whole.

The management team was searching for possibilities to detect the causes for the lack of cooperation more clearly so that it could start an improvement project in the future. Power Supply asked Arthur Andersen to conduct a survey to determine the parameters for cooperation between Customer Services and Technical Services. At the beginning of the survey it was emphasized to interviewees that the purpose of this survey was *not* to rate current cooperation as good or bad, nor to give advice about how to improve cooperation. The survey's purpose was to provide a tool for measuring cooperation. It would help employees, together with their managers, to assess the degree of cooperation and to take measures for improvement.

The Results

Arthur Andersen was able to formulate strategic, functional, and operational CSFs and synergy indicators for cooperation. Exhibit 7.13 shows one of the strategic CSFs and its corresponding synergy indicator. The strategic CSF for alignment has been derived directly from the organization's mission. Alignment between Customer Services and Technical Services is of crucial importance for offering good service. Clients' complaints may well be a direct result of bad cooperation. For example, if Technical Services fails to return the meter charge ticket containing the message that the connection has become operational to Customer Services or returns it too late, Customer Services will not authorize the supply of power to the connection. As a consequence, the client will have to wait unnecessarily

Exhibit 7.13   Strategic Synergy Indicator for Power Supply Inc.

Aspect	Strategic CSF	Strategic Synergy Indicator	Definition
Alignment	Service quality as perceived by customers.	Responses by customers about quality of installation.	The number of negative responses by customers about the performed installations as a percentage of the total number of customer responses about the performed installations per period.

long for electricity and will not be pleased with the way the installation has been performed.

For the strategic CSF, the synergy indicator "Responses by customers about quality of installation" was developed. Measuring complaints can be done in a proactive or in a reactive way. Measuring customer satisfaction in a proactive way can be done via the telephone or written survey, as a Power Supply initiative. Some questions one can ask clients are: "Are you satisfied with the time in which the work was done?" "Was the information that you have received about the activities that were carried out adequate?" "Has Power Supply kept all its appointments?" Reactive measurement of complaints consists of registrations of clients' complaints that come in via letters or telephone.

Exhibit 7.14 shows one of the functional CSFs and synergy indicators. The functional CSF "Acceptance of organizational structure" deals with the fact that for their activities Customer Services and Technical Services need to share the information in the customer intelligence system. If one of the departments uses the system incorrectly or enters the information too late, the other department's activities may be affected. To install a connection to the electricity mains well, the first department has to enter the data correctly, on time, and completely before the second department can proceed carrying out its activities on time and correctly. It is

Exhibit 7.14   Functional Synergy Indicator for Power Supply Inc.

Aspect	Functional CSF	Functional Synergy Indicator	Definition
Structure	Acceptance of organizational structure.	Use of customer intelligence system.	The number of times that the customer intelligence system is used per period by both departments.

essential that both parties are prepared to use the customer intelligence system and to trust each other's input.

The cooperation between the departments is measured by examining the degree to which they make joint use of the system. This can be measured with the synergy indicator "Use of customer intelligence system," formulated as "The number of times that the client intelligence system is used." If one of the departments makes considerably more use of the system than the other does, then the departments may be using the system differently. Or it may be that the department that makes little use of the system underestimates the value of it, for instance, when the employees think that the information in the system is unreliable.

Exhibit 7.15 shows one of the operational CSFs and its corresponding synergy indicator. As an operational CSF, the "Handling of the application for installing a connection" was defined. Timely installation is important in that it directly influences customer satisfaction. A customer expects connection or repair services to be performed as quickly as possible. After all, living without electricity, gas, or heating can be very inconvenient. The corresponding synergy indicator is "Timely installation of connection," formulated as

Exhibit 7.15   Operational Synergy Indicator for Power Supply Inc.

Aspect	Operational CSF	Operational Synergy Indicator	Definition
Other	Handling of the application for installing a connection.	Timely installation of connection.	Average cycle time from moment of client application until installation, per period.

"Average cycle time from the customer's application to the actual connection, per period." This can be indicated by the number of days that passed from the moment the application was received until the moment of actual electricity supply to the customer by Power Supply Inc. For the activities that are performed consecutively by Customer Services and Technical Services, as shown in Exhibit 7.12, target times need to be determined so that not only the total period but also the time spent per step can be evaluated. Effective cooperation will reduce the total length of time needed and will indicate problem areas, for instance, when one department handed over deliverables to the other department that were not up to standard and that caused delays.

The survey results were well received by the managers of both departments. They concluded that the proposed synergy indicators were very appropriate and useful for measuring the cooperation between Customer Services and Technical Services. They intended to put the measurement of synergy indicators into practice. Unfortunately, they have not yet been able to actually do this because shortly after the survey's results were reported, it became known that Power Supply was about to merge with another power supply organization. Because of this, all new projects were halted in anticipation of the merger's effects. However, the management team has expressed their intention to start the implementing of synergy indicators after the turbulence surrounding the upcoming merger has eased up.

CASE: STIMULATING PERFORMANCE BEHAVIOR AT XEROX

This case study describes the management process that forms the core of Xerox's consistent high-quality performance. Xerox's performance measurement process is used to drive business results. Arthur Andersen visited Xerox to take a good look at Xerox's management model and the manner in which Xerox's strategy is deployed throughout the organization. The results of this case study were used for some of the ideas in this book.

Organization's Background

Xerox is the world's number-one copier company and the world's second-largest printer company. The company is also number one in high-end printing and production publishing systems and in providing document services. Xerox is one of the most recognized and valuable brands in the world.

Xerox is a global company that provides document solutions that enhance business productivity. The company's activities encompass developing, manufacturing, marketing, servicing, and financing a complete range of document-processing products and solutions. Currently, black-and-white light-lens copiers represent approximately 40 percent of the revenues. Some of Xerox's new digital products will replace part of the current light-lens equipment. Xerox is focused on turning paper information into digital information and vice versa.

Xerox consists of Xerox research and technology, business group operations, general market operations, industry solutions operations, developing market operations, and Fuji Xerox. Xerox has a matrix organization, combining a functional and a geographic structure. Revenues in 1999 amounted to US$19.2 billion with net income of US$1.4 billion.

Xerox Quality History

Xerox's performance management process has evolved significantly over the past 40 years. Initially the focus of the process was just on measuring profit. This focus endured almost 30 years, from 1960 until 1987. In the 1980s, Xerox was one of the first companies to embrace total quality management (TQM) by implementing a program called Leadership Through Quality. The emphasis of the performance measurement process was no longer on only profit but also on customer satisfaction. Gradually, this emphasis was widened during the 1990s to also include employee motivation and satisfaction and market share, while at the same time "profit" was replaced with the more encompassing "financial results." Next to multiple, national quality awards, Xerox won two Malcolm Baldrige National Quality Awards (1989 and 1997), and it was the first company to win the European Quality Award (1992). During this time, the Xerox Management Model was devised and implemented to strengthen the focus on quality and results and to enforce performance-driven behavior.

The Xerox Management Model

The Xerox Management Model (XMM) is a framework that incorporates all of the key business activities and shows how Xerox is run. The model is based on the criteria contained in the Malcolm Baldrige Award Model and has been in place since 1993, with several updates made since then (Exhibit 7.16). The reason for developing and implementing XMM was to align the many improvement initiatives that were at the time taking place within the company. XMM also would establish a clear and easy-to-recognize framework for employees so they can see how Xerox is run. Existing models like the EFQM model (the European quality model) and the Malcolm Baldrige model did not fit the Xerox company entirely, so the XMM was tailor-made for and by the company.

The relationships among the six categories convey important messages. At the center of the model is the "customer and market focus" category. First, the requirements of Xerox's current and potential customers have to be understood. Knowledge about Xerox's markets has to be gained in order to provide the products, services, and solutions that will make the customers more productive in their activities. Xerox's people (the "human resources" category) deliver these products, services, and solutions through "business processes" and by applying "knowledge and information." "Management leadership" provides vision and direction to the company and its people. Finally, business "results" are obtained after the organization has satisfied the requirements and needs of its customers and markets.

The XMM is used to support the annual cycle of the performance management process (as detailed in Exhibit 7.17). This case describes the enforcement of performance-driven behavior in the processes of policy deployment, performance planning, performance review, business assessment, and performance diagnosis.

Exhibit 7.16   Xerox Management Model

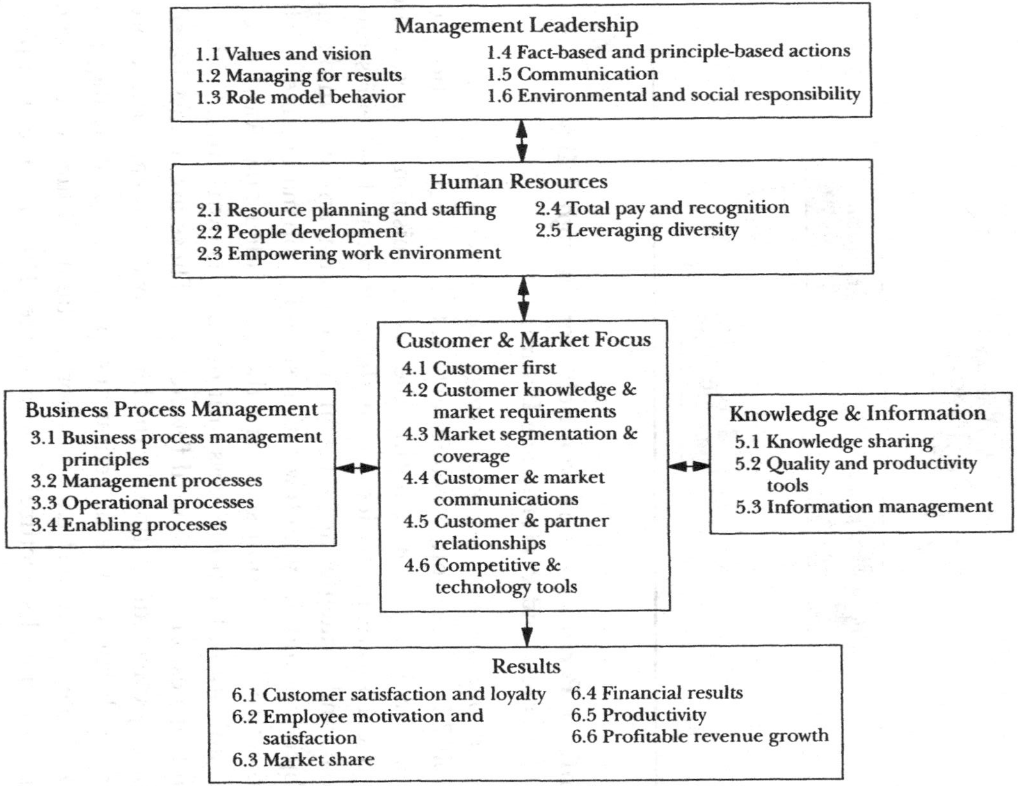

Management Leadership

1.1 Values and vision
1.2 Managing for results
1.3 Role model behavior

1.4 Fact-based and principle-based actions
1.5 Communication
1.6 Environmental and social responsibility

Human Resources

2.1 Resource planning and staffing
2.2 People development
2.3 Empowering work environment

2.4 Total pay and recognition
2.5 Leveraging diversity

Knowledge & Information

5.1 Knowledge sharing
5.2 Quality and productivity tools
5.3 Information management

Customer & Market Focus

4.1 Customer first
4.2 Customer knowledge & market requirements
4.3 Market segmentation & coverage
4.4 Customer & market communications
4.5 Customer & partner relationships
4.6 Competitive & technology tools

Business Process Management

3.1 Business process management principles
3.2 Management processes
3.3 Operational processes
3.4 Enabling processes

Results

6.1 Customer satisfaction and loyalty
6.2 Employee motivation and satisfaction
6.3 Market share

6.4 Financial results
6.5 Productivity
6.6 Profitable revenue growth

Exhibit 7.17   Xerox Management Processes

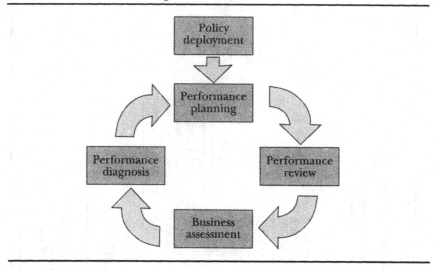

Enforce Performance-Driven Behavior through Policy Deployment and Performance Planning

The deployment of Xerox's strategy is depicted schematically in Exhibit 7.18. At corporate headquarters, the strategic direction of the company is set by articulating the vision, mission, values, beliefs, and corporate priorities. From these, three-to-five-year strategic goals and strategies are set, which are then translated into annual objectives and the vital few action steps for top management. These objectives and action steps are then cascaded downward into the organization. Each business unit defines its own annual objectives and agrees on its own vital few actions. These are always based on the objectives and actions of the level above it and are, therefore, in line with corporate's direction and priorities. The manager is responsible for a vertical and horizontal fit (due to the matrix organizational structure). The manager finalizes the group's and individuals' objectives and actions and then publishes the Blue Book (referenced in Exhibit 7.19). The Blue Book is an easy-to-read summary used to communicate the objectives and the actions on multiple levels in the organization. The entire process only takes three to four days for each manager to complete and about

Exhibit 7.18   Xerox's Policy Deployment Process

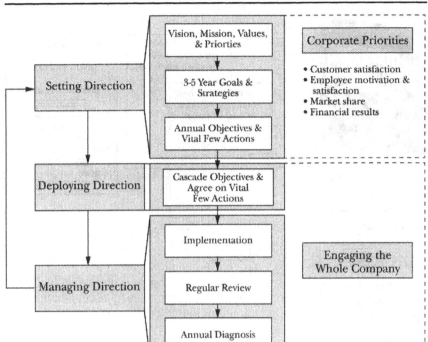

two months to deploy throughout the entire organization. During the year, regular review takes place, and an annual diagnosis is made of the results achieved on the objectives and actions.

A central, important part in the planning process is played by "the vital few actions," as they are called at Xerox. These are the actions that will deliver the improvements needed to achieve the annual objectives. The actions are divided into three categories:

1. *Breakthrough actions*, which will deliver discontinuous improvements. These are generated from the policy deployment process. Normally, one or two of these actions are formulated.

2. *Continuous improvement actions*, which will deliver continuous improvements. These are generated from the policy

Exhibit 7.19 Xerox's Blue Book

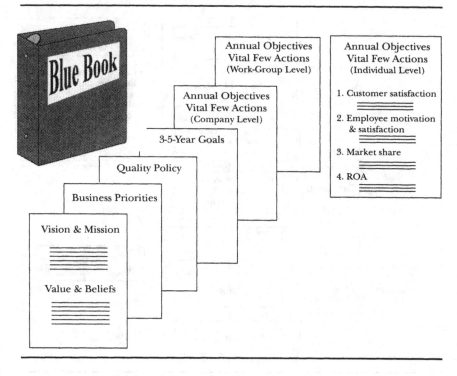

deployment process. Normally, three to five of these actions are formulated.

3. *Business as usual actions,* which will deliver day-to-day out-
puts. These are generated from daily management needs.

The actions are put in the personal policy deployment (PPD)
form of individual managers. The PPD contains basically the personal objectives of each manager for the coming year. The results
on the PPD are tied into the bonus reward scheme of Xerox.

Performance Review at Xerox

During the monthly performance review, the progress on and the
results of the vital few actions are discussed with the direct superior (Exhibit 7.20). Due to the many years of attention to TQM,

Exhibit 7.20   Monthly Review of Progress on Corporate
Headquarters' Priorities

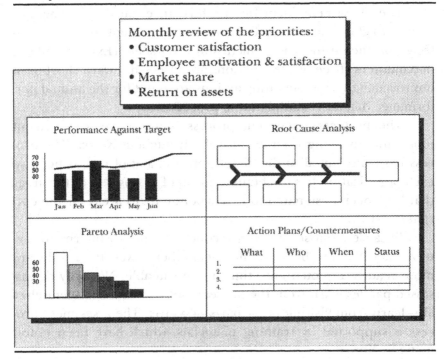

Xerox has built a strong performance management culture in
which people make sure they can come up with measured results.
As Xerox's quality manager puts it: "No facts, no decision." This
attitude is possible because Xerox employees hold each other accountable for the delivery and the analysis of performance indicators and action-driven management.

Self-Assessments

Global Xerox organizations conduct a business assessment against all
of the elements of the XMM. This business assessment is performed
by the employees and element owners and is validated by senior managers from other parts of the company. These senior managers typically look at a selection of XXM elements (see Exhibit 7.16),

reviewing the quality and the factual basis for these. Also, actions are challenged against the "to be achieved" improvements.

The assessment identifies performance gaps and generates actions to close these gaps. The business assessment results are collected on the business assessment summary sheet (Exhibit 7.21). A maximum of three of these actions are targeted toward short-term improvements. The remaining actions are input for the annual performance diagnosis and planning process.

The business assessment process is an active management tool, which is being used extensively throughout Xerox. The process has contributed to the direct improvement of results because each organization has to obtain a rating of at least "4" in the areas that have been designated to be corporate-focus areas for the current fiscal year.

Because the assessments are conducted not by internal or external auditors but by Xerox managers themselves, the results are more readily accepted and, thus, more valuable. Not only the assessed parties learn from the process, but the assessors themselves also learn from visiting other parts of Xerox. The assessment process is supported by training materials, which have been tailor-made by Xerox.

Performance Diagnosis

Annually, a diagnosis is made of the actual performance. The review is conducted at work-group level and is consolidated at the Xerox level. This review creates the starting point for the following year's setting of the objectives and vital few actions (Exhibit 7.22). The annual review starts after the third quarter (the results of the fourth quarter will hardly affect the diagnosis), when the business assessment has been performed. This continuous improvement process is depicted in Exhibit 7.23.

When results for certain elements are below the desired level, an analysis is made of the root causes for the gap. Based on this analysis, improvement actions are planned for the next year. For example, these actions might entail changing certain processes. The effects of these actions are then tracked and reviewed by monthly or (at a minimum) quarterly reports.

Exhibit 7.21   The Business Assessment Summary Sheet

Self-Assessment Summary "Quadrant"

Item:
Desired State:
Owner:
Rating: 99 ☐   00 ☐

Performance | Contributing Factors

Strengths | Improvement Areas

Actions

Assessment

	1 2 3 4 5 6 7	Results	Approach	Pervasiveness
	1	Anecdotal no generalization or gems.	Anecdotal no system evident or demonstrated.	Anecdotal, isolated, may not be of benefit. Theory not practice.
	2	Sporadic results.	Sloppy or over bureaucratic.	Some or most areas deployed.
	3	Some positive trends in some areas.	Beginnings of systematic prevention basis.	Some or of business Management employees the point.
	4	Positive trends in most major areas. Evidence that some results are caused by approach.	Sound systematic prevention that includes evaluation/improvement cycles. Some evidence of integration.	Core are business. Management or employees work the problem.
	5	Good in major areas. Positive trends then some to many supported areas. Evidence that most results are caused by approach.	Sound systematic prevention basis with some evidence of refinement through evaluation/improvement cycles. Evidence of integration into management process.	Core area business, some sup areas.
	6	Good to excellent in major areas. Clear evidence that most results are caused by approach.	Good integration.	From sort many sup area.
	7	Excellent (world-class) results in major areas. Good to Excellent in support areas. Sustained results (3-5 years).	Sound systematic prevention basis refined through evaluation/improvement cycles. Excellent integration.	Core area and support areas. Full deployment. Management employees and customers work the problem.

ML (Management Leadership)
1.1 Values and vision
1.2 Managing for results
1.3 Role model behavior
1.4 Face-based and principle-based actions
1.5 Communication
1.6 Environmental and social responsibility

HR (Human Resources)
2.1 Resource planning and staffing
2.2 People development
2.3 Empowering work envir.
2.4 Total pay and recognition
2.5 Leveraging diversity

BP (Business Process)
3.1 Business process management principles
3.2 Management processes
3.3 Operational processes
3.4 Enabling processes

CM (Customer Market)
4.1 Customer first
4.2 Customer knowledge and marketing requirements
4.3 Market segmentation and coverage
4.4 Customer and market communications
4.5 Customer and partner relationships
4.6 Competitive and technology trends

K (Knowledge)
5.1 Knowledge sharing
5.2 Quality and productivity tools
5.3 Information management

BR (Business Results)
6.1 Customer satisfaction and loyalty
6.2 Employee motivation and satisfaction
6.3 Market share
6.4 Financial results
6.5 Productivity
6.6 Profit revenue growth

247

Exhibit 7.22   Annual Review of Progress on Corporation's Priorities

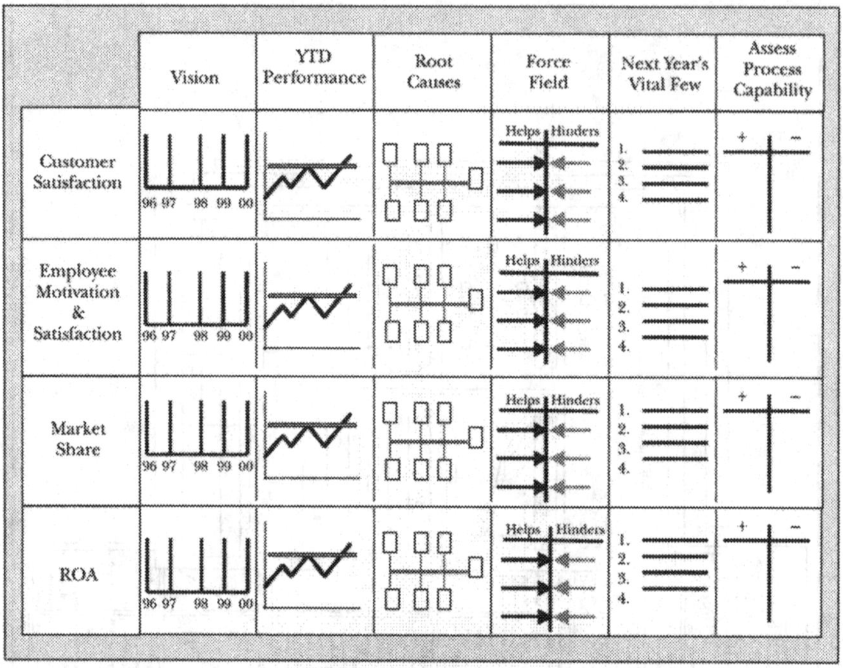

A lot of coaching takes place between senior management and employees to help obtain the desired results. If, however, an individual repeatedly does not perform at the desired level, this person will be asked to step aside.

Benefits of the Process for the Company

The XMM helps Xerox in many ways. Every new employee is trained in the meaning and the usage of the model, thereby explaining to them the way Xerox operates. The business assessments enable a continuous improvement process. Because assessments are executed by Xerox managers, they form a great learning experience.

Also, the resulting "areas for improvement" are used as input for the planning and control processes. Vital few actions ensure that the focus is on key issues and that valuable management time is

Exhibit 7.23   The Continuous Improvement Process

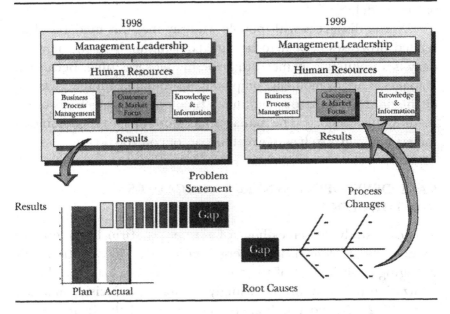

used efficiently. These vital few actions are put into the PPD form of individual managers. Because the results on the PPD are tied in to the bonus reward scheme of Xerox, everyone values what is important to the company.

Frequent tracking of the measured results and reviewing of the plans enable a strong performance-driven culture. Management can find the old results on the Intranet and can compare these with the actuals and the newly proposed action steps. When a manager has a review with a superior, the manager always brings additional information and examples, so he or she is sure to provide results supporting the proposed actions or for the actuals.

Xerox considers the attitude "agreement is agreement" as an important precondition for the XMM to work. Management not only has to speak out in favor of the model, but also has to stick to it and use it. Excuses (except for personal circumstances) for not using the model and its related processes are not accepted in the company. Also, providing all new employees with a rigorous training program ensures that everybody is aware of the benefits of the model.

Xerox disagrees with people who say that this model and its related processes appear to be time-consuming. In fact, the company is absolutely convinced that the model saves time. Because a manager is at any moment completely up-to-date with the facts, he or she does not have to spend much time on status meetings or on reading thick reports. The manager has more time to spend on customers and can also have a greater span of control.

CASE: DEVELOPING SYNERGY INDICATORS FOR THE CLOCK[11]

This case study describes how a fruit auction firm became more flexible by implementing synergy indicators. The continuously changing environment of the auctioneer The Clock forced the organization to act in an increasingly flexible and decisive manner. Until 1992 demand was higher than supply in the fruit marketplace. However, since then, the supply of fruit has grown considerably because growers increased their production substantially. This had a negative effect on prices. Also the competition among auctioning firms to obtain quality growers as clients increased. The Clock had to make its organization more efficient to maintain its competitive position. Arthur Andersen was asked to look at the possibility to implement synergy indicators.

Organization's Background

The fruit auction firm The Clock is a cooperative society of fruit growers. The auction firm functions as a link in the logistic chain from grower to wholesaler and has a commercial task because it is a marketplace where supply and demand of fruit products come together (Exhibit 7.24).

The Clock's mission is "to realize the highest possible selling price for the products offered by the fruit growers." To achieve this, the organization has formulated the following strategy: "To organize a marketplace where growers and wholesalers from around the

Exhibit 7.24   The Logistic Chain of Fruit Products

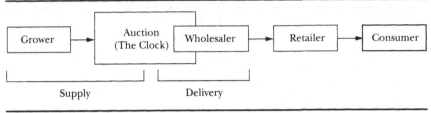

world can trade fruit products, with the lowest possible auction fees and an optimum level of customer service."

The Clock has two groups of customers: (1) the growers who want to get the highest possible price for their products with the lowest possible auction fees and with the quickest possible handling to preserve fruit quality (supply side); (2) the buyers who are interested in the range of products available and in a quick and efficient distribution system (delivery side).

The Clock strives to continuously strengthen the supply side by employing an acquisition policy of quality growers. It wants to strengthen the delivery side by increasing the efficiency of handling the products in the auction hall ("under the clock") and by offering buyers suitable spaces on the auction grounds for further handling of the fruit products (e.g., packaging and preparing for transportation).

The Clock has six departments Logistics, Operational Services, Commerce, Information Systems, Operations, and Society Affairs (Exhibit 7.25). The Logistics and Commerce departments are mainly engaged in the primary process of selling fruit by auction. The department managers are responsible for daily operations.

Need for Cooperation

This case study focuses on the cooperation between the Logistics and Commerce departments. Logistics is responsible for the logistic process that takes place on the auction grounds: efficient handling of the fruit supply process, auctioning preparations, transportation in the auction hall, and the delivery process. The

Exhibit 7.25   Organization Chart of The Clock

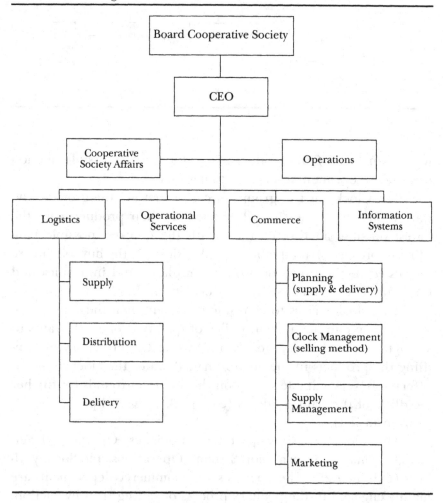

department is also responsible for all transportation vehicles, such as trolleys and electrocars. The department's primary objective is "to offer customers high-quality services at an acceptable cost level." Because of the nature of the logistics process, the department mainly focuses on the present rather than on the future: the goods need to be delivered as efficiently as possible, at the right time, and at the right place.

Commerce is responsible for The Clock's commercial management: the selling method (the so-called clock management), the supply of growers (range of products and number of growers), the delivery (number of buyers), and the planning and alignment of supply and delivery. The department's main objective is "to achieve the highest possible price for growers and the highest possible market share for The Clock." Because of the nature of the commercial process, the department is focused on the future rather than on the present: continuously increasing the supply and the delivery sides.

Because of The Clock's strategy, it is essential for the success of the firm that these two departments cooperate well. When for instance Commerce decides to improve commercial services by advocating quicker distribution, it may lead to an increase in Logistics' costs. Another example of the close interrelationship of the departments' activities is the portioning of the auction batches. By selling products in smaller auction batches, there will be more transactions, which is good for the selling price. But more transactions also mean more handling and, thus, involve higher costs for Logistics.

Developing the Synergy Indicators

Arthur Andersen consultants and The Clock employees together defined the strategic, functional, and operational success factors and synergy indicators for cooperation between Commerce and Logistics. Some of these are described in this section.

Strategic Synergy Indicators.   In order for The Clock to be able to provide customers with good service, Logistics and Commerce must cooperate well. Customers who defect to other auction firms will seriously affect the organization's long-term continuity. Providing good service strengthens the organization's position with its customers. This makes examination of how customers experience The Clock's service a strategic issue (Exhibit 7.26).

If the firm is to function optimally, employees must be prepared to jointly put the firm's strategy into practice. It is surprising, though, that the main objectives of Logistics and Commerce

Exhibit 7.26   Strategic Synergy Indicators for The Clock

Aspect	Strategic CSF	Strategic Synergy Indicator	Definition
Alignment	Quality of services, as perceived by customers.	Grade given by customers, during customer survey, for quality of service.	Average grade of appreciation given by customers for the quality of the service over a certain period.

contradict instead of complement each other. Achieving the highest possible price may result in higher logistics costs. Lowering Logistics costs may lead to a lower service level. Therefore, the objectives of the departments need to be aligned to ensure that The Clock's strategy is implemented in the best possible way. This alignment must be expressed in quantitative objectives: service levels, desired selling prices, distribution times, and logistics costs.

The degree of alignment will manifest itself also in the quality of the yearly plan for the expected growth in volume. Every year Logistics drafts this plan. Commerce has to provide the data needed for the drafting of this schedule, such as forecasts of expected developments in the market and the supply side. The yearly plan in turn is the basis for the budgets of various other departments. Finally, the plan will be translated into the required capacity per day. If the yearly plan is not accurate enough, the estimates of the required space, personnel, and transportation vehicles will be incorrect, which will have a negative effect on the provided service level and/or the logistics costs. The fewer mistakes that have been made in the planning, the smoother the operational process will be (Exhibit 7.27).

To cooperate effectively during the implementation of The Clock's strategy, it is necessary that departments accept one another. This is not about accepting responsibilities, but (and perhaps especially) about accepting each other's competence and added value. There must be mutual trust that the other department will perform its activities well without the need to check whether this is the case. This trust will reveal itself in people collectively

Exhibit 7.27   Functional Synergy Indicators for The Clock

Aspect	Functional CSF	Functional Synergy Indicator	Definition
Consensus	Willingness to jointly implement strategy.	Balanced quantitative objectives.	The desired budget levels for commercial and logistics objectives in a certain year.
	Quality of year plan.	Planning mistakes.	The number of times that actual volumes deviated from planned volumes, per week.
Structure	Acceptance of organizational structure.	Recognition of added value of other department.	The average grade of appreciation for the quality level of the other department over a certain period.
		Number of joint projects.	The number of projects in which both departments are involved, per period.
Communication	Acceptance of organizational structure.	Number of discussions and meetings between departments.	The number of times that members of both departments have qualiatively good meetings, per period.

working on projects and in the existence of joint meetings, at all managerial levels, about the current situation, possible problem areas, and expectations for the future.

Operational Synergy Indicators.   Every day, The Clock Management and Distribution Supply managers consult each other about the amount of merchandise that is scheduled to be sold by The Clock that day. On the basis of this, the Distribution manager can make a time schedule and inform buyers about the expected ending time before the auction starts. He or she will also indicate where possible logistics bottlenecks are to be expected. The Clock Management manager may remove these bottlenecks by, for example, introducing a short extra break during the auction. Thus the managers have a joint responsibility for reaching optimal logistics flows and "under the clock" prices (Exhibit 7.28). So every workday people have to cooperate to make sure that the fruit batches arrive within a certain time at the right place (Exhibit 7.29).

In a concluding session with the managers of both departments, it turned out that both parties regarded the proposed CSFs and synergy indicators as very useful for measuring and monitoring the cooperation between Logistics and Commerce. The management team wanted to implement these synergy indicators along with the ongoing development of KPIs for the other business processes. However, it was decided to delay the implementation until the reorganization, which was still ongoing at Commerce, was finalized.

Exhibit 7.28   Operational Process of Auction

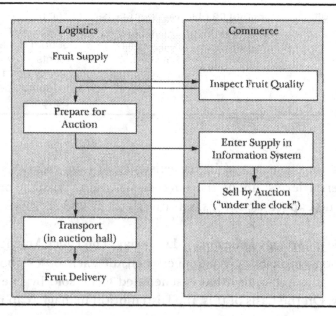

Exhibit 7.29   Operational Synergy Indicators for The Clock

Aspect	Operational CSF	Operational Synergy Indicator	Definition
Other	Fruit batches handling.	Correct handling of fruit batches.	The number of mistakes in the handling of fruit batches, per period.
		Handling speed of fruit batches.	The number of times that the planned ending time was exceeded, per period.

KEY POINTS

☑ Managers need to replace passive reporting performance *measurement* with proactive, results-oriented performance *management*.

☑ Every manager and employee in the organization should know what performance is expected from him or her. Individual responsibilities, targets, and incentives should be aligned with the strategic objectives of the organization. Employee performance is the single most important characteristic that stipulates whether an organization is successful.

☑ People should act on what was agreed. Management should set the right example by "walking the talk," consistently delivering on what was promised. This walk-the-talk culture should be focused on actions and should follow up on these actions.

NOTES

1. Maguire, B., Journal for Quality and Participation, June 1996.
2. Fentener van Vlissingen, P., in: S.G. Simsek, Met visie aan de top [transl. 'With vision at the top'], Kluwer BedrijfsInformatie, 1998.
3. Maguire, B., Journal for Quality and Participation, June 1996.

4. Cascio, W.F., Costing human resources, the financial impact of behavior in organizations, 4th edition, South-Western College Publishing, 2000.
5. Gubman, E.L., The talent solution, aligning strategy and people to achieve extraordinary results, McGraw-Hill, 1998.
6. Cascio, W.F., Costing human resources, the financial impact of behavior in organizations, 4th edition, South-Western College Publishing, 2000.
7. Cascio, W.F., Costing human resources, the financial impact of behavior in organizations, 4th edition, South-Western College Publishing, 2000.
8. Rucci, A.J., S.P. Kirn, and R.T. Quinn, The employee—customer—profit chain at Sears, Harvard Business Review, January–February 1998.
9. Rucci, A.J., S.P. Kirn, and R.T. Quinn, The employee—customer—profit chain at Sears, Harvard Business Review, January–February 1998.
10. At the company's request, the company name has been changed. This case study is somewhat older than the other case studies in this book. It was first described (in Dutch) in de Waal, A.A., and H. Bulthuis, Cijfers zeggen niet alles! [transl. Managing beyond the figures, improvement methods for internal management reporting]. Kluwer Bedrijfswetenschappen, 1996. However, we feel the case study gives a good example of an organization developing and using synergy indicators.
11. At the company's request, the company name has been changed. This case study is somewhat older than the other case studies in this book. It was first described (in Dutch) in de Waal, A.A., and H. Bulthuis, Cijfers zeggen niet alles! [transl. Managing beyond the figures, improvement methods for internal management reporting]. Kluwer Bedrijfswetenschappen, 1996. However, we feel the case study gives a good example of an organization developing and using synergy indicators.

8

Balance Integration with Simplification

CHALLENGE OF KEEPING IT SIMPLE

> The builders of visionary companies tend to be simple—some might even say simplistic—in their approaches to business.
>
> *J.C. Collins and J.I. Parras*[1]

> Really complex organizations will be crushed by their own weight at some point.
>
> *P. Fentener van Vlissingen*[2]

> In many organizations the annual budgeting exercise is now a thing of the past, having been replaced by a monthly or quarterly event, or rolling forecast.
>
> *A. Gurton*[3]

In many organizations there is a tendency to make the performance management process too complicated. This is understandable because there are many conflicting challenges that have to be addressed all at the same time. The long-term focus has to be balanced with the short-term focus; financial information has to be supplemented with nonfinancial information; strategy has to

259

be linked with operations; individual objectives have to be aligned with organizational objectives; and a clear parenting style and structure have to be defined. It is not easy to devise a clear, simple, practical, and concise performance management process that works. But it can be done!

A LIMITED SET OF KEY VALUE DRIVERS PROVIDES THE LINK

When a simple, integrated performance management process is created, many of the ideas described in the preceding chapters can be used. The main concepts to be applied are the use of a limited number of key value drivers, the definition of contingencies areas, and the use of exception and action reporting (see Exhibit 8.1).

The performance management process provides a powerful tool for aligning the organization. By linking strategy, budgeting/target setting, performance measurement, performance review, and

Exhibit 8.1   The Integrated Performance Management Process

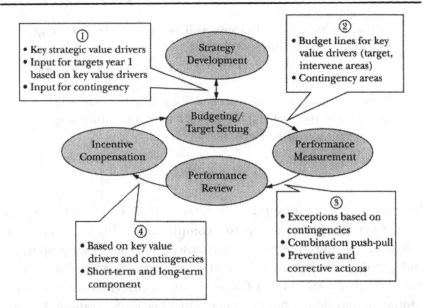

incentive compensation subprocesses into one integrated process, an organization not only achieves excellence in each subprocess, but also aligns the information flows and activities between the subprocesses. If every part of the performance management process refers to the same value drivers, then the potential for confusion, misunderstanding, and error is minimized. This consistency also supports the organization's need for simplicity and speed.

The key concept is that a limited number of key strategic value drivers provide the link between the stages in the performance management process. These key value drivers, which include lagging financial and leading nonfinancial value drivers, are identified during the strategy development process as being the most important, critical items on which the organization has to focus to achieve success and create value. The strategic action plans are centered around these key value drivers. The strategic plan becomes less complicated because it focuses only on the key items. For each key value driver, targets are set for all the years in the strategic horizon. The financial budget is made only for the limited number of key financial drivers. A complete, detailed budget for profit and loss (P&L) and balance sheet is not needed. The financial targets for year 1 of the strategic plan make up the budget for the coming year (① in Exhibit 8.1).

For each key value driver, the contingency areas are defined, based on the sensitivity analysis made during the strategy development process. With the targets (defined in the strategic plan for the coming year) and the contingency areas, the budget lines and intervene areas can be constructed. Contingency areas (which stipulate when higher management levels should consider intervening) only need to be established for the key value drivers. The lines and areas determine what kind of information has to be reported when and to whom (② in Exhibit 8.1).

Management needs information only about results and forecasts for the key value drivers and can, therefore, focus strictly on exceptional results (positive or negative). When the results wind up in one of the intervene areas, exception reports are delivered to higher management levels (push). These management levels can obtain additional information, if needed, by surfing around on the management Web (pull). Corrective and preventive actions are formulated for the exceptions (③ in Exhibit 8.1).

Managers are rewarded on the results they obtained for the key value drivers. Because these key value driver contain both lagging financial and leading nonfinancial drivers, managers are evaluated on the short-term (lagging financial) and long-term (leading nonfinancial) components of organizational performance. The deviation of the actual results from the targets on the budget lines stipulates the amount of bonus and compensation (④ in Exhibit 8.1).

INTEGRATION OF THE IDEAS

Another way of looking at integrating the performance management process is by combining some of the ideas described in this book. So far, many ideas have been put forward. You may very well ask how one specific idea combines with other ideas. Some ideas are mutually exclusive, but others can be implemented alongside each other. In Exhibit 8.2 we address the impact that a corrective action for one challenge may have on another challenge.

ONE STEP FURTHER: BEYOND BUDGETING

> The budget is the bane of corporate America. It never should have existed. Making a budget is an exercise in minimalization. You're always getting the lowest out of people, because everyone is negotiating to get the lowest number.
>
> *J. Welch*[4]

> Traditional budgeting sets not only a ceiling on costs but also a floor. It promotes centralization of decisions and responsibility, makes financial control an annual autumn event, absorbs significant resources across the organization, and acts as a barrier to customer responsiveness.
>
> *B. Bognses*[5]

Exhibit 8.2   Relations Between the Challenges

	Enforce Performance-Driven Behavior	Focus on What Is Truly Important	Embrace Information Transparency	Make Value-Based Strategies Operational	Balance Long-Term and Short-Term Focus
Establish consistent responsibility structure	Responsibilities are clear and are consistently applied to manage expectations.	Content and timing of exception reporting to corporate headquarters varies, based on the chosen contingency areas.	Content and volume of information provided to corporate headquarters by lower levels varies, based on chosen parenting style.	Involvement of corporate headquarters in making the strategy operational for lower levels varies, based on chosen parenting style.	Involvement of corporate headquarters in defining the Operational Action Plan varies, based on chosen parenting style.
Balance long-term and short-term focus	Reward structure has short-term and long-term components. There is a focus on short-term and long-term actions.	Strategic plans are more action-oriented. Strategic actions do not stop after year 1.	Information on short-term and long-term key value drivers is available.	Strategies are translated in short-term and long-term targets. Some operational activities have long-term effects.	
Make value-based strategies operational	Focus on value exists throughout the organization, because of a common language.	Key value drivers, defined in the strategy, focus managers on the core of the business.	Information to fill the balanced scorecard and value driver tree is available.		
Embrace information transparency	Clear, transparent information enables managers to act. Transparency creates trust, needed for empowerment.	Only information about key value drivers is pushed through the organization.			
Focus on what is truly important	Clear accountability and proactivity, supported by exception + action management, make it possible to "walk the talk."				

There are developments that take the integration and the simplification of the performance management process even further (see Exhibit 8.3). The two most important ones are:

1. *Integration.* Much more focus on the external world, especially during the strategic planning, targets (benchmarks, etc.), and management reporting processes. This combats the still frequent practice of companies being too focused on the "inside world." By focusing more on the external world, an integrated and balanced view of all relevant issues can be obtained.

2. *Simplification.* Abandoning the traditional budgeting process, which is considered too detailed, only financial, setting boundaries on performance, always outdated, and so forth. In the remainder of this section, we will look at the new developments in this area.[6]

Budgets were developed in the 1920s to help organizations manage their assets and plan their capital requirements. In the 1960s, budgets began to be used to control processes and to evaluate management performance. Nowadays, budgets are predominantly used to set strategic and operational targets, to monitor strategy implementation, and to manage business processes. However, both in the professional literature and in practice, there are

Exhibit 8.3   Further Developments and Simplifications?

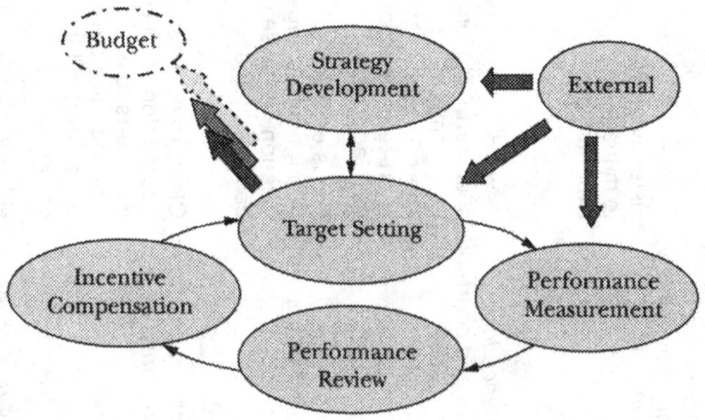

more and more signs that organizations are not satisfied with the results produced by budgeting. These organizations do not realize or insufficiently realize their budgeting objectives. The main shortcomings of budgets are the following:

o Budgets reinforce the command-and-control management model and thereby block initiatives such as decentralization, empowerment, management by exceptions, and team-based management.

o Because budgets are fixed for the entire financial year, they automatically impose limits to growth expectations as well as limits to cost reductions. And when budgets are met, there is not enough stimulus for managers to go for additional turnover or cost reductions. Instead of breakthrough performance, budgets encourage marginal improvement.

o Budgets insufficiently take into account the real value drivers of an organization: knowledge and intellectual capital. Strong brands, skilled people, excellent management processes, strong leadership, and customer loyalty are assets that do not appear in traditional accounting.

o Budgets do not provide the chief executive officer (CEO) with reliable figures and forecasts. Budgets are usually extrapolations of current trends and thus do not take into consideration changes in the organization's environment. Many organizations put together their budgets at the beginning of the year, which makes them almost immediately outdated and not fit for use later in the year.

o Budgets block synergy opportunities between the organization's departments and business units. They encourage working for one's own targets because reviews and subsequent rewards mostly focus on realizing departmental and business unit targets. Thus budgets do not or insufficiently include cross-departmental cooperation.

o Budgets contain too much detail and parameters. This makes compiling budgets a time-consuming exercise. Reaching consensus on the numbers in the budget takes too many iterative rotations between managers from different organizational levels.

If budgets have so many shortcomings, why then do so many organizations still use them? The answer to this question lies in the prominent position that budgeting has acquired in accepted management practice, caused by a long history of usage by many organizations. This does not mean there have not been efforts to improve the budgeting process. Many alternatives have been tried, such as rolling forecasts, balanced scorecards, quarter-end combined with year-end prognoses, three-dimensional accounting, activity-based management, economic profit models, zero-base budgeting, and activity-based budgeting. In practice, these alternatives often turned out to be too difficult or too labor-consuming and thus not efficient enough. Also, in many cases the behavioral problems related to the budgeting process remained.

Beyond Budgeting Round Table

In 1998, 33 mainly European organizations formed a group named Beyond Budgeting Round Table (BBRT), a part of the CAM-I non-profit research consortium. The BBRT performed research into alternatives to the budgeting process. The task of the group was to find organizations that had abandoned budgeting, visit those organizations, and report their findings to the BBRT members by way of case studies and presentations. In this way, the group gradually developed a model for organizations to work without budgets. Some of the ideas described in this book can be found, in somewhat altered forms, in the BBRT model. This makes it possible, in principle, to combine implementing the ideas with part of the BBRT model at the same time.

The first organization identified by the BBRT that abandoned budgeting was Svenska Handelsbanken, Scandinavia's most profitable bank, with the lowest cost of all the European banks. It abandoned budgeting in 1970, and its managers attribute the bank's success to this visionary move. Some of the organizations that recently abandoned budgeting are Volvo Cars, IKEA, SKF, Borealis,

Schlumberger, and Boots. These organizations are all successful without, or partly without, the use of budgets.

As a result of the visits to the aforementioned organizations and an extensive literature study, the BBRT discovered a leitmotiv: There was a need to change the focus of management. Managers had to acknowledge that "people are assets, not (expendable) tools," "profit comes from customers, not from products," "quality is a religion, not a series of ad hoc decisions," and "striving for value is more important than reducing costs." In the Exhibit 8.4, more details are given about this change of focus, arranged according to the different activities that are performed during the budgeting process.

Outlining the Model

The BBRT currently works on the development of guidelines for developing a new performance management model that does not use budgeting. This resulting model, called the Beyond Budgeting Performance Model (BBPM), serves only as a guide and is not a general-purpose blueprint. There are many possible variations of the model, and each organization has to determine which elements of the model are the most suitable. The BBPM does not replace the ideas described in this book, but the model might act as a supplement to these.

The BBPM encourages ambition and innovation, by combining the setting of stretch targets, developing innovative strategies, striving for radical changes, and enhancing peer pressure. It allows senior management to develop an all-encompassing overview of the organization and helps coordinate resources and manage action plans. The model emphasizes both value creation and cost reduction by encouraging employees to question why certain costs are made. Finally, it enables managers to look ahead and to manage future developments. A depiction of the model is shown in Exhibit 8.5. The model includes the following eight steps:

1. *Set stretch targets.* Set targets not to exceed the budget, but to maximize value in the long run and to surpass competitors.

Exhibit 8.4   The Change of Management Focus Needed for
Beyond Budgeting

Activity	Traditional Focus	New Focus
Set targets	• By negotiation • Fixed throughout the year • Focused on financial targets • Focused on marginal improvements	• Continuous adjustments throughout the year • Relative, compared to competitors • Focused on maximum improvements
Translate strategy	• Top-down • No/little input from lower management levels • Fixed in certain period • Cautious, conservative	• Adjusted to the management level • Flexible and reacting to the environment • Radical and full of initiative
Strive for improvements	• Yearly cycle • Aimed at accelerating and improving current processes • Focused on functional improvements	• Continuous cycle • Aimed at working differently • Focused on process improvements
Manage resources	• Based on yearly budget • Decision making long before resources are needed • Focused on tangible resources	• Based on the latest forecasts • Decision making just before resources are needed • Focused on intangible resources
Coordinate budgets	• Based on closely linked (departmental) budgets • Alignment occurs only once • Hindered by the "not invented here" syndrome	• Based on closely linked (departmental) action plans • Continuous alignment • Focused on synergy and best practice
Manage cost	• Focused on defending the cost budget • Overhead allocated • Costs managed through the budget	• Focused on lowering costs • Internal market determines service costs • Elimination of costs without added value

Exhibit 8.4   Continued

Activity	Traditional Focus	New Focus
Make forecasts	• Based on adjusted budgets • Overdetailed and time-consuming • Focused on staying on track	• Based on rolling forecast models • High-level and efficient • Focused on achieving strategic objectives
Measure and control	• Focused on central control • Budget variations must be explained • Information widely available and not timely	• Focused on learning and action planning • Trends and exceptions must be explained • Information widely available and timely
Determine rewards	• Based on achieving the budget • Focused on individual performance • Belief that money motivates people	• Based on relative performance • Focused on business unit performance and performance of the entire organization • Belief that peer pressure motivates people
Delegate	• Central decision making • Emphasis on rules and procedures • Risk taking not stimulated	• Local freedom to make decisions • Emphasis on learning and gaining experience • Risk taking stimulated

Fixed, rigid budgets are replaced by relative or stretch targets. These are set in comparison with internal or external competitive benchmarks. The targets are set not for each item in the P&L account and balance sheet, but for a limited number of key value drivers. Managers on all organizational levels are informed about how they are performing as compared to their fellow managers. As a result of peer pressure, the overall performance level of the organization is improved. Minimum targets are also set, and results that do not meet the minimum levels are unacceptable. There are several techniques and tools available to determine targets, such as value-based management, critical success factors (CSFs) and

Exhibit 8.5   The Beyond Budgeting Performance Model

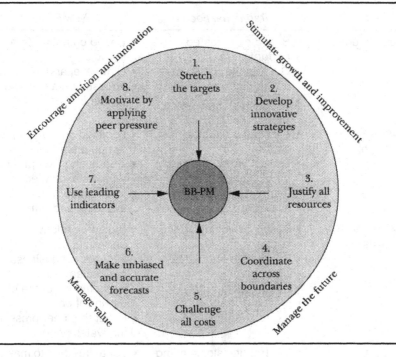

key performance indicators (KPIs), the balanced scorecard, and benchmarking.

2. *Develop innovative strategies.* Translate strategy to the lowest levels of the organization, and change the strategy development process from a yearly top-down event to a continuous, open process. Senior management defines the strategic guidelines, targets, and business limitations for the complete organization. Strategy formulation is then performed by local managers, with senior management at corporate headquarters having right of veto. Senior management discusses the formulated strategies with local management and tests the validity of underlying assumptions of the plan. The feasibility of the action plans is also discussed. Tools that can be used for strategy development are scenario planning and risk management models.

3. *Justify all resources.* Manage resources not on the basis of short-term budget allocations, but on the basis of expected value creation during the life span of the investment. Senior management approves strategic initiatives and the investments required for these. For this, they need to have an overall view of the organization to be able to balance the deployment of scarce resources, such as capital, human resources, and information technology. Long-term investments still need to be justified, but the evaluation should be as flexible as possible: It must be possible to quickly revise decisions if the underlying assumptions of the initial investment request change.

4. *Coordinate across boundaries.* Manage and coordinate not through departmental budgets, but through causal relations across business units and processes. Senior managers continuously evaluate the organization's portfolio. During this process, they look at strategic initiatives and the accompanying risks from a different, higher-level perspective than local managers do. They help local managers to find best practices and synergy opportunities within the organization, and they encourage the sharing of knowledge throughout the organization. The use of techniques such as the balanced scorecard and the implementation of knowledge and project management systems provides support for building an organization-wide network.

5. *Challenge all costs.* Do not discuss whether costs were raised or reduced compared to the past year, but discuss and question continuously whether costs lead to added value for the organization. The focus of cost management shifts from costs to value. Each activity is subjected to a so-called value test: Does the activity add enough value to customers, products, or strategic initiatives? The starting point is no longer the past year's cost level but the resources required to execute this year's plan. Activity-based models can be used in the value test.

6. *Make unbiased and accurate forecasts.* Use forecasts not to just stay on track, but to manage the strategy implementation and to take strategic decisions. Forecasts play an important part in decentralized organizations. They continuously provide senior management with a

view of the current and expected performances of business units. This enables senior management to predict the year-end result and thereby to manage shareholders' expectations. Because the rolling forecasts are not linked to managers' performance reviews, local managers can provide an honest and accurate picture of their business unit. Several advanced forecasting systems are available in the market that can automatically change crucial variables, such as prices and currency fluctuations, and then calculate the consequences on future results.

7. *Use leading indicators.* Do not use a vast amount of detailed (historical) reports, but use a limited number of crucial "leading" (forward looking) and "lagging" (backward looking) indicators to monitor the organization's performance. KPIs provide local managers with the information needed to quickly take corrective or preventive actions. The emphasis is on understanding the underlying causes of the problems. If the data are stored in a data warehouse, all management levels can quickly and efficiently access the information. This way, management at corporate headquarters can detect specific trends and patterns instead of looking at an overload of details. Thus management can focus on exceptions and special issues that demand an explanation. Competitive benchmarks and rankings help to compare the results internally (between departments or business units) or externally.

8. *Motivate by applying peer pressure.* Base rewards not on individual performance, but on business unit performance and the performance of the organization as a whole. Performance discussions no longer focus on negotiated targets, but on the required minimum performance and performance compared to other managers. This competition among managers is more powerful than traditional financial motivators.

Beyond Budgeting in Practice

Several of the organizations visited by the BBRT have implemented parts of the BBPM. For example, Volvo Cars evaluates and adjusts its strategy and forecasts several times a year (steps 2, 4, and 7 of the BBPM). Every month flash forecasts are produced with the expected quarterly results; quarterly rolling forecasts are used to predict the year-end result; and the yearly rolling forecast looks four years ahead. The Vice President (VP) Finance of Volvo Cars expressed it as follows: "Managers build competence by visualizing the future. And in the future there are opportunities and threats that traditional budget-driven processes cannot detect until it is too late."

Borealis uses an advanced activity accounting system and rolling moving averages to get a clear picture of causes for costs and cost trends. The costs of central departments are subjected only to trend analyses and, if necessary, to exception-based control (steps 3, 4, and 6 of the BBPM). For example, the central service costs had to meet the "zero increase" criterion. The VP Corporate Control of Borealis said: "The traditional budgeting process sets not only a ceiling but also a floor to the costs level. The process enhances centralization of decision making and accountability, turns the financial control process into a yearly event in the autumn, absorbs significant resources from the entire organization, and is a barrier to responding quickly to changing customer demands."

Handelsbanken uses three fairly straightforward indicators: return on capital employed, income-to-cost ratio, and profit per employee. These indicators are understood by every employee and are used to stimulate internal competition between branch offices as well as to build a shared concept of what is important for the organization. The employees know that by looking at the degree of improvement of the indicator results, they have an insight into how much their rewards will increase. The final reward is linked to the result of Handelsbanken in comparison to competitors (steps 1, 5, 8, and 9). Jan Wallander, visionary architect of the Handelsbanken management model, emphasized the following: "Relative targets are more effective than fixed targets because they are always up-to-date and continuously improve the average. We communicate only the average to our people and a ranking list that shows those branch offices that scored above the average and those that scored below the average. The system is completely self-supporting."

CASE: SIMPLE BUT EFFECTIVE PERFORMANCE MANAGEMENT AT BUSINESS SYSTEMS CORPORATION[7]

This case study describes a management culture that is open-minded and focused on the long term, while continuously questioning the current status and looking for new improvement opportunities. In general, employees and customers characterize Business Systems Corporation's (BSC) culture as inspiring. Arthur Andersen visited the corporate headquarters in the United States and focused on specific elements of the management process that, according to the company itself, contribute to much of its culture.

Organization's Background

BSC designs, manufactures, and services electronic products and systems. The product line is used by people in various industries. In 1999, the company's revenues amounted to more than US$40 billion. The strategy of the company contains the following elements: grow from profit, listen to customers, grow the company by trusting in people, and care for the society.

Balance the Long Term with the Short Term: "Flexible Coupling"

The strategic planning process of BSC is called the Business Systems Strategy Review (BSSR), which results in a Business Systems Strategic Summary (BSSS). The process starts in the second quarter of each fiscal year by defining a set of strategic guidelines. The guidelines are based on scenarios and business models and address general macroeconomic trends and developments. The guidelines look at the financial implications of these trends in terms of growth of revenue, margin, expenses, assets, and economic value added (EVA) for each division. Each division, after discussing the strategic guidelines with BSC's CEO and CFO (chief financial officer), will use the guidelines as input for its strategic planning process. The divisions are autonomous in the way they develop their own strategic plans. In general, the process consists of bottom-up strategic planning, in which the divisions give targets to the business units. Then the division makes the BSSS, which is a three-year plan with last year's actuals, this year's expectations, the next three years' estimates, and descriptions of strategic activities. The corporate team acts as a facilitator and checks the viability of the BSSS that is presented by each division vice president, controller, and some of the business unit general managers. This happens during the BSSR to share information. The BSSR is not intended as a session to seek approval for the strategic plan from the executive committee.

Linking the annual BSSR process to the budgeting process is what BSC calls "flexible coupling." To better understand how this works, insight into BSC's budgeting process is necessary. BSC's budgeting process had been changed just before Arthur Andersen visited the company. The change was mainly driven by shortened product-life cycles and by business becoming more volatile, making budgets less and less reliable. As a BSC manager put it: "Once you have made the budget, it is already outdated."

BSC introduced the SCALE process, which stands for "Short-term Contract And Long-term Estimate," to increase the frequency of the budgeting process, while simultaneously shortening the time span of the budget. The results are enhanced reliability, achievability, and value of the budgets. In order to maintain a longer-term focus, the budgets are accompanied by forecasts to stretch the time period of operational management attention. The short-term contract is the budget agreement for the first half-year. It is the division's financial commitment to the CEO. It is also linked to the management compensation program. The long-term estimate is a forecast for the next 12 months. In the second half-year, the SCALE process is repeated, resulting in budgeting twice a year. The SCALE process has a planning horizon of 18 months.

The flexible coupling pertains to the two-way information exchange between strategy and budget. On one hand, the BSSS provides input for the contract made between the division and the

CEO during the budgeting process in the first half-year. On the other hand, the insights gained during budgeting in the second half-year provide valuable input for the strategic planning process.

Focus on What Is Truly Important

BSC is able to create and to maintain focus in its performance management process by using a limited set of key financial value drivers and by using the business balanced scorecard selectively.

Selective Use of the Business Balanced Scorecard. BSC uses a balanced scorecard with key financials and nonfinancials of each division and its underlying business units. Initially, the company used a prescribed corporate set of KPIs with standard definitions. Each division had to report this scorecard on a quarterly basis to the senior management team. After some time, BSC decided to change the reporting process around the balanced scorecard, based on the following considerations:

- Reporting of divisional scorecards to the senior management team was considered to be too mechanical. The process was mainly focused on proper execution of the reporting process steps and on adherence to the reporting guidelines. The scorecard was not really used at the corporate level for management and steering purposes.
- The added value of reporting balanced scorecards to the corporate level was not clear. It was felt that the information in the scorecards was of more value to the divisions and the business units than to corporate. This was due to the limited involvement of corporate in operationally steering the business units.
- Divisions found that a standardized corporate set of performance indicators did not focus enough on their own specific strategic issues. They needed more flexibility in the layout and content of the scorecard, as "one size does not fit all."

BSC decided to implement the following changes:

o Only the limited set of 20 mandatory KPIs has to be reported to corporate. The diversity of the divisions and their autonomy in managing the business units is so substantial that only select financial indicators can be used for all divisions and business units to measure performance in a standardized way. This limited set of financial indicators is complemented with a few nonfinancial indicators that measure employee satisfaction, overdue performance evaluations, and safety. The divisions and the business units now have the freedom to decide on the content of their own balanced scorecard.

o Divisions can decide for themselves if they want to report their balanced scorecard to the executive committee. The scorecards are no longer meant for steering purposes at the corporate level; they serve as extra background (explanatory) information during review meetings.

o Divisions and business units now use their specific balanced scorecards for their own management and control purposes.

Fixed Set of Key Financial Value Drivers.   Senior management has selected a fixed, standardized set of 20 key financial value drivers. This set is used throughout the company. Each region, division, and business unit reports this set on a monthly basis, comparing actual performance with SCALE targets. This encourages BSC managers to include only these 20 items in the budgets. Managers and controllers can access more details by drilling down into the chart of accounts on value drivers. Before doing this, managers have to think about BSC's credo: "You must not dig in the numbers, before you know the question."

Important key financial value drivers are return on sales (ROS), return on assets (ROA), earnings per share (EPS), and economic value added (EVA). EVA has a rather special position in the company. Although it is the most important indicator, it is used only at the corporate level, mainly for strategic portfolio analysis purposes. One reason for this high-level use is the fact that the company shares many resources across divisions. This can lead to major efforts in allocating assets if EVA has to be measured accurately per division. Also, as one BSC manager described the challenges with divisional EVA: "You can then put up a smoke screen," thereby creating ownership problems.

Embrace Information Transparency: Not Only with Technological Means

In order to stimulate transparency of information throughout the company, BSC uses an Intranet, a common chart of accounts, and open-book management.[8] In this way, the company strives to obtain a balance between the information that is collected and stored structurally and regularly in a standardized way and the information that has to be available to lower management levels and that is accessed on an ad hoc basis. This latter type of information is typically not standardized.

All managers have at their disposal an Intranet that provides access to multiple data warehouses that store different types of information, such as expense reporting, budgets, consolidated financials, accounts receivable, human resources, costs (up to the invoice level), orders, and revenues. Supporting information and reporting tools enable detailed analysis of the data in these data warehouses. The Intranet is used for communication purposes, especially for the finance organization. The information that can be accessed includes closing schedules, reporting formats, accounting and consolidation instructions, data management rules, and a tool that tracks the monthly closing process.

Especially within the finance process, BSC established a great deal of standardization. In addition to the implementation of one chart of accounts, standardized reporting has been implemented through standardized line items, language, processes, and financial and data management reporting tools. This not only leads to more clarity and credibility around the finance process, but it also improves comparability and efficiency in the closing and consolidation process. To allow divisions and business units some flexibility to adapt these processes to their own reporting needs, extra accounts can be set up on lower levels of the chart of accounts. Consolidation takes place through a one database concept, consolidating data bottom-up to the corporate level.

In optimizing the transparency of the performance management processes, the finance organization plays a crucial role. Not only does this organization formulate and define the formats and guidelines for the process, but it also is the watchdog over the proper implementation and execution of the performance management processes. The finance organization catches signals, brings problems forward, and is a major communicator in sharing experiences and changes. It has the following characteristics:

○ A strong functional tie exists among the finance associates throughout the company. This functional tie is established by conducting joint finance meetings with corporate, division, and business unit controllers working together on analyzing specific issues. Functional analyses made by corporate control are shared with the other controllers to create a better and deeper understanding of certain issues, and close informal communication occurs several times during the week between corporate control and divisional controllers. Finance professionals rotate jobs frequently throughout the organization, increasing their knowledge about the various parts of the business. Finally, controllers help each other when they have problems. If necessary, divisional controllers can block time on their own in the CFO's agenda.

○ BSC implemented eight shared-service centers worldwide, which provide accounts payable, billing, general ledger, and fixed assets services to the divisions and the business units. The centers have taken over low-value-added, financial transaction processes from the business controllers. This allows a controller more time to become a business partner with his or her CEO. Implementing these centers forced the finance organization to work closely together, thereby fostering a cultural change with respect to the role of controllers within the organization.

KEY POINTS

☑ To establish an integrated performance management process, the long-term focus has to be balanced with the short-term, financial information and then supplemented with nonfinancial information. Strategy has to be linked with operations. Individual objectives have to be aligned with organizational objectives. A clear parenting style and structure have to be defined—and all this in a simple and concise way!

☑ The main concepts that need to be applied to obtain an integrated performance management process are the use of a limited number of key value drivers, the definition of contingencies areas, and the use of exception and action reporting, all supported by an integrated information technology architecture.

☑ Some of the ideas described in this book are mutually exclusive; others can be implemented alongside each other. The possible impact of ideas to overcome an individual challenge on the other challenges is addressed in this chapter.

NOTES

1. Collins, J.C., and J.I. Parras, Built to Last, HarperCollins, 1997.
2. Fentener van Vlissingen, P., in: S.G. Simsek, Met visie aan de top [transl. 'With vision at the top'], Kluwer BedrijfsInformatie, 1998.
3. Gurton, A., Accountancy, 01-03-1999.
4. Welch, J., in: J. Hope and R. Fraser, The BBRT guide to managing without budgets, version 3.1, CAM-I Beyond Budgeting Round Table, 1999.
5. Bognses, B., in: J. Hope and R. Fraser, The BBRT guide to managing without budgets, version 3.1, CAM-I Beyond Budgeting Round Table, 1999.

6. This section consists mainly of a translation of the article by de Waal, A.A., J. Hope, and R. Fraser, Beyond budgeting, Tijdschrift Financieel Management, 1999/12. For the latest information, visit the BBRT website at: www.beyondbudgeting.org.

7. At the company's request the company name has been changed. Since the time of the case study visit, the management, the organizational structure, the processes and even the culture of the company have been significantly changed. This also meant the company had to reconsider its performance management process. This case study describes best practice ideas which were used before these changes. We feel these ideas are very interesting and can be useful to the readers.

8. For a description of open-book management, see Case, J., the Open-Book Experience, Lessons from Over 100 Companies Who Successfully Transformed Themselves, Addison-Wesley, 1998.

9

Implementing the Ideas

GETTING IT ALL TO WORK

> So when all is said and done, no matter how sophisticated and
> expensive an organization's information system, the key ques-
> tion is: do they provide the right information about the right
> things to the right people at the right time? . . . How you an-
> swer this question will determine nothing less than your orga-
> nization's ability to create and communicate value in the New
> Economy.
>
> *R.E.S. Boulton, B.D. Libert, and S.M. Samek*
> Cracking the Value Code[1]

On the basis of the experiences of organizations that have implemented ideas described in this book, we have formulated a number
of useful guidelines and described a plan for your implementation
of the ideas. Also, we have listed a number of barriers you can encounter on your way to world-class performance management. We
discuss the role of the finance function in the transition toward
world-class performance management. Finally, we describe the Feasibility Analysis, a tool that can be used to gauge the readiness of
your organization for world-class performance management.

IMPLEMENTATION GUIDELINES

Implementing these ideas to improve your performance management process is not done overnight. It is a gradual process in which

managers, who are often reluctant to change, need to be convinced of the merits of the ideas and of the new process. Fortunately, as the case studies described in this book show, it *can* be done, and the rewards for your organization can be great. In this section, several guidelines are given that can help you when starting the improvement project.

- *Make sure your organization understands the objective of the improvement project.* Before starting the project ask yourself: Are improvements necessary? What do we want to accomplish? Who has to partake in it? How much time and money is it going to cost? Is it the right time to start the project? The last section of this chapter, "Feasibility Analysis" will help you answer these questions.

- *Evaluate the performance improvement potential.* Map the expectations of senior management in regard to the desired performance improvements, and compare these with the performance improvement potential of the organization and its business units. At the same time, map the organization's key value drivers. Also map the willingness of senior management to act as sponsor of the improvement project and its willingness to be actively involved in the project.

- *Determine improvement targets.* Determine the targets and reasonable expectations for the improvement project, given the organization's current situation and its improvement potential. Agree on these targets. Determine the gap between the current and the desired performance levels, and discuss the time and the resources required to bridge this gap. Set the starting date and the end date of the improvement project.

- *Formulate alternatives.* Determine possible alternatives for the project approach as well as for the places in the organization where the project can be executed. Determine the consequences of these alternatives for the needed resources, experience, employee quality, timing, and so forth. Make sure that senior management gives its consent for the final choice.

○ *Agree on priorities, and coordinate plans.* Decide which improvement initiatives will be implemented first and the order of implementation. Use the support of senior management during the coordination of the implementation across business units.

○ *Appoint project teams.* Appoint project managers and establish cross-functional teams. Provide these with connections to the electronic network for swift information exchange.

○ *Make detailed action plans.* Add details to previously made action plans in order to take special project requirements into account. Determine relevant key performance indicators (KPIs) for and the timing and milestones of the project, and identify required information systems. See the next section, in which a possible project plan is given for developing a balanced scorecard.

○ *Manage the projects as if they are in one integrated portfolio.* Make sure that the right knowledge management systems are available and that progress reports and progress procedures are present and easily accessible.

○ *Review.* Determine the when, the how, and the who for the evaluation of the improvement project results.

PROJECT PLAN FOR DEVELOPING A BALANCED SCORECARD

Improvement of management reporting, by means of critical success factors (CSFs), key performance indicators (KPIs), and a balanced scorecard requires a structured project approach. Exhibit 9.1 depicts the eight main phases of such a project.

Exhibit 9.1   Project Phases

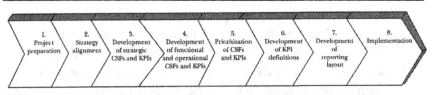

Phase 1: Project preparation. The purpose of this phase is to inform and to prepare the organization about the planned CSF/KPI development project. Information meetings are organized, and information memos are distributed. In this phase, a project team, which consists of people from all the functional areas that are relevant to the project, is established. Also, a project plan and a communication plan are made.

Phase 2: Strategy alignment. In phase 2, the organization formulates or reformulates its strategic objectives. During this process, the management team should reach consensus on the objectives to be achieved, because without consensus, it is impossible to develop a coherent set of CSFs and KPIs that is sufficiently supported by the organization. In addition to strategic objectives, functional objectives are formulated for each functional or process area or department. It is essential that the functional objectives and the strategic objectives are aligned; the two types of objectives should not contradict one another.

Phase 3: Development of strategic CSFs and KPIs. In phase 3, the strategic CSFs and KPIs are developed based on the strategic objectives that were developed in phase 2. This is done in a workshop in which all the management team members should partake to create support in the organization and to prevent the "not-invented-here" syndrome. In the workshop, CSFs are identified for each strategic objective, and then the accompanying KPIs with the draft definitions. Finally, environmental measurements that are relevant to the organization are determined.

Phase 4: Development of functional and operational CSFs and KPIs. In this phase, functional CSFs and KPIs are identified for each business function/department on the basis of the functional objectives that were developed in the phase 2. This is also done in a workshop in which all the managers of the business function/department should participate. The activities in this workshop are very much the same as those in the strategic workshop. Again, it is essential that the developed functional CSFs and KPIs are in line with the defined strategic measurements. In addition, operational CSFs and KPIs are developed for the crucial business activities. The crucial business activities should have been identified prior to the workshop.

Phase 5: Prioritization of CSFs and KPIs. The workshops of phases 3 and 4 result in a "brainstorm list" of CSFs and KPIs. In phase 5, this list is reduced until a manageable set of measurements remains. This is necessary because otherwise managers would get an overload of information and lose control. During the workshop, the management team decides on the CSFs and KPIs with which they want to start in the first year. These will be included in the organization's management reporting. Each objective has to be measured with at least one result CSF and at the most two effort CSFs, with their accompanying KPIs.

Phase 6: Development of KPI definitions. During the workshops of phases 3 and 4, a start was made with drafting definitions for the KPIs. In phase 6, only the definitions of the remaining (prioritized) KPIs will be detailed until there is only one possible interpretation of the KPI. In addition, the reporting procedures and the managers responsible for specific indicators are determined. Finally, the targets are determined for each indicator. These are all put in a so-called KPI definition document (Exhibit 9.2).

Phase 7: Development of reporting layout. In phase 7, a reporting layout is made. This layout must allow inclusion of the results of KPIs as well as analyses and actions. In addition, a timetable is made that mentions the dates by which reports should be delivered to the managers. A frequently used reporting layout is the balanced scorecard (see Chapter 4).

Phase 8: Implementation. Phase 8 consists of implementation of the new management reporting, which is based on CSFs and KPIs. The implementation process includes measurement of KPIs, reporting of the results, and discussion of the reports. After the reports have been used for a period, an evaluation of the measurements and their use is made. This may well lead to adjustments of the CSF/KPI set, the reports, the accountability, the reporting procedure, or the targets. The evaluation

Exhibit 9.2　KPI Definition Document Example

Key Performance Indicator 1

CSF

Quality of personnel

KPI

Training days

Definition of KPI

$$\frac{\text{Total number of training days attended by employees in the department since January 1}}{\text{Total number of training days that have been planned as of January 1}}$$

- *Attended training days:* the days on which an employee attended a training. The attended training should have been conducted by a qualified trainer (internal or external) and should be relevant for the position of the employee.
- *Personnel:* all people employed on a permanent basis (temporary employees are not included).

Reporting Procedure—Activities to Be Performed	*Data File*	*By*
Make a training plan for all employees, and register all the planned training days.	Training	Business unit manager
Register in the file the attended trainings and the number of training days attended by the employee. The updated information must be approved by the business unit manager.	Training	Business unit manager
Count all the attended training days of all employees in the department in the last quarter (= X).	Training	Business unit manager
Count all the planned training days of all employees in the department for this quarter (= Y).	Training	Business unit manager
Calculate $X/Y \times 100\%$.	Training	Business unit manager
Enter the resulting percentages in the report.	Report	Business unit manager

Exhibit 9.2   Continued

Target

The target for 2000 is that 100 percent of the planned training days have been attended before year-end. Expected is a linear increase of 25 percent each quarter. The number of planned training days for 2000 is 10 per employee.

Explanation of the KPI

If the result of the KPI is below target at the end of one of the first three quarters, a corrective action is needed to make sure that employees can attend the planned training days in the next quarter(s). If this does not happen, the employee will not be sufficiently trained to function in his or her present or new position. If in a certain quarter the result turns out higher than the target (perhaps more training was attended than planned), corrective actions are only necessary if it is expected at that year-end the number of attended training days will be higher than the number of planned training days. Otherwise, the training budget will be exceeded.

Data File

CSF: Quality of personnel
KPI: Training days
KPI def: Total number of training days that have been attended by employees in the department since January 1 *divided* by the total number of training days that have been planned as of January 1.

Quarter	Target	Attended Training Days
I	25%	22%
II	50	44
III	75	74
IV	100	80

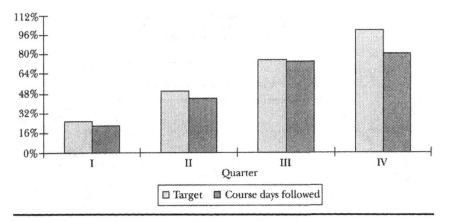

takes place periodically, at least once a year, preferably during the annual strategic planning process. This way the performance pyramid is integrated into the organization's planning and control cycle (Exhibit 9.3). After all, the organization's strategy is translated into CSFs and KPIs. The planning is expressed in the targets of the KPIs. The execution of activities is measured and monitored with the results of the KPIs. Finally, evaluation takes place by comparing the targets with the results of the KPIs.

Exhibit 9.4 provides a global overview of the activities that have to be performed successively in a development project.

Exhibit 9.3   The Performance Measurement Pyramid as an Integral Part of the Planning and Control Cycle

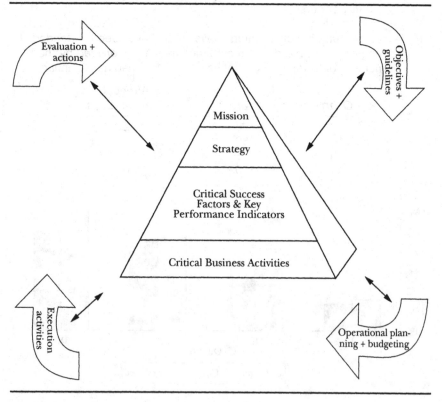

Exhibit 9.4   Activity Plan for the Development and the Implementation of CSFs/KPIs

Phase	Activities
1. Project preparation	• Establish the project team. • Draw up the project/activities plan. • Inform the project participants. • Draw up the communication plan.
2. Strategy alignment	• Collect and study relevant information. • Formulate and streamline the strategic objectives. • Set a date for the strategy alignment workshop. • Discuss the strategic objectives with the management team. • Document the workshop results and give feedback to participants. • Perform the aforementioned activities in this phase again for the functional/operational workshop.
3. Development of strategic CSFs and KPIs	• Set a date for the strategic workshop. • Prepare the strategic workshop. • Conduct the strategic workshop. • Document the workshop results and give feedback to participants.
4. Development of functional and operational CSFs and KPIs	• Set a date for the functional/operational workshop. • Prepare the functional/operational workshop. • Conduct the functional/operational workshop. • Document the workshop results and give feedback to participants.
5. Prioritization of CSFs and KPIs	• Compile the CSF/KPI table. • Ask participants to arrange the CSFs/KPIs in the table according to priority. • Collect and summarize the completed tables. • Organize feedback meeting and reach consensus on the prioritization of CSFs/KPIs. • Document meeting results and give feedback to participants.

(continued)

Exhibit 9.4   Continued

6. Development of KPI definitions	• Draw up a timetable that indicates when participants have to work on the KPI definitions. • Determine definitions, reporting procedures, reporting frequency, and targets. • Check quality of content and layout.
7. Development of reporting layout	• Determine graphic representation. • Determine reporting layout. • Develop action-oriented reporting. • Finalize new reporting layout.
8. Implementation	• Develop communication and reporting structure. • Determine KPI responsibilities. • Inform managers on the start of the new reporting. • Train managers in how to use the new reports.

BARRIERS TO CHANGE

Forewarned, forearmed! Now that it is clear how the performance management process in your organization can be improved, it is time to get to work. In practice, the implementation of the ideas might turn out not to be quite as easy as you might have thought. When you start a performance management improvement project, using CSFs, KPIs, and a balanced scorecard, you should take the following issues into account.

○ Clearly analyze beforehand what the *bottlenecks in the current performance management process* are. If this is not done, there is a real risk that the improvements do not deal with these bottlenecks in a satisfactory manner. The consequence will be that people are not motivated to really implement the "improvements," thereby carrying on in their same old ways.

○ To successfully finalize a performance management improvement project, the *involvement and the commitment of the future users* is needed. When the project has too low a priority for them, the project will be doomed. It is important to continuously communicate the advantages of the improvements to them and also to show them the benefits in practice. Also, the execution of the project has to be as efficient as possible and should not take up too much of the manager's time.

○ A *structured approach* of the performance management improvement project is important for the acceptance of the project by the managers. Such an approach, which has been used successfully before at other organizations, can save a lot of unnecessary problems and hiccups. Also, a proven approach makes it possible to see the expected end result beforehand, which not only motivates the managers but also makes it possible to track progress toward these end results.

○ One of the biggest changes that result from implementing an improved performance management system is that *managers' performance becomes much more clear and transparent.* This also makes such a system threatening to managers. If there is a culture of severe repercussion in an organization, managers will try to delay the improvement project and/or to manipulate the result of the KPIs ("how to lie with statistics"). If at the time of the performance management improvement project sufficient attention is paid to changing the management style from punishing to coaching and focusing on improvement (if the improved performance management system is primarily used to measure performance and not to blame managers), the new system will be less of a threat, and people will more easily accept it. This type of change in management style appears to be one of the most difficult elements of an improvement project.

○ During the improvement project, *information systems* play a crucial role in collecting and reporting the data that are required to calculate the new measurements. If it turns out that managers have to produce most data manually, they will see this as just more work. The willingness to put in this extra effort every month or quarter will quickly diminish. It is, therefore, important to schedule enough time for research, adjustment, and improvement of the information and reporting system architecture within the organization. In practice, the creation of a performance management portal can turn out to be one of the most delaying factors in implementation process, when the development of the portal has not started in time.

○ By making the *new measurements part of a manager's daily operations,* there is a better chance that the balanced scorecard will continue to be used in the future. The daily work of a manager consists primarily of taking action on information that he or she has received. The original balanced scorecard layout left out an important element, namely future and action orientation. Or, in the words of one of the chief executive officers (CEOs) we interviewed: "Do not give me overviews, but issues. I want to know what is happening, what we are going to do about it, and what is going to happen next." This indicates that it is not sufficient to include only future-oriented indicators in the balanced scorecard; actions and forecasts on the expected results of the actions taken also need to be incorporated. This will help to diminish the noncommittal attitude that is present in many organizations when it concerns action taking, and it will turn the balance scorecard into a living instrument. Therefore, make sure to implement action management alongside the balanced scorecard.

○ The customer perspective ("What do the customers think of us?") and the financial perspective ("What do the shareholders think of us?") of the balanced scorecard only focus on the external. But the *internal aspects* should also be taken into consideration. For example, a customer may think a 100-percent-on-time delivery is important, but that does not necessarily mean that the organization has to agree with that. It should be a conscious decision that the organization is going to meet this customer need or that, for instance, this customer will not be served. In other words, organizations should constantly look at the external as well as the internal factors. By letting managers partake in this decision, there will be more support in the organization and the balanced scorecard will be more relevant.

○ Every project in which behavioral changes are involved is difficult, and there are many *obstacles on the way to continuous improvement*. The matrix depicted in Exhibit 9.5 might help identify the status of the organization and the possible remaining barriers in the project. If one of the components mentioned in the matrix is missing, an organization cannot proceed with the implementation of the desired changes. Only if all components are at the right place can an organization reach its desired goals.

ROLE OF THE FINANCE FUNCTION

One of the challenges in the next few years for the finance function of an organization is this function's ability to play a leading role in the improved performance management process, thereby growing

Exhibit 9.5   Components of Successful Change: If One Is Missing, the Outcome of the Project Will Not Be Satisfactory

Pressure to change	+ Involvement	+ Communication	+ Training	+ Support structure and process	+ Reward/ recognition	=	Continuous change
⊘	✓	✓	✓	✓	✓	=	No action
✓	⊘	✓	✓	✓	✓	=	No emotional tie
✓	✓	⊘	✓	✓	✓	=	Quick start; quick ending
✓	✓	✓	⊘	✓	✓	=	Concern and frustration
✓	✓	✓	✓	⊘	✓	=	Fight symptoms instead of causes
✓	✓	✓	✓	✓	⊘	=	No long-term change
✓	✓	✓	✓	✓	✓	=	Continuous change

to a position of "business partner" to the CEO. This challenge can only be met by increasing the efficiency and the skills of the finance organization. In this section some of the examples encountered during the visits to the benchmark organizations, regarding improving these skills, are listed.

- Establish for the controller of each division/business unit a decision-support function and reporting function within the division/business unit as well as a functional reporting relation with corporate. In this way, division/business unit controllers can keep their objectivity toward their CEO.
- Create a strong functional tie between the finance people throughout the organization. This can be realized by conducting joint finance meetings and by corporate control contacting division/business unit controllers several times during the week. Also, corporate, division, and business unit controllers should work together in the analysis of specific issues. If functional analyses are made by corporate control (like finance costs) these analyses will be shared with all division/business unit controllers.
- Install job rotation of finance people throughout the organization.
- Conduct special training programs that increase the skills of financial and controlling people. A possibility might be to establish your own training institute.
- Use planning teams to coordinate both the strategic planning and the budgeting processes. In these teams the controllers of corporate, divisions, and business units work together to solve problems, to align business plans, and so forth. The division/business unit controller is responsible for the coordination of planning and control within the division/business unit.
- Reduce the time spent by division/business unit controllers on financial transaction processes, for example, by installing shared service centers. This way, controllers get more time to perform value-added activities for their CEOs.

○ It will take effort not only to develop the finance function into a high quality business partner for the CEO, but also to train functional managers to enhance their financial skills and knowledge so they can communicate properly with finance managers.

This fits in with the results of research done in 1998 by the Economist Intelligence Unit and Arthur Andersen into the role of the finance function in the twenty-first century.[2] The main conclusions of this research were that high-performing organizations demand superior financial management capabilities and that an innovative, well-equipped finance organization forms a powerful strategic weapon that helps the enterprise generate growth and sustain shareholder value (Exhibit 9.6).

As Exhibit 9.6 depicts, the research showed that the traditional activities of the finance organization, like transaction processing and reporting and measuring and controlling risk, not only will change in nature but also will diminish. In its place, the finance organization will spend more time on analyzing data and on

Exhibit 9.6   Vision of the Finance Organization of the Future: Adding More Value at Lower Cost

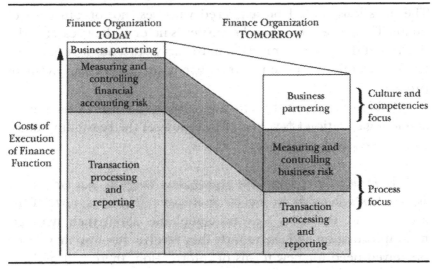

partnering with the managers in the organization. In short, the finance organization will add more value for less cost.

FEASIBILITY ANALYSIS

Not every organization is ready for a performance management improvement project and a balanced scorecard—for some organizations, the time is not yet ripe for starting such a development project. Particularly when there is a turbulent situation, such as a reorganization, disappointing financial results, and chronic overtime, managers have to focus on the problems of that moment. In such a situation, there is only little support for another drastic improvement project. Thus, before an improvement project is started, an organization has to determine whether its current situation is stable enough and ready for such a project and for implementation of the balanced scorecard.

A tool that can be used to assess the readiness of an organization for a new performance management process is the Feasibility Analysis we developed and have used at numerous organizations.[3] The Feasibility Analysis consists of 10 questions that must be answered before an improvement project is started. These questions constitute criteria that an organization must meet before the project can be started and before CSFs and KPIs can be developed. The questions should be answered with yes, no, or ± in case of doubt. The more often that the answer is no or ±, the greater is the likelihood that the organization must carry out a number of activities before initiating the performance management improvement project.

Exhibit 9.7 shows the Feasibility Analysis filled in for the example organization CNS. The 10 questions of the Feasibility Analysis are described as follows:

1. *Do managers within the organization recognize that the current information systems do not provide them with sufficient support?* If the answer is no, the users have no complaints about their management information and the reports they receive. Because there is no perceived need for new forms of information, there will be little

Exhibit 9.7   Feasibility Analysis

Feasibility Analysis Questions	Y/N/±	Remarks
1. Do managers within the organization recognize that the current information systems do not provide them with sufficient support?	Y	Managers complain a lot about the information they do not receive.
2. Is the organization stable?	N	Reorganizations have been started, some personnel will be laid off.
3. Is the management team sufficiently involved in the improvement project?	Y	The CEO has pledged her support for the project.
4. Is the organization's working environment stable?	N	Everyone already works very hard. A new round of reorganizations has started, some personnel will be laid off.
5. Does the organization have clear insight into the market and its position in it?	Y	Recently, customer satisfaction surveys were held.
6. Has the organization formulated a mission and an organization strategy?	Y	Strategic objectives are relatively clear and recent.
7. Does the organization have insight into its business processes and departmental structure and into the relationship between them?	±	CNS consists of four departments, which only partly cooperate with each other and which do not have a good knowledge of each others' activities.
8. Are there enough resources available for the improvement project?	±	Currently, CNS is not making a profit.
9. Are there any other change processes in progress within the organization that have a relation with the improvement project?	Y	No other change processes are under way.
10. Does the organization have an open communication structure?	±	Employees were more willing to share information with us than with their management. Negative results are seen as threatening.
Start the performance management improvement project?	**N**	CNS is much too engaged in organizational changes.

incentive for users to put efforts into developing them. In such cases, initiating an improvement project makes little sense.

2. *Is the organization stable?* The improvement project will require the organization to devote much of its attention to it. If the answer to this question is no, the organization has to focus its attention on other, more urgent matters, such as reorganizations, mergers and takeovers, excessive personnel turnover, or financial problems. There will be too little time and attention left for an improvement project.

3. *Is the management team sufficiently involved in the improvement project?* An organization's management has two important responsibilities during the improvement project. First, management must continuously incite people to develop, realize, and use the new performance management process. Second, management has an important exemplary function. If, for examples, employees see that the management team is frequently using the new balanced scorecard and is discussing it with other people, it becomes clear to them that the scorecard is taken seriously. If the answer is no, there is not enough support among the other managers for the improvement project. As a consequence, managers will not live up to their responsibilities, and it is unlikely that the organization will complete the project successfully.

4. *Is the organization's working environment stable?* If the answer is no, within the organization there is a tense situation characterized by conflicts, a lot of overtime, unfinished business, or serious stress. The employees will then focus their attention on other things or will lack the energy to work on the improvement project until the end.

5. *Does the organization have clear insight into the market and its position in it?* As the organization's strategy is formulated, the characteristics of the market in which the organization operates must be taken into account. If the answer is no on this question, the organization does not have sufficient insight into this market. The organization's mission and strategy will be incomplete or inaccurate. This will mean that the information in the performance management process, like the strategic and functional CSFs, will be incorrect or irrelevant.

6. *Has the organization formulated a mission and a strategy?* If the answer is no, the organization's strategic objectives are not clear. Due to this, it is unknown what should be measured, and the strategic and functional CSFs and KPIs cannot be determined.

7. *Does the organization have insight into its business processes, its departmental structure, and the relationship between these?* In order to be able to determine the critical business processes from which the operational CSFs will be derived, the organization must have clear insight into the business processes that it performs and their added value to the organization. To allocate the KPIs to the correct areas of responsibility and the correct people, the organization must have proper insight into the structure and the position of departments and business processes in it. If the answer is no to this question, the quality of the formulated CSFs and KPIs will be insufficient.

8. *Are there enough resources available for the improvement project?* If the answer is no, the amount of resources available in the organization is insufficient to execute the improvement project and to implement the results in an efficient and effective manner. Some examples of resources are the time needed of management and employees and the financial resources to pay for consultancy, renewal, and/or modification of current information systems.

9. *Are there any other change processes in progress within the organization that are related to the improvement project?* It is very well possible that multiple change processes are simultaneously in progress in the organization. If the answer to this question is no, the change processes are not related to the performance management improvement project. As a result, the projects will compete with each other for scarce resources. The more the unrelated processes coincide, the greater the chance is that there will not be sufficient resources for the improvement project. An example of a change process that is related is the restructuring of a department in which tasks and responsibilities are changed and reallocated. Subsequently, its performance management process and management information system will also have to be changed to depict the new situation adequately.

10. *Does the organization have an open communication structure?*
A world-class performance management process makes it easier to
see how an organization functions. If the answer is no to this question, there is no open and honest communication about the
achieved performances, and employees, out of fear of reprisals, will
be reluctant to use the new process.

There is no absolute number of "no" answers that indicates
that an organization should better not initiate a performance management improvement project. In some cases, it is possible to carry
out a number of corrective activities during the improvement project. In other cases, a single "no" can mean that it would be wise for
an organization to postpone the start of the improvement project.
The decision of whether to start a project strongly depends on an
organization's specific circumstances.

In a recent study,[4] 68 organizations were asked to fill in an
adapted version of the Feasibility Analysis. The results of the study
showed that relatively many questions in the Feasibility Analysis
have to be answered positively before an organization decides to
implement the balanced scorecard. From the study results, it was
not possible to say how many answers have to be positive; however,
it became clear that some questions are more important than other
ones. The main blockages for the start of a balanced scorecard implementation were the instability of the organization (because of
various reasons), the expectation that the management team would
not be sufficiently involved in the implementation project, and the
expectation that there would not be enough resources made available for the project. Main preconditions for a successful start of the
project turned out to be that the organization has formulated a
clear mission and organization strategy, that the organization has
a clear insight into the market and its position in it, and that management would be sufficiently involved (among other things, by
providing a sponsor for the project). The study concluded that
there is no generic recipe for the outcome of a Feasibility Analysis
but that it is important for every organization to fill in the ques-
tionnaire and to place the answers in the context of the specific situation of the organization.

KEY POINTS

☑ Practical guidelines that help you when starting an improvement project are the following:
  ○ Make sure your organization understands the objective(s) of the improvement project.
  ○ Evaluate the performance improvement potential.
  ○ Determine improvement targets.
  ○ Formulate alternatives for the project approach.
  ○ Agree on priorities, and coordinate plans.
  ○ Appoint project teams.
  ○ Make detailed action plans.
  ○ Manage the projects as if they are in one, integrated portfolio.
  ○ Review the results of the project regularly.

☑ One of the challenges in the next few years for the finance function of an organization is this function's ability to play a leading role in the improved performance management process, thereby growing to a position of business partner to the CEO. This challenge can only be met by increasing the efficiency and the skills of the finance organization.

☑ Not every organization is ready for a performance management improvement project and a balanced scorecard. A tool that can be used to assess the readiness of an organization for a new performance management process is the Feasibility Analysis.

NOTES

1. Boulton, R.E.S., B.D. Libert, and S.M. Samek, Cracking the value code, how successful businesses are creating wealth in the New Economy, HarperBusiness, 2000.
2. Economist Intelligence Unit & Arthur Andersen, Excellence in finance, transforming the business, The CFO Knowledge Series,

E.I.U., 1998; and: Economist Intelligence Unit & Arthur Andersen, The evolving role of finance, charting a strategic cause for the future, The CFO Knowledge Series, E.I.U., 1997.
3. de Waal, A.A., M. Bulthuis, Cijfers zeggen niet alles! [transl. Managing beyond the figures], Kluwer Bedrijfswetsenchappen, 1996.
4. Helden, G.J. van, and C.P. Lewy, Barrières voor de balanced scorcard [transl. Barriers for the balanced scorecard], Management Control & Accounting, no. 3, 1998.

Appendix

Management Information and Reporting Analysis

MANAGEMENT INFORMATION AND REPORTING ANALYSIS (MIRA) RESULTS

The 50 organizations that were examined in the MIRA varied in size, organizational structure, and industry and were both for-profit and not-for-profit organizations. The radar diagram in Exhibit A.1 presents the average scores of those organizations graphically.

On the basis of the MIRA, we compiled a list of strengths and improvement opportunities. For each aspect in the radar diagram, a description is given of the most important scores, both "positive" (+) and "requires improvement" (–). The points given can function as a mirror for your organization's management information process.

Internal Financial

+ Most organizations had a financial budget that was divided into subbudgets for the various organizational departments, products, and services. Exceptions were, in some cases, new products/services or new businesses that were recently acquired.

– In the reports, only limited use was made of financial ratios (e.g., return on invested capital and working capital). The use of ratios can make inclusion of the complete balance

Exhibit A.1   MIRA Radar Diagram Depicting the Average Scores

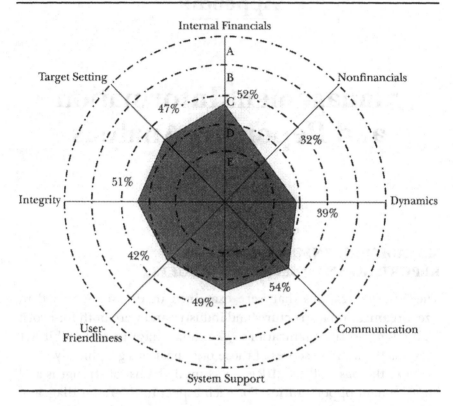

sheet and profit-and-loss account unnecessary. Advantage of this is that focus is only on critical aspects.

– During the budget period (usually a year), the financial budgets were seldom adjusted to changing circumstances. In a number of cases, this was counterbalanced by making latest estimates or forecasts.

Nonfinancial

+ The managers interviewed expressed a real need for using nonfinancial key performance indicators (KPIs).

Unfortunately, they were seldom involved in the development process of these measurements.

- The examined organizations did not use nonfinancial critical success factors (CSFs) and KPIs to monitor the extent to which they had achieved their strategic objectives. To monitor critical business activities, nonfinancial CSFs and KPIs were also sparsely used.

- In a large number of cases, no people had been made explicitly accountable for the results of the KPIs. This made it virtually impossible for organizations to address the responsible manager in the case of disappointing results and to force the manager to define corrective actions.

- The use of nonfinancial KPIs was usually limited to personnel files (number of staff and sick rate), project information (progress reports on large investment projects), and external information (market shares). Information on customer satisfaction, vendor performance, and product quality was usually not available.

- The level of cooperation between various divisions of the organizations was not measured or reported, even though divisions often had to cooperate to provide good service to customers.

Dynamics

+ A majority of the interviewed managers said that reporting was used as input for decision making and for defining actions to improve future results.

+ The reports showed a number of future and action-oriented elements, like explanatory notes and forecasts.

- The quality of the analyses of the results was often insufficient. In many cases, the explanatory notes dealt only with the deviation between actuals and budget. Most of the time, an analysis of the underlying cause of a certain result or development was not included in the reporting.

- Corrective actions were often not included in reporting, nor was the effect of these actions on future results. As a consequence, people hardly looked forward in time and responded too late to unexpected developments.

Communication

+ On the whole, managers were well informed about the organization's mission statement and strategy.
+ Managers thought they were informed on time regarding recent developments within the organization.
- Managers often gave different interpretations to the organization's mission statement and strategy. As a result, different managers focused on different (nonrelevant) aspects.
- Managers of different divisions were insufficiently informed about the results of other divisions.
- Only a few organizations had documented the reporting and communication process properly. As a result, the reporting process was often unstructured: meetings were postponed, data were not delivered on time, and the outcome of meetings was poorly documented.
- Meetings and memos were usually the only communication tools that were used to inform managers and other personnel. E-mail, organization magazines, and bulletin boards were sparsely used. With these tools, personnel can become better informed on the organization's results. These instruments contribute to personnel's willingness to become more involved.

Systems Support

+ Most organizations were improving their systems support for the management reporting process or had plans to do so.
- Virtually all the examined organizations supported their primary and supporting processes by information systems that were, more or less, integrated. However, the reporting

system was often not linked to the operational systems that collected the data. Consequently, a lot of manual labor was needed to generate the reports (often more than 10 working days for each reporting period).

- Most of the managers interviewed hardly used the reporting facilities of operational systems and management reporting systems. In many cases, the planning-and-control department had to distribute hard copies of the reports.

- In most organizations, the finance departments used spreadsheet-like programs to produce reports. Executive information systems were rarely used, even though these systems are especially meant to make reporting more accessible.

- Often, the e-mail system was not yet used to communicate the actual and the expected results. The use of e-mail can speed up the communication process because managers do not have to wait until the next meeting and because analyses and meetings are automatically documented. Thus, e-mail will improve the efficiency of the management reporting process, especially when an organization operates from different geographical locations.

User-Friendliness

- In the MIRA, none of the organizations scored really well on the user-friendliness of management reporting and of the reporting/information system.

- Managers were only moderately satisfied with the user-friendliness of the generated management reports.

- Hardly anyone used graphic charts, colors, and standard layouts in the reports. Also, the volume of the reports was too large.

- In some organizations where managers themselves had access to reporting systems, the score on user-friendliness was extremely low. The system could only be accessed by entering multiple passwords and could only be operated by easy-to-forget commands. In addition, the system was time-consuming and inflexible and had minor graphical facilities.

Integrity

+ The interviewees stated that the reported figures in management reporting were highly reliable.

+ The data that were included in the reporting were fairly consistent. Managers hardly made use of self-made "shadow" systems.

− Many reports were incomplete. Management often had to ask departments for additional information.

− An inventory of the information needs of managers was seldom made. As a result, reporting was often not attuned to management's needs and to the objectives that were set in the strategic plan.

− Reports were usually distributed too late. Organizations needed, on average, 10 working days after the reporting period to produce the reports and to deliver these to management. As a consequence, the value of the information in reporting diminished. Corrective actions could only be started late.

Target Setting

+ The accountable managers accepted the targets that were set and used them to evaluate their own performance.

+ In most organizations, seasonal patterns were taken into account during the target-setting process. As a result, targets remained realistic throughout the year.

− In most of the examined organizations, target setting took place in an unstructured manner. Only financial targets in the form of budgets were annually set. If target setting is done in a structured manner, targets can be evaluated and adjusted periodically. This should be done in consultation with the responsible managers so that the targets are and will remain realistic and obtainable.

- The targets were primarily based on the organization's own experiences in the past. Little use was made of customer information and benchmarking (internal and external) to set the targets.

MIRA RECOMMENDATIONS

On the basis of the MIRAs, a number of recommendations can be made, of which the main ones are listed in the following sections. It is not a complete list, and other recommendations can be made as well.

Formal and Informal Steering and Control Tools

The examined organizations used both formal steering and control tools (e.g., management reports and regular management team meetings) and informal steering and control tools (e.g., informal meetings and unstructured information sharing, such as telephone calls and e-mail) (Exhibit A.2). In many of the organizations the emphasis was put primarily on informal control because the management reporting was considered unsatisfactory. Management

Exhibit A.2   Steering and Control Tools of an Organization

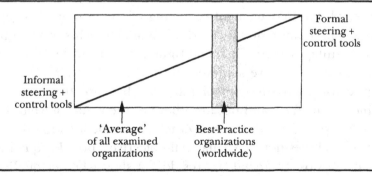

reporting was mainly used for accountability instead of for management purposes. Informal control has at least two disadvantages. First, there is no guarantee that everybody receives all the information. Second, there is no guarantee that messages have been received without distortion. The formal role of management reporting in the planning and control cycle was often not clear. There were various reasons for this: There was no standard reporting set available, or managers used their own reporting set and ad hoc reports.

Recommendation: Improve formal steering and control tools.

The MIRA study showed that best-practice organizations use a combination of formal and informal steering and control tools, with strong emphasis on the formal. In these organizations, formal information is always supplemented by informal information sources because certain types of information cannot be included in formal management reports (e.g., strategic information about a merger) or because action is required earlier than the reporting frequency allows.

Formal steering and control tools can be improved significantly by focusing structurally on improving the management information and reporting function. This can be done by designing a standardized reporting set and by structurally planning reporting meetings.

Incomplete Information

In general, the management reporting of the examined organizations was predominantly focused on financials. This has a number of disadvantages. First, financial figures only provide information about results that were achieved in the past. Financial figures are of little use for daily control purposes because they are always behind on the facts and because they are the result of what has already happened in the organization. Second, an organization's strategy includes not only financial objectives, but also qualitative objectives. Most financial figures do not show whether qualitative objectives have been achieved. Finally, managers often do not recognize their own results in the financial figures. The following information was often missing in the reports:

○ *Structural information on external and internal customers.* Customer satisfaction and needs of customers should be continuously monitored on a structural basis in order to anticipate customer behavior. This applies not only to external but also to internal customers. The quality, timeliness, and added value of products or services that are delivered by a staff department to other departments has to be regularly evaluated.

○ *Structural information on the organization's innovativeness and ability to adapt to change.* These two factors are crucial to an organization's survival. If there is no information available on this, lagging performances in these areas will show up in the financial figures only after a significant time delay. But by then, it is already too late to recognize unfavorable developments.

○ *Better quality information about personnel.* Virtually every organization says people are its main asset. However, many reports include information only on the number of full-time employees and the sick rate. Reporting generally provides little insight into the quality, motivation, and satisfaction level of personnel. Thus we cannot speak of real "people management."

Recommendation: Include nonfinancial information in reports.

By including nonfinancial information in reports, managers get a broader and better picture of the performance of the organization. This information makes it possible for managers to respond more quickly to changing circumstances than financial figures permit. However, it is important to find the right balance between nonfinancial and financial information. When an organization's main focus is on nonfinancial information, there is the risk of managers losing track of the financial bottom line.

Strategic Relevance

The MIRA showed that management reports include insufficient information on whether the organization's strategic objectives have been achieved. There were at least two reasons for this:

1. The strategy had not sufficiently been translated into concrete objectives for lower organizational levels. In most of the examined organizations, top management had formulated a corporate strategy; but no substrategies for the divisions had been derived from that. And even if these were substrategies, there was no alignment between the strategies of higher and lower organizational levels. This could lead to various organizational levels working toward conflicting objectives.

Management reports contained predominantly operational information from lower organizational levels because of the lack of strategy alignment. Because it was not clear what exactly had to be measured and reported, management did not know the extent to which these lower levels contributed to the achievement of strategic objectives.

2. CSFs and KPIs were often not included in management reporting. A CSF provides a qualitative description of an element of the strategy in which the organization has to excel in order to be successful. A KPI is the standard with which to measure a CSF. The use of CSFs and KPIs enables measurement (and thus control) of strategic objectives. If these measurements are not included in management reports, the extent to which strategic objectives have been achieved is insufficiently apparent.

Management reporting was also insufficiently used as a communication tool to inform personnel about the strategy execution. This is a shame, because one of the major problems of organizations was, and still is, to get and to retain support within the organization for the selected strategy and to have all employees contribute to its execution.

Recommendation: Formulate objectives based on the strategy, and translate these into CSFs and KPIs.

In order to make management reporting more relevant to the organization's strategy, managers first have to formulate concrete objectives that are derived from the strategy. These strategic objectives make the strategy more tangible because they can be measured by means of CSFs and KPIs. On the basis of the strategic objectives, objectives are formulated for each department/division. These objectives are then also translated into CSFs and KPIs. Finally, action plans are initiated based on the results of the CSFs and KPIs.

Performance Management

To measure performance just for the sake of measuring is not interesting. What is really important is what management does with the outcomes of measurement. Do they make analyses, and do they translate these into actions? The MIRA showed that management reporting insufficiently supported and activated managers in this so-called performance management. The reporting layout was mainly designed to report the results and to identify who was accountable for these results. It was not designed to keep track of actions. In addition, the reports contained little future-oriented information on expected results. Therefore, many managers were noncommittal on the measurement outcomes. Sometimes, the actions that had to be taken were discussed in management team meetings and recorded in the minutes. The actions then might be discussed in one of the following meetings. But by that time, the relation between results, actions, and new results had usually disappeared. Furthermore, managers had often not been made accountable for registering and taking action on receiving specific nonfinancial information. As a consequence, no one continuously monitored these data, and managers responded too late to a disappointing result—after all, it was not clear who was supposed to take action first. Often, the reason people gave for this lack of accountability was that they trusted each other and thus did not have to check one another with figures and reports. But this is a false sense of trust. Real trust is the willingness to share information and results openly and to learn from each other's experiences without fear of criticism or retribution.

Recommendation: Implement performance management.

To make effective use of management reporting, organizations should have a culture of openness/transparency and self-improvement. This culture has to be supported by reports that contain future-oriented information (because this supports pro-active and anticipating behavior) and that can be used to monitor actions (agreements, accountable persons, expected results, and actual results).

Alignment of Reporting and Management Team

In most of the examined organizations, the organization's management reporting and the activities and the responsibilities of the management team were not sufficiently aligned. (The management team is the highest management level of an organization, including the managing director/chief executive officer, the financial manager, etc.) There were several reasons for this lack of alignment:

○ The management team had little involvement in determining the content of reports. Reports were primarily compiled by the financial department. This department did not check sufficiently with the managers to learn if the information provided in the reports was relevant.

○ Too much time was spent on discussing the reliability of data. In recent years, a lot of time and energy was put into improvement of the information architecture (implementation of new information systems, etc.). This was often accompanied by discussions on how to improve the accuracy and the reliability of data. Meanwhile, very little attention was paid to the relevance of these data in relation to managers' activities.

○ The role of the management team was not always clear. It was unclear whether the management team was primarily a "group of department and division managers" that shared information every once in a while or whether it was more a "board of directors" that determined the organization's strategy. This uncertainty made it difficult to align management reporting with the role and the activities of the management team.

○ The management reports often contained operational data that were of no interest to nonoperational managers or managers of other departments. This was especially the case when activities of departments and divisions differed greatly. In addition, the profit-and-loss account was often of limited use to department/division managers because it predominantly contained aggregated data.

Recommendation: Formulate the role of the management team clearly, and involve the management team in the development of key performance indicators.

It is essential for an organization to have a clear description of the management team's role in the steering and control process. The focus should be on the strategic function. Management reporting then should be aligned with this role by including organization-wide cross-departmental information. The operational information should be discussed bilaterally by the manager who is accountable for the department/operating organization/division and the managing director. An absolute prerequisite for success is involvement of all management team members in the development process of a new reporting set.

Insufficient Focus on Improvement

The question arose as to why organizations had not already begun to or had not done more to improve their management reporting, because their managers were so discontent with the current reporting. There was a lack of focus on improvement because:

○ In the past years, organizations have concentrated on total quality management (TQM) projects. As a result of this, many companies put a lot of time and energy into the improvement of operational processes, procedures, standards, and documentation. Due to this, there had been little attention and few resources for further development of the reporting side of the management process.

- The organization's culture was neither ready for nor receptive to better reporting, possibly because:
  - The management culture primarily focused on accountability, not improvement.
  - Figures were threatening because they provided more transparency, thereby destroying "little kingdoms."
  - There was not yet a culture of efficiency and accountability.
  - There was little enticement to improve management reporting because the compensation structure was linked not to the total management results, but strictly to the achievement of the financial budget (or as one manager said: "No one has ever been laid off because he had achieved his financial budget").

Recommendation: Make the improvement of management reporting an integral part of the self-improvement culture.

To create a favorable climate for the improvement of management reporting, it is essential for an organization to have a self-improvement culture. In this context, you are actually dealing with a chicken-and-egg problem: Where do you start? Should you first change the culture and along with that the organization's management style? Or should you first change management reporting? In practice management, style, and culture only change when there is an urgent cause to do so. Implementation of action-oriented management reporting is such a cause because it is not without its consequences. This means that managers have to discuss the reported results regularly and structurally, that actions are evaluated on their relevance and accuracy, and that the results of actions are examined. Top management should be an example to others in this respect. They should talk to managers about the results and actions in the reporting. If management visibly uses the new reporting, personnel will become aware of the importance of the new approach to reporting.

Notice, however, that even when there is the right culture in an organization, improvement may still turn out to be a difficult process. The effort that is required to improve management reporting is usually underestimated because (1) managers have, during their professional career, become used to financial reporting, which makes it more difficult for them to understand the concept of nonfinancial information; (2) nonfinancial data are less clear, more organization-specific, and less standardized than financial data, which makes them more difficult to develop and to report.

Index